The Visitor's Guide
to
Northern Ireland

GW00401634

THE
VISITOR'S GUIDE TO
NORTHERN IRELAND

Rosemary Evans

MPC

HUNTER
PUBLISHING INC

British Library Cataloguing in
Publication Data:

Evans, Rosemary
  The Visitor's guide to Northern
  Ireland.
  — (MPC visitor's guides).
  1. Northern Ireland —
  Description and travel — 1981-
  — Guide-books
  I. Title
  914.16'04824   DA990.U46

Author: Rosemary Evans

Published by:
Moorland Publishing Co Ltd,
Moor Farm Road,
Airfield Estate,
Ashbourne,
Derbyshire DE6 1HD
England

ISBN 0 86190 182 7 (paperback)
ISBN 0 86190 183 5 (hardback)

Published in the USA by:
Hunter Publishing Inc.,
300 Raritan Centre Parkway,
CN94, Edison, NJ 08818

ISBN 1 55650 037 8

Printed in the UK by A. Wheaton
and Co. Ltd, Exeter, Devon.

Cover photograph: Downhill Strand
and Mussenden Temple, County
Londonderry.

The cover photograph and all other
colour and black and white
illustrations were kindly supplied by
the Northern Ireland Tourist Board.

For J.D.G.E.

Acknowledgements:
The author is grateful to the
following kind people who gave
assistance in the preparation of
this book:
Maureen Cunningham, Catherine
Fitzpatrick of Kilkeel, Ian Hill,
Rev. W. R. D. McCreery, Marion
Meek, Lexie Mitchell, Eric
Montgomery, Meta Mayne Reid,
Roger Weatherup, Betty Wilson,
and Peter Connolly of Sheeptown
Road, Newry.

CONTENTS

Foreword   6
Introduction to Northern Ireland
    1. Climate   9
    2. On the Road   10
    3. Ulster at Work   11
    4. Historic Monuments   14
    5. Towns and Architecture   18
    6. People and Places   19
    7. Art and Culture   22
    8. Hospitality for the Holidaymaker   25

Exploring Northern Ireland
1 In and Around Belfast   30
2 The Ards Peninsula and St Patrick's Country   57
3 The Mournes and Mid-Down   83
4 County Armagh and Newry   106
5 Fermanagh Lakeland and the Clogher Valley   133
6 The Sperrins and the North West   161
7 The Causeway Coast and the Glens of Antrim   195

    Further Information   224
    Index   237

FOREWORD

Northern Ireland covers an area of only one-sixth of the island of Ireland but its population is over a third of the total. As everyone knows, *the North is different.* How and why takes some explaining but the cliché contains a truth that resonates at every level among people who understand or think about or visit Ireland. It expresses a fact about the history of the island and reflects the attitudes of many of its inhabitants.

However, this book focuses on things to see and do. Historical events are mentioned when relevant which, it must be said, is fairly often. A few saints get a mention and one or two giants, but no leprechauns. Remember to pack a light raincoat. A hearty appetite to tackle the Ulster breakfast is useful and, if you are touring by car, a non-combative driving style. Cattle, sheep, tractors, pony-trekkers, dozing dogs, parades and pipe bands are just some of the many other road users you may encounter, and all of them expect to take priority over motorists.

People living in Great Britain are unlikely to wonder, as Americans sometimes do, how long the train journey is from London to Belfast. Still, many of them have only a hazy idea of where Northern Ireland is. Tell them Ulster, as it's often called, is as close to Britain as Kew Gardens is to Tower Bridge and they won't believe you.

But geography isn't everything. Events in Ulster in recent years, certainly the way they are often manipulated in presentation, have obscured the essential character of this interesting and pretty country, with its great variety of landscape, huge lakes and small towns, blue mountains and viridian grass. They have also made it appear geographically remote — even to the people on the larger island next door. This of course is all bonus for visitors who want a leisurely vacation away from crowds and noise. It means that accommodation is not under pressure and outdoor activities like cruising, sea fishing and golf always have spare capacity. Even so, the fact is that at its closest Northern

Ireland is only 13 miles from Scotland, the shortest sea crossing is about 2 hours, and flying time from London — more than a dozen flights a day from Heathrow and Gatwick — is an hour.

It is not necessary for visitors to read up on background. The carloads of dedicated anglers who spend their entire holiday wading into rivers after salmon certainly do not bother, and neither do most of the 900,000 or so people who visit each year. However, even a modest insight into the country's heritage will bring its own rewards.

Rosemary Evans

Map and text symbols

Symbol	Description
	Towns/Villages
	Motorways
	Main roads
	Rivers
	Lakes/Reservoirs
	Building
	Archaeological site
	Church/Ecclesiastical site
	Forest Park/Country Park
	Garden
	Nature Reserve/Trail
	Other Places of Interest
	Castle
	Museum/Art Gallery

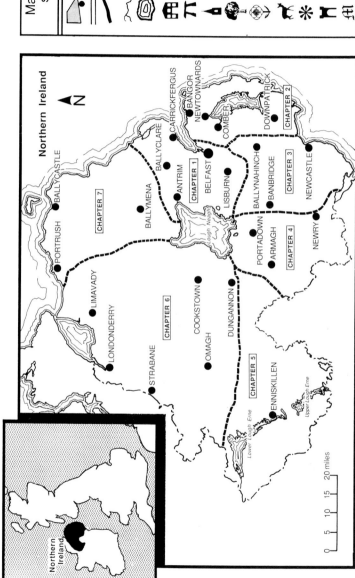

Northern Ireland

N

PORTRUSH
BALLYCASTLE
CHAPTER 7
LIMAVADY
LONDONDERRY
STRABANE
BALLYMENA
BALLYCLARE
ANTRIM
CHAPTER 1
BELFAST
CARRICKFERGUS
BANGOR
NEWTOWNARDS
COMBER
DOWNPATRICK
CHAPTER 2
LISBURN
BALLYNAHINCH
CHAPTER 3
BANBRIDGE
NEWCASTLE
CHAPTER 6
COOKSTOWN
OMAGH
DUNGANNON
Lough Neagh
PORTADOWN
ARMAGH
CHAPTER 4
NEWRY
CHAPTER 5
ENNISKILLEN
Lower Lough Erne
Upper Lough Erne

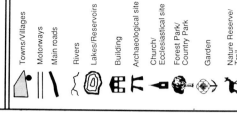

Northern Ireland

0   5   10   15   20 miles

INTRODUCTION

The six counties of Ulster which form part of the United Kingdom of Great Britain and Northern Ireland are Antrim, Armagh, Down, Fermanagh, Londonderry and Tyrone. The province is 5,500 sq. miles in area, barely 85 miles from top to bottom and about 110 miles wide. Right in the middle is Lough Neagh, largest lake in the British Isles. This huge expanse of water is impressive seen from an aircraft coming in to land at the international airport but is almost invisible at ground level because the surrounding land is so flat.

To the north-west are the wild Sperrin moors, good walking country frequented by golden plover and red grouse, with the lava-capped Antrim plateau in the north-east reaching the coast in magnificent cliffs. Most of the small lakes and rivers of the forested south-west drain into Lough Erne, a 50-mile-long waterway which is popular for fishing and boating holidays. The lowlands of south Down and Armagh are liberally sprinkled with small whale-backed hillocks called 'drumlins' which stick up through the peaty bogland in a wide belt right over to the Atlantic west coast, in reckless disregard of the 250-mile border with the Irish Republic to the south.

The shapely Mourne mountains tucked away in Ulster's south-east corner dominate the south Down landscape and Strangford Lough. Highest of the twelve peaks over 2,000ft is Slieve Donard (2,796ft). From the top you can clearly see the Isle of Man, the Belfast hills and the pale line of Lough Neagh. On a lucky day, it is said, you can also see the Scottish coast, Snowdon in Wales and the Cumbrian hills in England. The Irish Sea is quite wide here but drive up the coast to Torr Head and you are hardly 13 miles from the Mull of Kintyre in Scotland.

1. Climate

Visitors are instantly struck by the greenness of the countryside and the big cloudy skies that seem to press down over the fields

The Mournes from Dundrum Castle, County Down

even in a comparatively dry summer. Ulster's weather is often abused, and certainly it rains a lot. Ferns and plants like sedges and reeds grow luxuriantly in ditches and other mossy places and the grass is an emerald green. What makes it palpably different from, for example, England, is the combination of water vapour in the atmosphere and slow natural drainage.

Clouds drift in from the Atlantic over Ireland all year round, an island only a third the size of Britain. Much of the moisture discharged has nowhere to go. A lot hangs in the air and casts a soft misty light over the landscape, giving it a curious dreamlike quality, especially in the mountains and across in the west. But the north of Ireland is also breezy. When the south-westerly winds drive the clouds out to sea, the scene can change dramatically. The sky turns blue and the air is suddenly clear and sharp. 'The Blue Skies of Ulster' is a favourite phrase with some graffiti artists and can often be seen scrawled on walls and in public telephone boxes.

2. On the Road

Travelling by car is the most efficient and agreeable way of getting to see the country. The road network is outstanding, with 70 miles of motorway for those in a hurry, about 1,500 miles of dual carriageway and 'A' roads, and very low traffic density. The only route that could be called remotely busy starts at Larne which is a major port for container traffic to all parts of the island. It runs south via the Belfast Westlink dual carriageway, where more container lorries, from Belfast port, join the road, along the M1 to Lisburn and down the A1 to Newry and the border with the Republic.

The two main motorways striking out from Belfast skirt Lough Neagh to the south and north. The M1 goes deep into County Tyrone, to the edge of the Clogher Valley and points west to the Fermanagh Lakeland. The shorter M2 ends in the middle of nowhere just beyond Antrim town, but by then you are well on the way to the north Antrim coast and Londonderry City. Minor roads are smooth, well signposted and remarkably free of traffic. If you miss a turn it is reasonable to assume that the next turn will take you to the same place since even a hamlet can have half a dozen ways in and out. With nearly 15,000 miles of road to fit into such a small country, they all have to go somewhere. The rush hour in the Belfast area apart, it is hard to mention Northern Ireland's roads without hyperbole. They really are very good.

Compared with the rest of Ireland, the province gives a general impression of neatness. If the County Down farmer tends to trim his hedges too severely, at least there is no wholesale uprooting for prairie-style agriculture. In Down and Antrim especially, the country roads are tidy-looking, with pavements and stone kerbs, cut verges, and marking the high ground beyond the tonsured hedgerows, the towers and steeples of parish churches. In leafy inland parts like Armagh, unruly thorn bushes laden with blossom in summer run round the edges of tiny sloping fields, sometimes containing a pony, or a cow with her calf, munching buttercups. Fuchsia hedges are common and purple rhododendrons grow wild on the Antrim plateau and in the Mournes. Golden whin (gorse) grows everywhere in great profusion, in fields, gardens and banked in bright masses on stony ridges. The blossoms smell like sweet coconut. Boiling eggs in whin to dye them yellow is an Easter custom, and some farmers pound the prickles to feed to horses. It is said to keep their coats glossy.

3. Ulster at Work

With just over 1½ million people, Northern Ireland's population density is 286 per sq. mile, about 2½ times greater than that of the Irish Republic. For more than 150 years there has been a steady shift into industrial east Ulster and now most people live on the eastern side of the province. Apart from Londonderry City, west of the Bann river there are only four towns with over 10,000 inhabitants.

Outside the industrialised area around Belfast the country has stayed rural. Agriculture remains the most important industry, with one in ten working on the land. Nearly all farmers own their farms though many are too small to provide a living. The average size of the 25,000 biggest farms is 72 acres, half the UK average. Cattle, sheep and dairying account for at least 60 per cent of farming, with pigs and poultry (like the famous north Antrim turkey) making up most of the rest. The beef goes mostly to Britain, lamb to France, and a quarter of all UK bacon is Ulster bacon. Though pig rearing is now nearly all in indoor production units, the occasional (accompanied) porker can be seen snuffling along the road verge. Farm animals in the province have an excellent health record. Land quality, the weather and also the distinctive field patterns which give the countryside an attractive patchwork appearance, do not favour large-scale crop production. The main crops are grass, barley and oats for animal feed, and potatoes. Seed potatoes in bulk go to Mediterranean countries.

In addition to the bigger farms, there are thousands of tiny units — 20,000 at the last count — some no more than a couple of fields with a few heifers, a pet donkey and perhaps some geese being fattened for Christmas. 'Conacre', the custom of seasonally letting some or all of your land to someone else, is widespread. The field adjoining the farmhouse may be let for grazing while the farmer, and his wife too, work in the nearby town. Many of these smallholders have full-time jobs in every kind of business, from telephone engineers and shipyard workers to policemen and bus drivers. Ask them what their main occupation is and the answer is usually 'farmer', for the Ulsterman has a strong attachment to his land, however little it may be. With high unemployment and general uncertainty about the future, official efforts to curb 'double jobbing' make little impact.

The biggest social event of the farmer's year is the Royal Ulster Agricultural Society Show in May, with sheep shearing and horse-shoeing contests, goat and foxhound parades and other diversions going on late into the long, light evenings. Heavy horse shows and horse ploughing matches at Fair Head, Ballycastle, are held every year. There is also an established autumn competition when, if they can find a field large enough, fifty ploughmen on fifty tractors plough a hundred acres in unison. The Ulster Folk Museum near Belfast has regular demonstrations of vanished or vanishing rural skills but, despite the fact that farming generally is highly mechanised, you can observe ploughing with horses as well as turf cutting, scything and occasionally, thatching, being done at the side of the road.

Linen
The flowers of the pretty flax plant may soon be seen again in Ulster after a gap of more than 30 years. Linen exports have been on the increase recently, mainly to Japan and Italy for high fashion garments, but all the flax has had to be imported for processing. Since 1984 small acreages have been grown, not of the old blue variety but modern white-flowering strains. The flowers last for just a week, usually early in July depending on the weather, but the attractive seed heads linger a while longer. A field of flax in full flower is a glorious sight.

A hundred years ago 240,000 acres were given over to flax growing and as early as 1787 the province had nearly 400 bleach greens, where the woven linen was spread on the grass to bleach in the weather. When the agriculturalist Arthur Young visited in the 1770s, he was dismayed by the size and extent of the linen industry. He thought it had destroyed the country's agriculture: 'A whole province peopled by weavers!' While the Irish Linen Guild does not contemplate anything on that scale, the flax plant on the reverse of the Northern Ireland £1 coin may be more than nostalgia. In the meantime, the industrial archaeology of linen, the most important of all Ulster's industries during the eighteenth, nineteenth and early twentieth centuries, is preserved in parks and museums and found on river banks.

Fishing
Pleasure angling — game, sea and coarse — has a strong attraction for visitors but fishing is also a sizeable industry. Ulster people seem to prefer a good beef steak, a pity in a country where all the rivers are full of fish. The Foyle and Bann are big salmon rivers and there have long been rich salmon fisheries along the north coast. On one extraordinary day in 1635, sacred in the annals of Ulster fishing, 62 tons of salmon was taken from the Bann at Coleraine. Trout, freshwater herring and especially eels are caught commercially in Lough Neagh. William Laud, the

archbishop of Canterbury who was executed by the Puritans in 1645, rated Lough Neagh eels 'the fairest and the fattest'. Salmon and trout are widely available in restaurants but eels are hardly ever on the menu. You can buy them at some fishmongers but they mostly end up, smoked, on Dutch dinner tables.

The principal fishing ports, Kilkeel, Portavogie and Ardglass are on the east coast. Apart from cod, herring, mackerel and whiting, some 5,000 tons of shellfish are trawled each year from the Irish Sea, including lobsters and the very large 'Dublin Bay' prawns. As the boats come in, small knots of residents and caravanners with plastic bags gather at the harbour ready to strike a quick bargain before the main catch is landed. Restaurateurs have regular orders, some have their own lobster pots and nets. There are a dozen or so trout farms and oyster farming in Strangford Lough is big business. The UK's largest oyster producer is based here, and the Pacific kind are sold in pubs.

4. Historic Monuments

More than most, the Northern Irish are intensely interested in and knowledgeable about their historical heritage. Anyone living near

Monea Castle, County Fermanagh

*Carved figure,
Boa Island,
County Fermanagh*

a ruined castle, for instance, will be able to tell you how it came to be that way. From Stone Age tombs to seventeenth-century castles, there is a pleasant informality in the way Ulster's historic monuments sit in the corner of a field, at the end of the high street or in someone's front garden. The early Christian farmsteads called 'raths' — interesting if unspectacular circular earthen banks with ditches — are so common in Ireland that archaeologists can do little more than count them and mark them on maps. There are 1,300 in County Down alone. Much rarer are 'cashels', stone-built defended homesteads of the same period, and their watery equivalent, the 'crannog', an artificial island in a shallow lake.

Monuments with immediate eye appeal are the Neolithic tombs, 'dolmens', where one huge flat stone is balanced on three or more unhewn upright ones. The capstone is usually slightly tilted, sometimes with one end resting on a pair of tall stones and a shorter stone supporting the other end, like a shaky three-legged stool.

Ruined Abbey and Round Tower, Devenish Island, County Fermanagh

Though not so big nor so thick on the ground as in Britanny, the dolmens of Ulster have a special charm because they occur in some delightful places. Many of these, and later monuments too, from early churches to 'plantation' castles, are in state care. From the tenth to the thirteenth century the monks built round towers — the one at Devenish Island is especially fine. From the seventh to the twelfth century, crosses and high crosses went up all over Christian Ireland — the crosses at Ardboe and Donaghmore, both in County Tyrone, are good examples of this peculiarly Irish religious art. Early monasteries and primitive churches, Anglo-Norman mottes and castles, Elizabethan tower houses and plantation 'bawns' (fortified enclosures round castles and manor houses) are also part of the cultural past.

The twelfth-century castle at Carrickfergus was in continuous military use from its foundation until 1928 and is a complete building — most unusual in Ireland. Almost all the medieval buildings that survive are in ruins, having been destroyed in fighting or abandoned, and then robbed for stone. These often splendid remains are being conserved, unspoiled by 'restoration', and there are good information boards at the sites. About a dozen properties have year-round custodians, and there are guides on a

The Friary, Armagh City

number of other sites in summer. Some seventeenth-century castles, much altered, are in use as private homes, one is a hotel, another does bed and breakfast, and the pretty William and Mary house at Springhill near Moneymore is a National Trust property open to the public. Like the ruined castles round Lough Erne and on the Tyrone-Armagh border, they were built by the Scottish and English 'planters' who settled in the north of Ireland following the submission of the Gaelic chieftains to Elizabeth I in 1603.

After simmering and fuming for a few years, the defeated chieftains fled to Europe in 1607 to rally support against England, and never came back. Their abrupt departure, known as 'the Flight of the Earls', was the final blow to the old clan social system, and the Roman Catholic interest in Ireland submerged for several hundred years. The Gaelic lands in Fermanagh, Tyrone, Coleraine and elsewhere were seized and granted to Protestant settlers in return for a commitment to invest capital and labour, plus, of course, allegiance to the Crown. The companies of the City of London were much involved, not always enthusiastically, in providing men and money to build whole towns. Several junior branches of the departed O'Neills and Magennises survived as large landlords, though not as chiefs. Fortresses like Monea, Balfour and

Harry Avery's Castle, Newtownstewart, County Tyrone

Castlecaulfield, built by the farmer-colonists right in the middle of the forfeited estates, inevitably came under attack. In the 1641 rising they were sacked, some were patched up and changed hands several times before being finally abandoned. Few had as brief a heyday as Tully Castle, built in 1613 by a Berwickshire knight on the shores of Lough Erne, burnt on Christmas Day 1641 and not touched since. An on-site information board gives the melancholy details.

5. Towns and Architecture

The towns planned and built by the London companies, including Coleraine and Londonderry, shared most of the following features: a ditch and earthen rampart, or a fortified town wall, a grid street pattern with two main streets intersecting in the middle to form a square or diamond, a market house, a church, a mill by the river, and the planter's residence, often with a bawn round it. These towns differ from others in Northern Ireland which typically have a single, straight, wide street (Cookstown's is 1¼ miles long and 130ft wide), and also from the nineteenth-century mill villages, like Bessbrook and Sion Mills, which were planned round greens.

Bawns or sections of bawns are quite common, particularly in isolated parts outside towns. They were built to protect the family and livestock of the planter. His poorer neighbours could find shelter inside in the event of an attack, and the bawns doubled as a base for a small garrison. Look out for the massive flanker towers built at the corners of the walls. An unusually well preserved one, Dalway's Bawn (1609), is on the B90 3 miles north-east of Carrickfergus and easily reached from Belfast.

Hardly an original building in the little plantation towns has survived but the street pattern is still apparent, and is particularly noticeable in Moneymore because everything is on a small scale. The 1817 reconstruction of this village by its seventeenth-century founders, the Drapers' Company of London, has given Moneymore some delightful buildings.

Minor Georgian houses, and farmhouses of the same period, are dotted here and there around the countryside. Some have lost their sash windows, sprouted modern extensions and gained practical if ugly front porches. Armagh has groups of Georgian townhouses and public buildings and so has Hillsborough. The visitor with an interest in how the other half lived will want to see the big country houses that escaped the depredations of weather, war and time and are now looked after by the National Trust. Best of all the demesnes dating from the Age of Enlightenment (often, in Ireland, called the 'Age of the Anglo-Irish Ascendancy') is Castle Coole built for the Earl of Belmore by the English architect James Wyatt. The Trust's only other truly 'stately' stately homes are Florence Court (1764), seat of the Earls of Enniskillen, and Castle Ward, built by Lord Bangor in 1765. Other Trust houses in the province have an appeal for visitors who like the intimacy of the smaller scale, for example, a thatched seventeenth-century rectory, an early nineteenth-century gentleman's house and a manor house with an eighteenth-century cobbled working farmyard. Unfortunately, several Trust houses cannot be visited mid-week except in high summer.

6. People and Places

Differences in accent are intriguing for newcomers. It takes time to tune in. The systematic settlement of a Gaelic-speaking country where there were few roads and fewer bridges, and when the English-speaking colonisers were from all over Britain, was bound to affect the way people spoke, and still speak. The vigorous dialect and accents of the Presbyterians and other dissenters from the Scottish lowlands, who settled along the valley of the Lower Bann river, can be heard in the shops and pubs of Bally-mena, principal town of Antrim county. These dissenters built a large number of plain 'barn' churches. East of the Bann valley, the Glens of Antrim accent is soft and well modulated. The Glens people are descendants of the native Irish and of their Scottish Hebridean cousins from across the narrow Sea of Moyle. The long isolation of the Glens, cut off by rivers and without a proper road until after 1834, helped preserve the language — this is one of the last places in Northern Ireland where Gaelic was spoken. The small English-style parish churches in the Lagan Valley, and the Vale of Evesham-style apple orchards of Armagh, indicate set-tlers originating from the English west country, and the voices are different.

Nowadays everyone living in say, Ballymoney, seems to speak with that robust mid-Antrim accent, and a soft-voiced farmer from Fermanagh is as likely to have settler as native ante-cedents. In the larger villages and towns, churches of all denomin-ations cluster together, the halls of the nonconformists cheek-by-jowl with the single spire or tower of the Church of Ireland, and the French-Gothic towers (often twin) of Catholicism. As is often the case in Northern Ireland, however, generalisations can mislead. For instance, the tall three-tiered Lombard-Gothic tower opposite Queen's University, Belfast, is a Presbyterian church of 1862, now used for concerts and students' exams, and Newry has one of similar Italianate inspiration.

Place Names

Ulster may be the most British part of Ireland but it has more Gaelic place names than any other region. The explanation for the paradox is that while other parts of the island came under English influence in the Middle Ages, the 'woodie and boggie' province of Ulster remained thoroughly Gaelic, with powerful chieftains and without agriculture or internal trade, right up to the seventeenth century. The planters who took over the land also took over the place names and anglicised them. A glance at the index of this book shows that a common one is Bally (from *baile* — townland) as in Ballynahinch, Ballywalter and so on, Drum or Drom (*druim* — ridge) as in Dromore, Ard (*ard* — height) as in Ards Peninsula, Ardboe, Ardress and also Armagh (*ard Mhacha*). Dun (fort) as in Dungannon and Dungiven, appears in literally hundreds of town, village and townland names. A townland is the smallest of Irish land divisions, no bigger than 300 acres, and there are 60,462 in Ireland as a whole. We know that because the Ordnance Survey recorded them all on the famous 1846 series of 6 inch:1 mile maps. People are much attached to their particular district and, so far, townland names have survived the Post Office's introduction of postcodes and dreary postal areas.

The American Connection
Curiosity about their ancestry brings many people to the province. The North American connection is especially strong. However you look at it, the Ulster contribution to the foundation and development of early America seems to have been disproportionately great for such a small country. About 250,000 Ulstermen, mostly dissenters, took a one-way ticket to America in the eighteenth century. Five of them signed the Declaration of Independence, which was printed by John Dunlap from Strabane in County Londonderry. The printer's shop where he learned his trade is open to the public. Another Ulsterman, Charles Thomson, who was born at Upperlands, north-west of Lough Neagh, was secretary to the first Congress. At least a dozen US presidents had Ulster ancestry. They include Andrew Jackson, hero of the Battle of New Orleans, Ulysses S. Grant, commander of the Union army, and Woodrow Wilson. Wilson's grandfather left County Tyrone in 1807, at the beginning of a century in which 4 million Irish people emigrated. The founder of the American Presbyterian Church, Francis Makemie, sailed for Virginia in 1682, and John Hughes, first archbishop of New York (Roman Catholic) went in 1817.

Americans with Ulster roots, as recorded at the Ulster-American Folk Park near Omagh, include Davy Crockett, Sam Houston who avenged the Alamo, Mark Twain, and Neil Armstrong, the first man on the moon. The first American potato patch was planted in New Hampshire in 1720 by a Gaelic-speaking Presbyterian minister from Limavady, and Catherine O'Hare, mother of the first white child born west of the Rockies (delivered by Indian midwives in 1862), was a native of Rathfriland in the Mournes. The tourist board has developed a heritage trail which includes four US presidential ancestral homes that have been restored. Genealogy is one of Northern Ireland's growth industries, and although most people's ancestors were neither famous nor especially brave, visitors who have come to trace their own roots in libraries, or to

hunt through dusty parish records, are glad of a few hours off to
visit places on the trail.

World War II provides more recent links with the US.
Londonderry was the largest UK escort base for transatlantic
convoys, and there are remains of many American training
airfields. Outside the city hall in Belfast an obelisk commemorates the arrival of the first US troops in Europe — in
Northern Ireland in January 1942.

7. Art and Culture

Fairs and Festivals

Being so far west and north, the country has long winters with
short daylight hours. The compensation is long summer days and
everyone makes the most of them. There is always a *feis* (pronounced 'fesh') or a *fleadh* ('flah') — traditional Irish music and
dancing — or a horse fair, agricultural show, regatta or folk festival going on somewhere. If you miss a fête in one place, you are
likely to catch one at the next village. Sheepdog trials, terrier
races and gun dog scurries are popular, and there are medieval
pageants in the grounds of castles such as Carrickfergus, Hillsborough Fort and Gosford.

Traditional Irish dancing — a 'fleadh', in Londonderry City

Ulster Hall, Belfast

An annual fixture for at least the last 200 years has been a curious pageant at Scarva on the Upper Bann river. On 13 July thousands of 'Blackmen' (cousins to the 'Orangemen' — members of the Orange Order, a Protestant society that has a high profile in Northern Ireland) converge on this picturesque village (population 250) for a parade and symbolic re-enactment of the Battle of the Boyne in 1690. Highlight of the day is a joust (the 'Sham Fight') between two horsemen in period costume representing James II and William III. 'James' always obliges by falling off his horse amid good-natured applause. The previous day, 12 July, Orangemen celebrate William's victory (which established the Protestant succession in Britain) by marching to a central meeting place, usually an open field, to listen to religious and political speeches. These colourful parades take place simultaneously in about twenty towns. The marchers wear an orange sash, good walking shoes and, if they own them, a bowler hat and white gloves. In addition to bands and banners, some of the country parades have a few 'Lambegs'. These giant drums, with vividly painted goatskins and hoops, weigh over 30lb and their 'blattering' can be heard for miles across the countryside.

'The Twelfth' is a general holiday in Northern Ireland. There are about 2,000 parades every year, mostly small ones, and many of them are a kind of practice run for mega-parades like 12 July and another big one at the end of August. The Feast of the Assumption (15 August) sees the Hibernians donning their finery to walk in similar processions with bands and painted banners. The Hibernians' sashes are green, the banners bear different images and the bands play different tunes but the style closely resembles the Orangemen's. An uninitiated onlooker can find it all rather confusing. The big parades are impressive but there is more fun at a small one. Friends and families at the roadside cheer on the marchers and then there is a rush to get ahead of the parade to have the picnic spread out at 'the field' and a pair of clean socks ready. The socks are needed for the long march home after the speeches.

The province is well provided with bands of all sorts — pipe, flute, silver, brass and accordion — and they are hard worked. Popular music of all kinds, folk, authentic country, traditional Irish, punk, rock, jazz and gospel, has an avid following. Rock star Van Morrison, flautist James Galway and pianist Barry Douglas, as well as various punk bands that made the big time, are homegrown talent. Folk and gospel concerts draw especially big crowds. You can still buy an Irish harp made locally but you have to go to a concert to hear one. However, the *uilleann* pipes (Irish bagpipes), fiddle and *bodhran* (small single-skin drum) can be heard for the price of a pint of Guinness in 'musical' pubs once or twice weekly (check which days), and certainly at a Saturday night *ceili* ('kaylee' — dance) in nationalist areas.

Apart from star names at the international arts festival in November in Belfast, autumn festivals in Armagh, Derry, Omagh, Enniskillen, Newry and other towns have chamber music and theatre, with ballad singers coming up from the Republic to reinforce local talent. The province has a good-sized orchestra, the Ulster Orchestra, based in Belfast. The city is well off for theatres and has an opera house (1894) designed by Frank Matcham. Bear in mind that after the 'proms' in June, the orchestra takes a month off. The opera house and Belfast theatres also close in July and August but there is light comedy at Portrush; Newcastle has theatre mid-week and Irish nights at weekends, and the waterside theatre in Enniskillen has a summer programme.

Literary Associations
Northern Ireland's literary associations are interesting and, although some of its writers do not 'travel' well, modern poets

such as Louis MacNeice and Seamus Heaney have international reputations. Oscar Wilde and Samuel Beckett were educated at Portora School, Enniskillen; William Congreve, master of Restoration comedy, and Jonathan Swift are associated with Carrickfergus; Anthony Trollope wrote the first of his 'Barsetshire' novels in Belfast, where he worked for the Post Office; the novelist Joyce Cary and dramatist George Farquhar (who wrote *The Beaux' Stratagem* in 1707) were born in Londonderry. Thackeray enjoyed himself travelling around in Ulster in 1842 and wrote memorably about the Giant's Causeway; and Walter Scott, Wordsworth and John Keats also visited long before the days of one-hour air hops to Belfast International. The best known religious writer born in the province is C. S. Lewis, who 'made righteousness readable', but there are others, especially hymn writers, like the Rev. H. F. Lyte ('Abide with me'), Joseph Scriven ('What a friend we have in Jesus') and the prolific Mrs Frances Alexander, wife of a bishop of Derry. Mrs Alexander wrote scores of children's hymns. The best known are 'Once in royal David's city', 'There is a green hill far away', and 'All things bright and beautiful'.

8. Hospitality for the Holidaymaker

Accommodation

Visitors touring by car without accommodation reservations will find there is a good choice of reasonably priced bed-and-breakfast farmhouses, seaside guesthouses and private homes scattered across the country. Breakfasts are large, and an evening meal in one of these comfortable houses is good value. Unlike England, Scotland and Wales, which have no official rating scheme, Northern Ireland has a registration system covering all establishments which offer tourist accommodation. The booklet *All the Places to Stay*, published annually, lists all accommodation approved by the Northern Ireland Tourist Board. Hotels and guesthouses are graded and inspected regularly, so you can be sure of acceptable physical standards, cleanliness and so on. Very few guesthouses have a licensed restaurant but many (though not all) will serve your own wine at table. Family-run hotels have an informal, friendly atmosphere and meals are generous. Tourist information centres will make overnight reservations.

Self-catering accommodation is still rather scarce though what there is is good. New chalet and apartment complexes are spring-

Waterworld — an all-weather amenity at Portrush on the north coast

ing up in the main holiday areas, and there are cottages and houses on private estates, island cottages, youth hostels along the coast and in the mountains, and caravans for hire. Cruising on the Fermanagh lakes is perhaps the most popular kind of self-catering holiday. The cruisers are well equipped and are good value. You can stock up at handy provision shops around the lough shores. Self-caterers should resist the ubiquitous pre-packed hamburger for supper, since local beef, lamb, ham and home-made sausages are all good.

Food and Drink
Bread-making is something the Northern Irish excel at. Every little town has its home bakery with laden shelves of 'farls' — soda farls, wheaten farls, treacle farls and potato farls. This rather odd word is from 'fardel', fourth part or quarter. Shaped like triangles with one rounded side, farls are baked on a griddle. Soda and buttermilk, instead of yeast, provides the leavening, and wheaten flour is often used. Potato bread is eaten cold or fried in bacon fat for breakfast. Other bread specialities are soft and crusty baps, wholemeal cobs, bannocks and brown barmbracks with fruit and spices. As in northern parts of Britain, high tea is an institution, and moderately priced. Served from about 5.30pm to 7pm it consists typically of cakes and scones with, say, a lamb cutlet,

roast chicken, ham or fried fish with chips and several varieties of bread. Fully-fledged dinner in the evening is still not universally available in hotels, and in some restaurants the meal can be expensive and undistinguished though helpings will be hefty. In some country areas cafés serving afternoon tea are hard to find but a pot of tea with biscuits or fresh scones is available in many pubs at any time during the day, sometimes at amazingly low cost. The pubs are open all day long, Monday to Saturday, which is some recompense for the fact that at the time of writing, they still close on Sundays.

Going out for Sunday lunch (usually after church) is another institution and always good value. Book if you can. Eating options on Sunday are few. It is the one day when you need to think ahead about meals. Some licensed restaurants are shut and others open for lunch only. *Let's Eat Out in Northern Ireland*, a list of about 1,500 eating places published annually by the tourist board, gives opening times.

Ireland's most famous drink is Guinness. Its particular taste and texture depends on how it is stored, and poured, so do not try to hurry the barman. 'Real ale' has made some headway in Northern Ireland in the last few years and several breweries welcome visitors. The distillery at Bushmills on the north Antrim coast has been making whiskey since 1608 and is billed as the world's oldest (licit) distillery. Irish whiskey is often drunk with a bottle of Guinness. The order 'a bottle and a half 'un' is frequently heard in country pubs.

A precondition of good whiskey distilling is of course good water. It is worth knowing that Ulster's ordinary drinking water straight from the tap is very good, cold and sweet. Survivors from Spanish Armada ships wrecked off the coast in 1588, remarked on the sweetness of the local water and could not understand why the Irish should want to drink anything else.

Outdoor Activities

Weekends and holidays find people pottering around the loughs and coast, boating, fishing or out on the golf links. Others go on family expeditions to the mountains and forest parks. Nine of the province's sixty-odd forests are established forest parks. Most were once part of great patrician estates and retain features of historical interest such as big houses, outbuildings and planned gardens. Usual amenities are an information/interpretative centre, shop, café, camping and caravan sites, signposted walks

Pony-trekking at Rostrevor, County Down

Golf at Royal Portrush, one of Northern Ireland's magnificent championship golf courses

and nature trails, fishing, and sometimes provision for boating, pony-trekking and orienteering. One or two country parks have similar amenities. Large areas of the countryside are designated AONBs (areas of outstanding natural beauty). They include almost all the coast, the Mournes and the Sperrin mountains,and the Lagan riverside parkland which extends into south Belfast and is much used and appreciated by the people of a city that has very little in the way of green areas in the middle. The AONBs embrace National Trust-owned coastal stretches, whole fishing villages, beaches and sand dunes — to all of which there is year-round access. The Ulster Way, one of Europe's great long-distance footpaths, is waymarked for a large part of its 500-mile circular route, reaching all the scenic corners of the province.

1 IN AND AROUND BELFAST

In a country where cities are the size of small English towns and many towns are hardly larger than an English village, Belfast stands out as a true metropolis.

Half a million people — a third of the province's population — live within 10 miles of Belfast city hall. The city, when you walk round it, has the air of being distinctly more prosperous than economic and political commentators suggest it ought to be. The centre has been redeveloped, with restaurants, cinemas, theatres, art galleries, and shopping arcades that echo to the music of buskers with fiddles and *bodhrans* (single-skin drums), or a lone tin whistle. A large statue of Queen Victoria in front of the city hall gazes regally down Donegall Place into the main shopping area. With chainstore names like Boots, British Home Stores, Littlewoods and Marks & Spencer you might at first glance believe yourself in Manchester or Liverpool. Like those breezy cities across the Irish Sea, Belfast was a phenomenon of the Industrial Revolution.

In a century when the population of Ireland was cut by half through emigration and famine, the town mushroomed from 20,000 in 1800 to a linen boom city of 387,000 by 1911, almost the size of Dublin and soon to overtake it. By the beginning of World War II the population had swollen to 438,000 but its traditional industries — shipbuilding, rope-making, tobacco and linen too — were already in decline. Even so, the giant cranes of Harland & Wolff looming up behind the Albert Memorial clock tower preside over what is still the UK's largest shipyard, with a repair dock taking ships up to 200,000 tons. Visitors interested in the history of the port of Belfast — only London and Liverpool were larger last century — will want to see inside the handsome old Harbour Office building. Across the river is Shorts' aircraft works, adjoining Belfast Harbour Airport.

If you fly into this small city-centre airport (not to be confused with Belfast International which is 20 miles west) you will probably

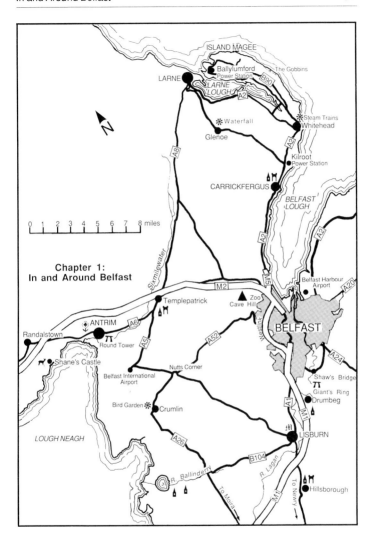

be sitting in a Shorts' 360 aircraft, on a domestic flight from Birmingham, Manchester, Edinburgh or Glasgow. The airport is based on the airstrip where Short Brothers have tested their aircraft for the past 50 years. The Sunderland flying boat was developed here, and so was the SC1, the first vertical take-off jet. The

Belfast City Hall and surrounding area

The Albert Memorial Clock Tower and Docks

SC1 prototype is in the Ulster Folk and Transport Museum a few miles away. Today the company is best known for its commuter aircraft and weapons systems. These two large employers, and engineering firms making textile machinery, micro-electronics and electrical goods, continue to draw people away from the country to the eastern seaboard, a region that has especially close historical links with Great Britain.

Belfast Grand Opera House — detail of ceiling panel

The City Centre

A walk round the city centre and a visit to the university and museum area provide a good introduction to Belfast for first-time visitors who are touring by car and have only limited time available. On-street parking is not allowed in the centre but finding space in a convenient (pay) carpark is fairly easy. The multi-storey carpark in High Street is opposite the tourist information centre.

The rather splendid **city hall** dominates Donegall Square and was meant to. Built of white Portland stone, the main façade is 300ft long with a copper dome rising 173ft above the traffic. After Belfast was declared a city in 1888 the city fathers set about demolishing the White Linen Hall of 1784 to build a city hall worthy of the new civic status. The architect, Brumwell Thomas, was knighted on its completion in 1906 but he had to sue the corporation to get his fees. Behind the railings is a statue of Sir Edward Harland, who came to Belfast from Yorkshire as a young marine engineer in the 1850s. Just behind him a marble figure commemorates the loss of the *Titanic* in 1912. *Titanic* was only one of many huge ships built here, including the P & O liner *Canberra* (1960) and the oil tanker *Myrina*, the largest vessel ever built in Europe when she was launched in 1967.

The dashing nobleman with handlebar moustaches and cocked hat in the little temple on the west side is the first Marquis of Dufferin who, among other things, was governor of Canada, ambassador to Moscow and viceroy of India. The statue was unveiled in 1906. Together with the city hall itself, it says much about Belfast's past imperial pretensions.

The city hall interior features colourful Italian marble, an oak-panelled banqueting hall, a large industrial mural, and an enormous crimson Smyrna carpet in the great hall. This room, 120ft long, was destroyed by a German bomb in spring 1941 when nearly 1,000 Belfast citizens were killed in the blitz. It was rebuilt in time for Queen Elizabeth II's visit in coronation year (1953).

Most of Donegall Square West is occupied by the massive **Scottish Provident building**, interesting for its voluminous stone decoration. There are dozens of lion's heads, queens, dolphins and sphinxes. Other sculptures, of ropes, spinning wheel, loom and ship, represent the industries that made Belfast prosperous. The city's street architecture includes many ornamental Victorian and Edwardian sculptures over doors and windows. Indians and Chinamen, gods and goddesses perch on the high ledges of shops and banks. Sculptured heads of famous men, Shakespeare, Homer, Michelangelo and George Washington, keep a beady eye on the back of the city hall from the façade of a pretty warehouse (no. 10 Donegall Square South). The front of the Venetian-style linen warehouse on Donegall Square North offers no clues to its present occupants, Marks & Spencer, behind the pink stone of this attractive building designed by W. H. Lynn in 1869.

The **opera house**, Great Victoria Street, designed by the celebrated theatre-architect Frank Matcham (1854–1920), was restored in 1980. It has a particularly gorgeous interior and comfortable seats. The reopening signalled a revival of evening entertainment in the city after the 'troubles' of the 1970s. Just opposite is a pub much admired by John Betjeman, the **Crown Liquor Saloon.** Its stained and painted glass and panelled snugs lit by the original gas lamps have been restored by the National Trust. Cosy atmospheric pubs are to be found in the narrow passageways called 'entries' in the High Street area. **White's Tavern** in three-cornered Wine Cellar Entry is the city's oldest pub. **Kelly's Cellars**, Bank Street, a haunt of the United Irishmen who rebelled in 1798, has traditional music sessions at night. There are a number of other 'musical' pubs.

Some of the city's best buildings are banks. The old National Bank with copper pinnacles is two doors down from the tourist office in High Street, near the **Albert Memorial clock tower** ✳ (a kind of mini Big Ben which subsidence has made lean more than a yard from the vertical). One of two fine banks in Waring Street is no. 2 on the corner, Belfast's earliest public building now surviving. Built in 1769 as a market house, it was the venue in 1792 for a famous assembly of Irish harpers.

You could probably visit a different church in Belfast every day of the year, though not more than a handful are architecturally distinguished. The oldest church (1737) is, strictly speaking, a bit outside, on the A24 driving south, just before the ring road. **Knockbreda parish church**, dark and bawn-like, is clearly visible on a hill (right). Its architect, Richard Cassels, designed Leinster House in Dublin, where the Irish parliament has met since 1923, and many other notable Dublin houses. The chancel has a starry blue ceiling. The Duke of Wellington's mother (Lady Anne Hill) worshipped here, and it was a fashionable place in which to be buried. The churchyard contains some superb late eighteenth-century tombs, big enough to live in.

Churches in the city centre to note include: **St Malachy's** (Roman Catholic, opened 1844), Alfred Street, with a fine fan-vaulted ceiling and romantic turrets overlooking the small Georgian terraces of the Upper Markets area. The nearby **May Street Presbyterian church** (1829) was built for the Rev. Henry Cooke, a formidable Victorian who campaigned against the theological errors of the time. Cooke's statue stands at the top of Wellington Place in front of the well-proportioned façade of 'Inst', the **Royal Belfast Academical Institution** where Lord Kelvin's father taught mathematics. Kelvin (1824–1907) invented the absolute scale of thermodynamics (the Kelvin Scale). He also made a fortune from his submarine cable patents. His birthplace in College Square East has been demolished but a statue stands inside the gates of the botanic gardens, appropriately placed midway between Queen's University and the Ulster Museum. 'Inst' opened in 1814 as an interdenominational school. The poet-physician William Drennan (1754–1820) saw the school as a place 'where the youth of Ireland might sit together on these benches and learn to love and esteem one another'. Son of a Presbyterian minister, Drennan helped found the United Irishmen Society and was inspired by the spirit of free thought sweeping through Europe. He was the first to call Ireland the 'emerald isle'.

St Malachy's Church, Belfast

The **First Presbyterian church**, Rosemary Street, completed 1783 and praised for its admirable elliptical interior by John Wesley, often has lunchtime concerts. **Sinclair Seamen's church** (1857), Corporation Square, is like a maritime museum inside. The organ has port and starboard lights and the pulpit is a ship's prow. The church (though not the interior) was designed by Charles Lanyon who was also architect of the handsome E-shaped **Custom House**, opened the same year. The twentieth-century Anglican cathedral, **St Anne's**, is in Donegall Street. Nearby are the offices of the province's two morning newspapers, the venerable *News Letter* founded in 1737 and unionist in character, and the *Irish News* (nationalist). There is one evening paper, the *Belfast Telegraph*, and one Sunday, both published in Belfast, and about forty weeklies. The number of shops selling religious books in Belfast, a city with rather few general bookshops, is striking — everything from evangelism to catechetics.

The area around **Queen's University** is good for moder-

Queen's University,
Belfast

ately priced restaurants, art galleries and theatre. The main college building, revived Tudor-style in mellow brick, with cloisters
and an entrance tower paraphrased from Magdalen, Oxford, was
designed by Lanyon in 1849 and stands at the centre of charming
little mid-Victorian terraces with magnolia trees in their front gardens. The university's arts and law faculties occupy most of the
houses. About 8,000 students with some 10,000 others on short
courses carry on the traditions of learning and science for which
Queen's has an international reputation. The film theatre attached
to Queen's shows art films.

Next door in the **botanic gardens**, the **palm house** is one
of the finest and earliest surviving examples of curvilinear glass
and cast-iron work in Europe. It was built between 1839 and 1852
by the Dublin iron founder Richard Turner. In the **tropical**

The Palm House, Botanic Gardens, Belfast

ravine opposite there is a view from the balcony down into a steamy sunken glen of exotic plants. The **Ulster Museum** faces into the gardens. Among its antiquities is the Spanish treasure from the Armada galleass *Girona* which sank in 1588 off the Giant's Causeway. Gold and silver jewellery and much else was salvaged in 1967–9 by Belgian divers.

There is also an interesting series of Iron Age bronze artwork. Irish paintings in the art department include works by Belfast-born artists Sir John Lavery, Andrew Nicholl and William Conor. Continental painters of the seventeenth and early eighteenth centuries are well represented and there is good silver, glass and Irish furniture. The museum's numismatics cabinet with 40,000 specimens is a major collection. Visitors to Belfast should not overlook the small **Transport Museum** in east Belfast. Steam locomotives, street trams, early fire engines, motorbikes, 'penny-farthing' bicycles and vintage cars are crammed into a tiny building close to Glentoran football ground.

On the lower slopes of **Cave Hill** to the north is **Belfast Castle**, a Scottish baronial pile presented to the city by the Earl

PLACES OF INTEREST IN THE CITY OF BELFAST

City Hall
The departure point for all city buses. In 1921, George V opened the first Northern Ireland parliament here.

Linen Hall Library (opposite city hall)
Established 1788 and still maintained by public subscription. Important Irish collection, scholarly atmosphere. Its first librarian, Thomas Russell, was executed.

Harbour Office
Belfast's seafaring history. Paintings, sculptures, stained glass.

Harland & Wolff Shipyard
The UK's largest shipyard. Two huge modern cranes, 'Goliath' and 'Samson', are familiar landmarks.

St Anne's Cathedral
Hiberno-Romanesque, begun 1898. Mosaics by Gertrude Stein. Lord Carson (1854–1935), leader of the opposition to Home Rule, is buried here.

Queen's University
Opened (as Queen's College) in 1849. Its central tower closely resembles the Founder's Tower, Magdalen College, Oxford. Queen's Film Theatre shows art films (public access).

Ulster Museum
Five departments — antiquities, art, botany and zoology, geology and technology (including flax and linen). Near botanic gardens and palm house.

Public Record Office
Includes private papers (1790-1822) of Lord Castlereagh. Public search room.

Transport Museum
Over 200 years of Irish transport. *Old Maeve* — biggest steam locomotive ever built in Ireland.

Crown Liquor Saloon
Formerly a railway hotel. Flamboyant interior. Built in about 1885 by Patrick Flanagan, a Banbridge student of architecture who was greatly influenced by what he saw on his travels in Spain and Italy.

of Shaftesbury in 1934. It has a square six-storey tower and a Baroque staircase snaking up from flowerbeds and lawns. Cave Hill itself is popular for walks and picnics in summer. The five caves near the top are man-made, carved out by Neolithic men and used as shelter by hundreds of later generations. At **McArt's Fort** on the summit, Wolfe Tone, Henry Joy McCracken and other United Irishmen in 1795 plotted rebellion for two heady days and nights and pledged themselves to the cause of Irish independence.

Parliament Building, Stormont

Here, you are at 1,200ft and it is a good spot from which to appreciate Belfast's fine setting, ringed by hills rising to nearly 1,600ft (Divis mountain), a deep sea lough and the valley of the Lagan river. Golf courses and parks on the city's outskirts are now visible, including the rolling parklands around the former parliament building at **Stormont** 4 miles east of Belfast. The green sward even at this distance is clearly divided by an impressive avenue, nearly a mile long, running up to the white portico. It is a splendid hilltop site. The building, which may be visited, opened in 1932. Stormont, and the Royal Courts of Justice completed the following year, are unmistakable architectural symbols of the Northern Ireland state. Also on Cave Hill, the **zoo** faces over the city. It is a real mountain zoo, getting steeper and steeper as you penetrate further. Once past the flamingoes on the lake, with a crannog (early Christian artificial island) in the middle, and heading for the polar bears, you are literally moving up the side of the mountain.

Around Belfast

Do try to visit the parks on the south side of the city along the **Lagan Valley**. International rose trials are held in **Dixon**

The Giant's Ring, Ballylesson

Cave Hill, overlooking Belfast Lough

Park — Rose Week is the third week in July. There are at least 20,000 rose bushes and trees, and copses and shrubberies on different levels.

Focal point of **Barnett's Park** is an attractive late Georgian mansion, Malone House, with views over the Lagan. Previously the National Trust's headquarters, gutted by fire in 1976, and now restored, the house is used for trade shows and other functions. It has a restaurant and tea room, a greenhouse, old paintings and watercolours and a permanent exhibition on Belfast parks. Beyond the demesne is the Mary Peters' athletics track established in honour of the province's gold medal winner in the pentathlon at the Munich Olympics (1972).

The steep slope from Malone House down to **Shaw's Bridge** carpark is favoured by tobogannists after snow. This is a convenient place to get on to the towpath. A wooden bridge was thrown across the river here by a Captain Shaw to transport the guns of Cromwell's army in 1655. The present picturesque bridge with five arches was built in 1709. Close by, too close, a concrete bridge carries ring-road traffic over the Lagan.

The nearby nineteenth-century mill village of **Edenderry** is hidden away in a bend on the river. Take the side road at the bridge and turn right after 200yd. An agreeable approach is to park here and walk along the bank (1^1/2 miles) though you can drive.

The road ends in a group of small terraces with slate roofs, tall red chimneys, footscrapers and minuscule front gardens. Two twelve-house terraces front the quay where lighters (flat-bottomed barges) delivered coal to the weaving factory, once famous for damask linen, now derelict. Two slightly longer terraces lead to a tiny gospel hall. Wedged between the river and the hillside with no through road, Edenderry is a tranquil spot. A circular enclosure known as the **Giant's Ring**, across fields to the east, is best approached via Ballynahatty Road (then signposted, large carpark). The enclosure is nearly 200yd in diameter, with an earthen bank 20ft wide and 12ft high, and a sort of dolmen in the middle. Refreshingly little is known about it. In the eighteenth century it was used for horse racing. A 2-mile race was six circuits and the punters stood on the ramparts. In 2,000BC it must have been a place for rituals too.

The towpath along the Lagan from Belfast to Lisburn starts in the university area. Joggers, birdwatchers, anglers, painters and boys on bikes are not quite so numerous as people out for a stroll.

Carrickfergus Castle

Even so, it must be the most crowded bit of the whole of the **Ulster Way**, a 500-mile footpath running all round Northern Ireland. The 9 miles of old locks and lock houses are the industrial archaeology of the Lagan Navigation that ran from Belfast to the shores of Lough Neagh where coal had been discovered. The Lagan was made navigable as far as Lisburn in the 1760s. In the 1790s the whole route was open. Its heyday was comparatively brief. Roads, and later the railway (1839), took much of the trade. Paradoxically, the canal provided the chief means of distributing coal imported through Belfast rather than moving Tyrone coal eastwards. It closed in 1958 and much of the waterway has disappeared under the huge rhubarb leaves of *gunnera manicata* and the pink and white flowers of wild balsam.

A lock-keeper's house at **Drumbridge** dated 1757 has been restored. Hidden below the level of the bridge, it is the only house designed by Thomas Omer, the Lagan Canal engineer, which is still lived in. There is a carpark here, across the road (B103) from the lychgate of **Drumbeg** church and the tombs of founders of the city. The church tower (1798) has a seventeenth-century

Chichester tomb,
St Nicholas
Parish Church,
Carrickfergus

bell. At **Drumbo** to the south-west is the stump of a twelfth-century round tower. (Reminder: *druim* means 'ridge'.) This village also has an attractive eighteenth-century parish church. Unusually it is nearly 2 miles away, at Ballylesson. In the graveyard is the huge tomb of a local worthy who rejoiced in the name Narcissus Batt. He rebuilt Purdysburn House nearby (now a psychiatric hospital). He was only sixteen years old when he helped form the Belfast Chamber of Commerce in 1783. The fifty-nine founder-members were not stuffy city-suited gents. Many were active in the Volunteers (the liberal movement in Ireland at the end of the eighteenth century). Their first president was commander of the Belfast Volunteers, and some were United Irishmen. Several went to prison and the grandson of one founder was leader of the United Irishmen, and went to the scaffold (Henry Joy McCracken). Narcissus Batt, more fortunate, died in his bed, rich and influential. Historically interesting, leafy and peaceful, this little backwater is only about 6 miles from central Belfast.

The road north to Carrickfergus and Larne runs through a quite

Round Tower, Steeple Park, Antrim

different landscape. A wide (ten lanes) strip of motorway between the crag of Cave Hill and Belfast Lough soon narrows and turns towards the north-west and the international airport. Traffic volume seems scarcely to warrant such a highway but it does carry motorists through the industrialised port area most efficiently.

Carrickfergus (population 18,000) grew up round the massive Anglo-Norman castle built by John de Courcy in 1180 to guard the approach to Belfast Lough. Fishing boats and yachts bob about in the marina, with the four-storey, 90ft keep an impressive backdrop. The castle, shaped to fit the rocky spur on which it stands, was crucially important to the Anglo-Norman toe-hold on Ulster. In June 1690 William of Orange landed on the pier beneath the walls on his way to the Battle of the Boyne. A plaque at the end of the quay marks the spot.

Defensive town walls were built in the early seventeenth century. At that time it was the only place in the north of Ireland where English was spoken. Medieval banquets in the castle are a tourist attraction, and the town's Lughnasa Fair, an annual event, is held around the battlements. Lughnasa (1 August) was a quarterly feast of the old Irish year. Wrestlers, archers, minstrels and 'monks' tending braziers between the gun platforms lend sound and colour to this fine example of medieval military architecture. In 1760 it was easily captured by a French squadron which appeared in the lough, and had to be hurriedly recaptured. In 1778 the American privateer Paul Jones sailed blithely past the castle and carried off *HMS Drake* in what turned out to be America's first naval victory. It is said that Belfast citizens ran to the shore to cheer the attackers. Ulster Protestants were generally sympathetic to the American Revolution though the French one was not at all to their liking.

St Nicholas parish church, off the market place, is contemporary with the castle, with late twelfth-century pillars in the nave. The chancel was finished in 1305 and is out of alignment with the nave, an unusual feature. It was damaged and burnt many times down the years and much restored in 1614. The north transept contains the kneeling figures of Sir Arthur Chichester, his wife and infant son in a marble and alabaster monument. Chichester was governor of Carrickfergus and, from 1605, Lord Deputy of Ireland. He was also the landlord of Belfast. A small effigy of his brother, Sir John, who had his head chopped off at Glynn (a small village near Larne) after a MacDonnell ambush in 1597, is part of the same monument. The Chichesters were the Earls of Donegall — a name which besprinkles the Belfast street directory. Their eventual bankruptcy coincided with the end of the great famine and allowed their tenants to become freeholders (a disaster for the family but a boon for the citizens of Belfast). Four stained windows are by Irish artists and the nave contains sixteenth-century glass. Only a short length of the old town wall is left, including

Irish Gate north of the church. In front of Gill's almshouses a sculpture commemorates Thomas Delaney, a young archaeologist who excavated the wall and died in 1979. A ghost is said to haunt seventeenth-century Dobbins Inn in High Street. The town hall, formerly the courthouse, is Georgian. Some of the town's numerous antique shops occupy attractive old buildings, and the market house (1755) is now a bank.

Literary associations with Carrickfergus are interesting. William Congreve's father was a soldier and the future Restoration dramatist came to live in the castle in 1678 when he was eight years old and Carrickfergus was a busy port 'filled with English sailors, rough and jovial fellows'. He put one of them, Sailor Ben, into *Love for Love* (1695). Jonathan Swift's first living was at nearby **Kilroot** where he wrote *Tale of a Tub* between 1694 and 1696. Though born in Belfast ('between the mountain and the gantries' as he put it), the poet Louis MacNeice (1907–63) spent his boyhood here. His father was rector of St Nicholas and the family lived in North Road at the rectory (demolished 1986, plaque at entrance). Another famous connection is Andrew Jackson, United States president, born in South Carolina in 1767. His parents emigrated from Carrickfergus in 1765. The **Andrew Jackson Centre**, a reconstruction of an eighteenth-century ✳ thatched cottage containing a little museum, stands near the site of their original home.

The port of **Larne** (population 18,000) is best viewed from a distance. To join a scenic road just outside Carrickfergus, turn left off the A2 opposite the huge chimney of Kilroot power station (Beltoy Road). At the top turn left (sharp turn) to go on up to **Glenoe** waterfalls but turn right, along the old Carrickfergus road, for a bird's-eye view of shapely Larne Lough with a lighthouse on the tip of the peninsula. The three chimneys of Ballylumford (another, even bigger power station), necklace-like Swan Island further up the lough and the dark shape of Olderfleet Castle, a sixteenth-century tower house down near the cluttered ♜ East Antrim Boat Club yard, are prominent features. A small ferry boat dashes across to Ballylumford on Islandmagee every hour or so, and the plangent hoots of the roll-on roll-off ferries float up the ridge. The port handles over half a million vehicles a year on the short sea crossing to Scotland.

Islandmagee is not an island but a 7-mile-long peninsula. It has a distinctive separate feeling about it. The last witches to be tried in Ireland (1711) were from Islandmagee. On the east side,

wild basalt cliffs called the **Gobbins** were the scene of a grue-
some incident in 1641 when soldiers from the Carrickfergus garrison threw the local inhabitants into the sea. The sea-level path
cut in the face of the rock is dangerous in places. To reach the
peninsula turn left off the A2 going back towards Belfast, and
drive up the west side along the B90. There is very little traffic,
lots of churches, signposts pointing to still more inland, some
(spotless) public toilets, and good places for picnics or camping.

Π Look out on the left for the **Ballylumford dolmen**, sitting for
the past 4,000 years overlooking Larne Lough and now
'incorporated' into the front garden of no. 91 Ballylumford Road.
The front door of the house is so close to this enormous Neolithic
monument that the occupants find it more convenient to use a
side entrance. The view across the lough is filled by container
ships and ferries that dwarf the harbour buildings and a modern
folly that looks like an Irish round tower. Fuel, groceries and
fishing tackle are sold above the sandy beaches at Brown's Bay
(campsite) and other beauty spots. The coast here is quite hilly,
with windswept palm trees towards Muck Island, and Portmuck
harbour on a promontory down a switchback road.

✳ **Whitehead** (population 3,500), a small resort with a pebbly
beach and long promenade, is the base of the Railway Preser-
vation Society of Ireland. The *Portrush Flyer*, a famous steam express, puffs out of the excursion station at holiday times. Some
miles west, at **Shane's Castle** near Antrim, is a narrow gauge
steam railway. It runs through woods along Lough Neagh's shore
and has two tiny stations. Once the seat of the Clandeboye
O'Neills, the estate contains a deer park and nature reserve. Cam-
ellias are grown in the conservatory, designed in 1812 by John
Nash.

The old county town of **Antrim** has trebled in population (now
23,500) over the past 15 years, with housing estates, shopping
centres and a ring-road bypass. A tenth-century round tower
stands in Steeple Park, a mile from the centre. This was the site
of an important sixth-century monastery (called *Aentrobh*, abandoned in 1147). Though over 90ft high, the tower is rather obscured in summer by even taller trees. Over the lintel is an unusual
cross-carved stone. At the base lies a giant two-hole 'bullaun' (hollowed stone). This tower and the twelfth-century one on Devenish
Island are among the finest intact round towers in Ireland. Their
purpose and function is not fully known, though they were
probably built in response to Viking raids. Certainly a sentry

monk onwatch at the high windows could sound his handbell if strangers approached, and a rope ladder to the raised doorway, 7ft off the ground, could be pulled up and the door slammed shut.

One of several famous battles fought around Antrim was in 1798 when royal forces fought off and defeated 3,500 United Irishmen. The plantation castle built (1662) by Sir John Clotworthy (later Lord Massereene) was burnt down in 1922. Opposite the courthouse (1726, still in use) in Market Square, the estate's Tudor-style gateway leads to magnificent gardens, now a public park and, unfortunately, somewhat vandalised. They were first laid out at the end of the seventeenth century and restored in the nineteenth century. Features include long ornamental fishponds flanked by high hedges, straight avenues converging on a round pool, a Norman motte with a hedged spiral path to the top, elegant memorial urns to departed Massereenes, inscribed stones to favourite dogs and horses, and a stone bridge over the Sixmilewater river. The stables and coach house (built about 1840) are used as an arts centre, Clotworthy House, with an open-air theatre in the yard.

Another historic building in the town is an eighteenth-century cottage in atmospheric Pogue's Entry off Church Street, birthplace (1863) of author Alexander Irvine, a newspaper boy who became a missionary in the Bowery, New York. His best known work is *My Lady of the Chimney Corner* set largely in this carefully maintained cottage. He and his parents are buried in the churchyard of All Saints parish church, dating from 1596. The church contains some Renaissance stained glass and many Massereene monuments. The steeple was erected in 1816. In summer there are cruises on Lough Neagh leaving from the marina.

At **Templepatrick** (population 750) on the airport road, Castle Upton stables are used as an art gallery. Designed in 1789 for Viscount Templeton by Robert Adam, the stables have a battlemented archway and clocktower, and another archway with a tower on top, leading to the rear courtyard where horses are still stabled. Peacocks roost overhead and groups of guanacos, a kind of llama, browse around the lake. Access to the manor house is by arrangement. Near the stables (but outside the estate), the triumphal arch of the Templeton Mausoleum (National Trust) is also Adam's design, though unfinished. John Knox's grandson, Josias Welsh, who was chaplain at Castle Upton, is buried in this graveyard. Robert Adam never actually came to Ireland.

Three miles west of Nutts Corner roundabout (where there is a

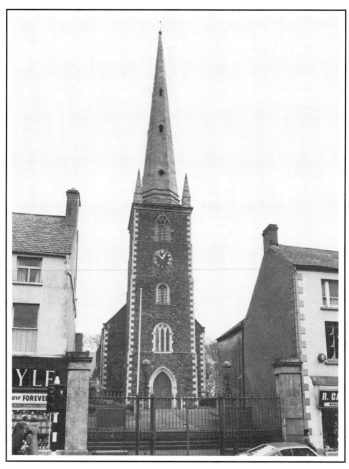

Lisburn Cathedral

big Sunday market) on the A52 at **Crumlin** (population 1,700) a
large collection of ornamental quail, pheasants, partridges,
grouse and ducks is kept in a walled garden adjoining eighteenth-
century Talnotry Cottage opposite an old mill chimney. A great
variety of wild birds nest in the ivy-covered walls. On side roads
about 5 miles south of Crumlin are the Ballinderrys, 2 miles apart
on a quiet little river of the same name. **Lower Ballinderry** has
a Moravian church and manse under one roof — church at one

PLACES OF INTEREST AROUND BELFAST

Ulster Folk & Transport Museum
Open-air museum and folk gallery. Original farmhouses, flax mill, smithy, church, whole village streets, rebuilt stone by stone, recreate Ulster's rural past. Traditional farming demonstrations. Exhibits in transport galleries extend from donkey creels to planes.

Carrickfergus Castle
The first real Irish castle, garrisoned continuously for 750 years.

Shane's Castle Railway & Nature Reserve
Closed and open carriages on a 3ft-gauge railway. Plantation castle ruins. Camellia house.

Pogue's Entry, Antrim
Historic eighteenth-century cottage in cobbled 'entry' featured in Alexander Irvine's *My Lady of the Chimney Corner.*

Talnotry Cottage Bird Garden, Crumlin
Quail and ornamental pheasant collection, with ducks, grouse and partridges, in walled garden. Craft shop.

Lisburn Museum
Wesley preached here 1756. Linen draper Henry Munro, United Irishmen leader, hanged outside after Battle of Ballynahinch (1798). His head was piked for a month. Permanent exhibition of development of linen industry in Lagan Valley.

Hillsborough Fort & Parish Church
Fort dates from 1650 though strategic site was occupied from ancient times. Custodian also has key to market house. Unspoiled Gothic-revival parish church: Snetzler and G. P. England organs (frequent recitals), Joshua Reynolds stained glass, memorial by Nollekens.

end, manse (with chimneys) at the other. At **Upper Ballinderry** is a barn church with bull's-eye glass in the windows, built in 1666 for Jeremy Taylor, the famous Bishop of Down and Connor, a descendant of Dr Rowland Taylor (burnt at the stake by Queen Mary), and one of the great prose writers of the seventeenth century. Theological tussles with local Presbyterians apparently made his bishopric 'a place of torment'. He died, aged fifty-four, the year before the Ballinderry church was consecrated and is buried in Dromore cathedral.

On the Lagan upstream from Belfast, **Lisburn** (population 40,000) is an industrial town with a Tuesday market. Few buildings survived a devastating fire in 1707. One that did was the assembly rooms, now a museum and exhibition centre. The development of the linen industry in the area is a permanent exhibition,

Hillsborough

appropriate for this town which was at the centre of the Linen Triangle (Belfast–Armagh–Dungannon), source of half Ulster's whole linen output throughout the nineteenth century. Yarn from all over Ireland was brought to the bleach greens along the banks of the Lagan, a river with a good head of water in summer — essential for the bleaching process — and with access to export markets via Belfast port. The first bleach green in Ulster was established before 1626 at **Lambeg** a mile downstream, a hamlet with a pretty suspension bridge and church. The hamlet gave its name to the big drums which came to Ireland from Holland with the army of William III. 'Lambegs' are seen — and heard — in Orange Lodge parades.

Louis Crommelin, appointed Linen Overseer of Ireland by William, also came from Holland. He found Lisburn an ideal headquarters. After the revocation of the Edict of Nantes in 1685, Huguenot families from Holland and France came to Ulster at Crommelin's invitation. Linen thread, made by twisting together two or more strands of yarn, is still made in the Barbour Threads factory at **Hilden** where John Barbour (a Scot from Paisley) set up Ulster's first hand-twisting mill in 1784. Nearby is a 'real ale' brewery (visitors welcome).

Louis Crommelin and other Huguenots who helped develop the industry are buried at Christ Church (1623, raised to cathedral

Hillsborough Fort

status in 1662), which is only the size of a parish church. The slen-der octagonal spire was added to the tower in 1804. The interior contains some significant tablets and monuments. But how squeezed it all is! The cathedral is almost invisible from the street and the grave of Crommelin, who brought such prosperity to the town, is squashed into a churchyard no bigger than a pocket handkerchief. In the market place a bronze statue with a pistol in one hand and a sword in the other is General John Nicholson, killed in the attack on Delhi during the Indian Mutiny (1857).

The village of **Hillsborough** (population 1,200) 10 miles south of Belfast, is something of a showpiece. Many of the Georgian townhouses along the steep main street are craft and antique shops. Across the square with its charming market house (built about 1760), the mansion visible through a pair of magnificent wrought-iron gates is Hillsborough Castle, formerly the residence of the governor of Northern Ireland, now used for visiting VIPs and occasional royal garden parties. The gates and screen (1745) came from Richhill Castle in County Armagh in 1936. On the other side of the square, beyond an oval lawn, Hillsborough Fort was built by Colonel Arthur Hill in 1650 to command the road from Dublin to Carrickfergus. The first Hill arrived in Ireland in the army of the Earl of Essex (sent by Elizabeth I to subdue the O'Neills). He founded one of Ireland's most powerful families. Bishop Jeremy Taylor lived with the Hills, his friends, in the 1660s and used to say his prayers in the fort. When it was remodelled for family feasts and parties, an ornamental gazebo was built in the middle of the north rampart in the bishop's memory. The windows resemble those of the parish church which he had consecrated in 1663.

Sir Hamilton Harty, called the 'Irish Toscanini' (1879–1941), is buried in the graveyard. He was born in Ballynahinch Street and his father was church organist here for 40 years. Characterful side-streets to explore include Arthur Street where terraces of one-and-a-half-storey cottages with slate roofs face each other in a cul-de-sac (1850). A lane behind the Shambles art gallery leads to a carpark by a beautiful artificial lake (fishing and canoeing permitted).

A prominent feature of the east and south approaches to Hillsborough is a 5-mile wall surrounding this lake and its adjoining forest. Built in 1841 by the third Marquis of Downshire, the wall has since acquired a concrete capping in parts. On a steep hill overlooking the town, an immense Doric column and statue of the said marquis appears to sprout from a cluster of bungalows. The present author ruined a pair of shoes going to examine the inscription *Per deum et ferrum obtinuit* on the base. It is the only ugly thing in this harmonious little place.

2 THE ARDS PENINSULA AND ST PATRICK'S COUNTRY

When St Patrick came to Ireland in AD432 he landed in County Down where the Slaney river flows into Strangford Lough. His plan had been to sail past the Ards, the long finger of land which separates this huge sea lough from the Irish Sea, but strong currents swept his boat through the tidal narrows and the historic landfall was made on the Down mainland

The Ards stretches 23 miles from Bangor to Ballyquintin Point and varies in width from 3 to 5 miles. Crossing west to east at the narrowest place, from Greyabbey to the breezy beach at Ballywalter, you see how effectively the peninsula shelters the lough. The people in the fishing villages along the seashore, and in farms among the low hills, are mostly of Scottish descent. The accession of James VI of Scotland to the English throne coincided with the first phase of the plantation of Ulster, and some of his countrymen were quick off the mark to take full advantage. Elizabeth I had previously granted land patents on the Ards to Sir Thomas Smith, an Englishman, but he seems to have been tricked out of them. In 1605 the king divided a big chunk of north Down into three lots — one stayed with Con O'Neill of Clandeboye (the original owner), and two entrepreneurial Scotsmen, Hugh Montgomery and James Hamilton, got one lot each. The Scottish adventurers quickly divested Con of his share, and soon control of 'the whole Great Ardes' was split between Montgomery, later Viscount Ards, and Hamilton, who was created Lord Clandeboye in 1622 and who owned all the land on the west side of the lough down to Killyleagh.

Hamilton brought men from Ayrshire to build the town of Bangor where Street Comgall had founded an abbey in AD558. **Bangor** (population 48,000) today hardly seems like part of the Ards proper, and its strongly Scottish character has been diluted as the town has grown. A pleasant traditional seaside resort with a little light industry, it is very much a dormitory town efficiently linked by road and rail with Belfast 12 miles away. Boating and

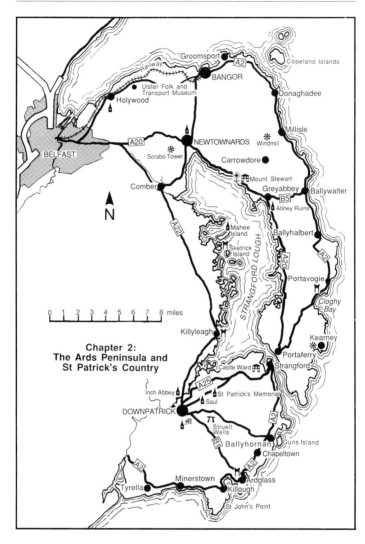

yachting (four yacht clubs), sea angling and golf are main leisure preoccupations. The sandy beaches are safe for bathing. The rather unlovely swimming pool near the marine gardens opened in 1931 and uses sea water. There are band concerts on the seafront in summer, amateur theatre, and an ice-rink. A ruined tower

Holywood Priory

house with Scottish corbelling on the seafront was built as a customs house in 1637. You can get tourist information inside.

Nothing remains of Comgall's famous abbey, nor of two twelfth-century monasteries — except possibly a fragment of wall near Bangor Abbey parish church. This church, which was altered in

1960, has kept its fifteenth-century tower and octagonal spire dated 1693. Memorials inside include a marble statue and cameo-busts of John Hamilton (died 1693) and his wife, Sophia Mordaunt, made in 1760 by Scheemakers. Most other buildings of any substance are Victorian — like Bangor Castle, now used as the town hall and for local history exhibitions. The jolly clock tower with four faces on the esplanade was put up during World War I and paid for by Mr McKee, the borough's rates collector. Churches of many persuasions flourish in the town — from Baptist to Bahai.

The train from Belfast to Bangor stops here and there to deposit commuters in the evening, at **Holywood** (population 9,500) for instance, which is bypassed by the main Belfast road. The clock tower of its old priory, dating from the thirteenth century, is floodlit at night. An abbey founded in woods (*Sanctus Boscus*) here in AD620 by St Laiseran was connected with the larger abbey at Bangor. The Normans first destroyed and then replaced this Celtic church with one of their own. The small Franciscan monastery established in the sixteenth century was one of several, including Bangor, Grey Abbey, and Movilla at Newtownards, burned in 1572 by Sir Brian O'Neill in case English troops tried to garrison them. At the bottom of Church Street is a 70ft mast with a weathervane at the top which, although it does not look like one, is known locally as 'the maypole'. Similar masts have stood here since a Dutch ship went aground nearby on the eve of May Day in 1700, though the tradition may go back even further. In High Street, a bronze statue of a boy playing an accordion, 'Johnny the Jig', is by Rosamund Praeger (1867-1954), sister of the distinguished naturalist, Robert Lloyd Praeger, whose home was in Holywood. Out on the main road, the Gothic mansion (now the Culloden Hotel) was formerly the Bishop of Down's palace.

Some trains (check which) stop at Cultra Halt for the **Ulster Folk and Transport Museum**. It has been developed over the past 30 years on the 136-acre Cultra Manor estate and deserves an extended visit. All the buildings dotted around the park have been removed stone by stone from the Ulster countryside and re-erected in a setting as close as possible to the original landscape. There are two main areas: a village which will grow eventually to a small Ulster town; and isolated farmhouses and the buildings of rural industries, including a flax mill from County Tyrone, a blacksmith's forge from Fermanagh,

Farmhouse from the Glens of Antrim, re-erected at the Ulster Folk Museum

and a County Down bleach green watch tower — a conical stone hut where the watchman sat with his musket, guarding linen laid out to bleach in the sun.

The village already has whole terraces carefully lifted from the streets of Belfast and the small town of Dromore, a school, a courthouse, a rectory and a church — all looking as if they have always been there. The houses from Tea Lane off Sandy Row in Belfast represent the oldest surviving terrace housing in the city. They were built in the 1820s. The oldest house so far erected is the rectory of 1717, from Toomebridge. The parish church stood in Kilmore, County Down, from 1792 until it was dismantled, re-assembled here in 1976 and re-dedicated. Each building has a guide inside, waiting to tell you about its history. The museum has a modern folk gallery with a souvenir shop. You can picnic anywhere in the open-air part, or go to the tea room in Cultra Manor — one building that started life in the right place.

Demonstrations of traditional farming methods go on all year. You may be lucky and arrive on a day when heavy horse harrowing is under way, or potato grubbing or wheat threshing. A road bridge across the main Belfast-Bangor road brings you to the

Watch Tower and Weaver's Cottage, Ulster Folk Museum

transport section. Exhibits include a lifeboat, a three-masted schooner, a vertical take-off jet, and a full-scale model of the monoplane that Harry Ferguson flew across his father's farm in 1909. Ferguson is more famous for his tractors but he was also the first man in Ireland to fly.

The part-thatched Old Inn at **Crawfordsburn**, there since 1614, was the main watering place on an ancient track from Holywood to Bangor Abbey. The sandy beach here, and the one at **Helen's Bay**, are part of Crawfordsburn Country Park where a glen walk under a five-arch railway viaduct (carrying the Belfast train) leads up to a waterfall.

Inland, the demesne of **Clandeboye** is the seat of the Marquis of Dufferin and Ava. A field sports fair is held in the wooded estate in June. Three-storey Helen's Tower (built in about1858), prominent on a hilltop at the far end, was erected in honour of Helen, Lady Dufferin, grand-daughter of Sheridan and composer of the popular ballad *The Irish Emigrant*. In 1915 and 1916, the 36th (Ulster) Division was camped at Clandeboye and drilled in sight of this romantic tower. A sad replica, called the Ulster Memorial Tower, was later erected on the Somme battlefield at

Scrabo Tower, Strangford Lough

Thiepval where nearly 6,000 Ulstermen were killed or injured in July 1916. *Helen's Tower*, a biography of the first marquis by his nephew, Harold Nicolson, is one of the tower's numerous literary connections. Nicolson (1886–1968) belonged to the Bloomsbury Group.

On a hill, 3 miles across the valley, and twice as tall as Helen's Tower, **Scrabo Tower** was built at about the same time in memory of the third Marquis of Londonderry. It has 122 steps up to a good view of Strangford Lough and beyond (open in summer). Part of it was lived in until about 1970. There is a golf course round the tower, with bluebell woods on the south side (off A21).

Newtownards (population 21,000), a manufacturing and market garden town a bit inland from the head of the lough, dates from the thirteenth century when a Dominican priory was founded by Walter de Burgh. The ruins with a seventeenth-century square tower in Court Square incorporate the nave of Walter's church. The family vault of the Londonderrys, who succeeded the Montgomerys as landlords of Newtownards, is in a corner. The nice old market cross at the end of High Street was smashed in 1653 and repaired in 1666 though not restored to its former height. A small chamber inside was used as a police cell.

The handsome market house (1765), now the town hall, has an

outsize market square (Conway Square) with a lively market on Saturdays. The harvest fair held here in September, has been going strong since about 1613. Many of Belfast's fresh vegetables come from around Newtownards (including Comber potatoes), and the horticultural firm of Dickson's (established 1836) is famous for its roses. The mayor's chain of office is fashioned from twenty-six gold medals won by the Dickson nurseries. The Ulster Air Show takes place on the Newtownards aerodrome by the lough in June. A commercial radio station (Downtown) broadcasts from here.

The name of **Comber** (population 7,600) is synonymous with early potatoes, molly-coddled in the rich soil around here. In a mild spring they are in the shops in April. A monument to a swashbuckling soldier, Sir Robert Rollo Gillespie, occupies a large part of the central square. He was a native of the town and was shot in action in Nepal. He died enunciating the words inscribed on the column: 'One last shot for the honour of Down.'

At **Groomsport** (population 900), where Marshal Schomberg landed with 10,000 Williamite soldiers in 1689, the harbour has a sandy beach on either side. Two eighteenth-century cottages close to the water, one still thatched, are used for art exhibitions (Cockle Row Gallery). The 'Row' was a row of fishermen's cottages that used to fringe the harbour. You can buy the paintings propped along the walls outside. Excursion boats go to the Copeland Islands in summer. Proximity to Bangor 3 miles west may account for the modern bungalow developments, and caravan sites. Some funny little brightly painted wooden prefabs with posh names at Fort Hill are holiday homes.

Donaghadee (population 4,000), an interesting seaside town with a lighthouse and a very big harbour, is the nearest Irish port to Great Britain. At a time when the only life insurance available on the Irish Sea crossing was said to be 'a bottle of claret to put the want of insurance out of your head', the shortest possible sea journey — namely the 21 miles from Portpatrick to Donaghadee — was obviously the most favoured. From the sixteenth to the nineteenth century Donaghadee was a major port that offered the only safe refuge from the treacherous reefs on this coast. In the expectation that the town would remain the mail packet station for Scotland, the harbour was greatly enlarged in 1820. It was a blow when the service was switched to the Stranraer-Larne route in 1849.

Local fishermen kept an unofficial ferry service going long

Donaghadee Harbour

afterwards. On calm days they rowed people across to Scotland for £5. At low tide, dulse-gatherers armed with small scythes go out in boats to cut at the purply fronds of this edible seaweed. It is left lying on the slope at the back of the harbour, shrinking and drying in the sun. Fresh dulse turns green when fried in bacon fat. Mostly it is dried and sold in little paper bags for eating raw. The lighthouse is the work of Sir John Rennie and David Logan (of ✳ Eddystone fame). The nineteenth-century castellated folly on top of a 140ft mound (the Moat) between the two main streets was used as a gunpowder store when the harbour was being constructed. Take the path to the top for the view.

Famous visitors landing here from Portpatrick were legion. James Boswell came in 1769, Keats came in 1818 (to walk to the Giant's Causeway but only got as far as Belfast). Daniel Defoe was acquainted with the town's hospitality, and so was Franz Liszt, who had a piano in his baggage, and was stuck here for some days in bad weather. The elderly Wordsworth made his cautious way back home via Donaghadee after a grand tour of Ireland in 1829. Grace Neill's Inn in High Street, now a pub, has been in business since 1611. A persistent claim on behalf of the old inn is that Peter the Great stayed there during his tour of western

Europe (1697–8) to learn shipbuilding and other technical matters. It is a story Brendan Behan would certainly have heard in this atmospheric pub during his stay in the town. After the last war, the Commissioners for Irish Lights gave Behan the job of painting the lighthouse.

Biggest of the three **Copeland Islands** to the north-east is, appropriately, **Big Isle**, a mile offshore. Beyond it is **Cross**, or **Lighthouse Island** where there was once a rogue lighthouse — a beacon that burned over a ton of coal a night. It was suspected of actually contributing to some of the many wrecks in these waters. The present lighthouse is on **Mew**, the outermost island. Cross Island is now an RSPB bird observatory visitable with National Trust permission. Garden herbs growing there are thought to have been part of a kitchen garden established by monks from Bangor Abbey.

On Big Isle in the eighteenth century, there was a thriving fishing and farming community of 'God-fearing Presbyterians' who rowed across every Sunday to attend church in Donaghadee. By the 1860s the population had fallen to about forty but they had a church and a school. The new teacher had to sleep in the classroom (there only was one) until people got to know him. Then he lodged with each family in turn, a month at a time.

The last islanders moved to Donaghadee in the 1940s. Sheep graze Big Isle now, narcissus, roses and fuchsia grow wild and the empty houses are used by weekenders. There are swimming races across the mile-wide strait, and excursion boats from several places on the coast, including Bangor.

Windmill stumps are a familiar sight in County Down, especially around the Ards. There used to be over a 100 windmills in the county. The cornmill at **Ballycopeland** is now the only working windmill left in the whole of Ireland. Built in about 1790, it stands on a drumlin a mile inland from **Millisle** (population 1,370), an unpretentious bucket-and-spade resort of fish-and-chip shops and acres of caravan sites. Ballycopeland is a tower-type cornmill, with a movable cap turned by an automatic fantail so that the sails always face into the wind. It was used for milling oats and wheat, and for making animal feed, right up to 1915, and was made fully operational again about 10 years ago.

South from Millisle, the A2 runs along the coast through a succession of shore villages. At **Cloghy** it slants inland towards Portaferry. To visit the National Trust's nineteenth-century fishing village, off the beaten track at **Kearney**, with a pebbly beach

Ballycopeland Windmill, near Millisle

and walks along the rocky shore, stay with the coast by leaving
the A2 at Cloghy. Though distances here are small, the scarcity
of places of refreshment on this whole stretch can be inconvenient, so plan your journey accordingly. After Kearney the road
west will take you quickly to Portaferry, or continue south to the
high grassy rath at Tara Fort, looking down over Millin Bay. From
there it is 2 miles to Portaferry.

North-west of **Ballywalter** village (population 1,000) are the
fragmentary ruins of medieval Templefinn ('white church') parish
church. Three Norman grave slabs lie at the east gable. The home

Strangford Ferry

of Lord Dunleath, Ballywalter Park is a magnificent Italianate palazzo by Lanyon, built in the 1840s for Andrew Mulholland, a Belfast textile tycoon. It has an open day only very occasionally. Burr Point at **Ballyhalbert** (population 250) is the most easterly place in Ireland, though some say Burial Island, the islet offshore where seals bask on the reefs, ought to count as being even more easterly! **Portavogie** (population 1,420) has one of Northern Ireland's three main fishing fleets. There is a modern harbour, boat-building yards and a fish auction on the quay most evenings. Giant prawns, already peeled, are sold in the village. There is intensive farming round here and at harvest time everyone has to pitch in. The secondary school closes while the children help to get in the potato crop.

A car racing circuit is a little inland, and at the north end of pebbly Cloghy Bay, near the golf course, is **Kirkistown Castle**, built by Roland Savage in 1622. The castle is in fact a tower house, one of the fortified private homes built from the fifteenth to the early seventeenth century by local landlords —

often as a protection from each other. This one has the remains of a bawn round it. The Savage family were the Norman landlords of the 'Little Ardes' and they built many of these small castles. Portaferry Castle is known to be an earlier one of theirs, erected in 1500.

Portaferry (population 2,150) has a beautiful site on the east side of the entrance to **Strangford Lough**. The long, low waterfront of cottages, terraces, pubs and small shops is best appreciated from the car ferry which takes you crabwise across the narrows to **Strangford** village in barely five minutes. It is a pity the crossing doesn't take longer since the views up the lough are worth savouring. Before the famines of the 1840s Portaferry was a busy coastal town with lively industries. Today it is a centre for yachting and sea angling — deep sea fishing outside the narrows and inshore fishing in the lough. Wreck fishing, for big conger eels and wrasse, is popular and there is a dive centre for wreck enthusiasts and underwater photographers. The lough is a great bird sanctuary and wildlife reserve. Queen's University, Belfast, has had a marine biology station here for the last 40 years, occupying two Georgian houses opposite the ferry slipway, and a marine aquarium is a recent attraction for visitors (1987). The Vikings called the lough 'violent fjord' (Strangford). Four hundred million tons of water rush through the gap twice a day.

The very ruined tower house is a prominent feature of the town. A typical small Georgian market house sits in the middle of the sloping triangular 'square' which has some incongruous buildings round it. On the south side is a modest redbrick Orange Hall of 1870, and on the north side a fire station and an ultra-modern Roman Catholic church, St Cooey's Oratory. Two stones outside the belfry are from the ancient church of Templecowey which stood on the shore below **Tieveshilly Hill**, 3 miles south-east of Portaferry. If you go there look out for three holy wart wells under the thorn trees. Portaferry House, in parkland on the lough shore to the north, is owned by descendants of the Savages. From the stump on top of Windmill Hill (east of the centre) you get a good all-round view. Several small castles on the far shore are prominent landmarks.

The drumlins, small rounded hills that cover north Down, extend into the lough. Dozens of drowned drumlins turn up here and there, mostly near the shore. These islands give Strangford the appearance of a freshwater lake, especially at the sheltered north end. The word drumlin, from *druim* meaning 'ridge', was

---

PLACES OF INTEREST AROUND THE ARDS

Ballycopeland Windmill
The only working windmill in
Ireland.

Grey Abbey
Founded 1193 by Affreca,
daughter of the king of Man,
and built by English monks.
Interesting memorials in the
ruined church.

**Mount Stewart House &
Gardens**
Home of the statesman Lord
Castlereagh. Huge central hall.
Fine gardens designed by
the seventh Marchioness of
Londonderry, political hostess
and friend of Ramsay MacDonald.
Exquisite eighteenth-century
garden building. (National Trust).

---

coined in 1833 to describe 'low ridges of superficial debris in the
North of Ireland'. There are thousands of these streamlined hillocks across the country. Many of the Strangford ones are breeding grounds for wildlife, including seals. The lough contains large
tope and some really huge skate. Anglers catching one of these
old and venerable creatures return it to the water after weighing. A
flock of brent geese winters here, feeding on sostra grass;
greylag and white-fronted geese visit from the Downpatrick marshes, and large numbers of surface-feeding ducks, like wigeon
and pintails, dabble and up-end in the shallows. Many species of
tern and gulls breed on the islands, there are oyster-catchers,
redshanks and curlews on the mudflats, and sea hares, sun stars
and curled octopus live around the shore. Predators include
buzzards, sparrowhawks and short-eared owls.

Of the four Cistercian monasteries in medieval County Down,
three were built round the lough — Grey Abbey, Inch Abbey and
Comber. A stone in the parish church is all that is left of Comber
Abbey but Inch (1180) and **Grey Abbey** (1193) have substantial
remains. All three foundations had filial connections with England,
and for nearly 400 years the monks carried corn, wheat, flour, fish
and salt to the beleaguered English abbeys in Cumbria and
Lancashire. Their boats, sixty-oar galleys, brought back Cumberland stone and iron ore.

Pause a while at **Kircubbin** (population 1,100), a boating and
fishing village where you can gather clean mussels and cockles
on the shore and there are always a few fishermen digging for lug-
worm. Grey Abbey ruins are further up the lough, on the edge of
Greyabbey (population 750), a pleasant old post-town. Founded by Affreca, daughter of the king of Man and wife of John de

Grey Abbey

Courcy, this was a daughter house of Holm Cultram in Cumbria.
Affreca followed usual practice in bringing monks from England,
since the Normans distrusted the Irish Church and its links with
clan chiefs. The abbey was burned in 1572 but the Montgomerys
later repaired the church and used it (interesting memorials) until
they built a new one nearby in 1778 (above the carpark). The ruins
of the abbey, in sheltered grounds with lawns and gardens, include triple lancet windows in the chancel and a fine west door,
looking much like one from an early twelfth-century English cathedral.

The National Trust property, **Mount Stewart**, on this same
scenic loughside road (A20), is most famous for its lovely gardens, ranked in the Trust's top six UK gardens, and created by
Edith, Lady Londonderry, from 1921. More historically interesting,
it was the Irish home of Robert Stewart, Lord Castlereagh
(1769–1822), foreign secretary of England during the Napoleonic
Wars. Many treasures in the house, like the painting of Hamble-
tonian by George Stubbs, were accumulated later but you can
see some of Castlereagh's personal possessions, portraits of his
political contemporaries, and objects connected with the great

Mount Stewart

Topiary in the Shamrock Garden

happenings in Europe during his brilliant career. These include the twenty-two original Empire chairs used by the plenipotentiaries at the Congress of Vienna (1814–15) which, after the defeat of Napoléon, established the 'balance of power' principle in international politics. They were brought from Vienna by the English ambassador, Castlereagh's half-brother, Charles.

Though Presbyterian, Castlereagh was educated under the auspices of the established church, at the Royal School, Armagh, a prudent choice since dissenters were still barred from military and civil office. He was a model landlord. He endowed schools, built a chapel, houses for his tenants, and a pier in front of the house for local fishing boats (aged seventeen, he survived a boating accident on the lough). He had an enigmatic and chilly personality and, despite his good works, hardly anyone seems to have liked him. As a politician, and an Irishman, who helped destroy the Irish parliament (Grattan Parliament) and who brought about the Act of Union (1800) he made himself one of the most disliked men in Irish history. Eighteen months after succeeding his father as second Marquis of Londonderry he committed suicide in mysterious circumstances.

Mount Stewart includes almost every style of gardening, and some of the inspiration of Gertrude Jekyll. The stone figures of dodos, dinosaurs, griffins, platypuses and other mythological creatures on the terraces, were made for the amusement of Lady Londonderry's children. An Irish harp is among the garden's imaginative topiary art. Special gardens include a Spanish garden, Italian garden, sunken garden and a paved shamrock garden surrounding a 'Red Hand' of Ulster (red-leaved plants). An octagonal garden building, the Temple of the Winds, was designed by 'Athenian' Stuart (1780).

North-east of Mount Stewart, in the churchyard at **Carrowdore**, is the grave of the poet Louis MacNeice (1907–63). The wide main street of the village (population 350) is closed off in September for a motorcycle race. The Northern Irish have a penchant for racing on their public roads. Apart from major occasions, like the Circuit of Ireland car rally, the Ulster Grand Prix motorcycle race and other big events, there are half a dozen small motorcycle races like the one at Carrowdore. The road surfaces in the host towns are said to be especially well maintained.

The west shore of Strangford, south of Comber, is a mass of small islands, submerged drumlins. The primitive monastic site of **Nendrum** is on **Mahee Island** at the end of a twisting causeway linking several of the larger islands together. St Mochaoi was its fifth-century founder-abbot. Three concentric stone walls (cashels) on top of the hill were excavated and restored in the 1920s. Finds from the digs, now in the Ulster Museum, Belfast, give a good idea of life in a tenth-century Irish monastery. The inner wall contains a ruined church with an unusual sundial, a round tower stump and a graveyard; the

Killyleagh Castle

second ring has the foundations of a rectangular schoolhouse and several little circular workshops. One was a smithy, another a pottery. The twelfth-century chancel in the church was built by Benedictine monks, brought from Cumbria by John de Courcy. You can leave your car at Nendrum carpark and walk back along the road to inspect a fifteenth-century ruined tower house, Captain Browne's Castle, at the west end of the island. The water level has changed since the days when the owners kept their boat locked up in a bay on the ground floor.

South of here, on **Sketrick Island**, the scanty ruins of a much bigger tower house also has a secure boat bay. The main reason for going to Sketrick, however, is the admirably-sited pub-restaurant behind the castle — and the **Hen Island** race, a quaint competition in October when a fleet of oil drums, crates and home-made rafts are paddled between Sketrick and tiny Hen Island.

Going south on the A22 to **Killyleagh** (population 2,100) a startling skyline of romantic turrets comes into view just before the village. Killyleagh Castle, home of the Hamilton family since the seventeenth-century plantation, acquired its fairy-tale silhouette in the 1850s when the turrets were added, but it is mostly the same castle that the second Earl of Clanbrassil rebuilt in 1666. In a lurid intrigue over ownership, involving a wicked wife and a secretly burnt will, the earl was poisoned in 1675. One of the towers is Norman. The castle has a massive fortified outer wall (bawn) and a Victorian gatehouse. A large stone at the gatehouse commemorates Killyleagh's most famous son, Sir Hans Sloane (1660–1753), physician to George II and founder of both the British Museum and Kew Gardens.

Sloane was a native of Killyleagh and, encouraged by the ill-fated second earl, educated himself in the castle library. His collection of 50,000 books, 3,560 manuscripts and cabinet of curiosities was the nucleus of the British Museum. Sloane settled in Chelsea in 1712. He gave his name to a Circle Line station on the London Underground as well as to Sloane Square and Hans Place. The Duchess of York's ancestral links with Killyleagh made this quiet little sailing centre headline news when Prince Andrew was created Baron Killyleagh on their wedding day in 1986.

The whole of the **Lecale** region between Strangford and **Dundrum Bay** has associations with the patron saint of Ireland and is often called St Patrick's Country. By taking the ferry from Portaferry you approach the area by water — as Patrick did. The road to Downpatrick has a number of sites connected with the saint. However, there are other places of interest on the route, not least Strangford village. The tower house that overlooks the small double harbour and ferry landing in **Strangford** (population 400) shared with Portaferry Castle the task of controlling traffic between the two shores and sea traffic through the narrows. South of the village is an early 'gatehouse' tower house, **Kilclief Castle**, which was the home of John Cely, Bishop of Down from 1413 until he was sacked in 1443 for living adulterously in the castle with one Lettice Savage, a married woman. No such colourful story attaches to three other tower houses nearby — Walshestown (sixteenth-century), Audley's (fifteenth-century), and Old Castle Ward (late sixteenth-century) standing in the farmyard on the National Trust estate of Castle Ward. There are more tower houses down the coast at Ardglass.

The designer of **Castle Ward** is unknown. Whoever he was, he did as he was told. The house was built after 1762 by Bernard Ward, later the first Lord Bangor, and his wife Anne, daughter of Lord Darnley. Ward favoured the Palladian style of architecture, Lady Anne preferred the Strawberry Hill Gothic which was fashionable at the time. The result is a compromise. The entrance front is in the Classical idiom, with a pillared pedimented portico, and the

Lady Bangor's Boudoir, Castle Ward

garden front facing Strangford Lough is Gothic, with seven bays of pointed windows and urns on the battlements. Inside, each style keeps strictly to its own side of the house — the exception being the staircase, in the middle. Mr Ward got that and so it is Classical. His rooms have Doric columns and restrained panelling, hers have quatrefoils, pointed doorways and amazing plaster fan vaulting in the boudoir. The stable yard contains a Victorian laundry and a converted barn for concerts and opera. A saw mill, cornmill and slaughterhouse are among stone buildings in the pleasant farmyard. Landscaped in the eighteenth century, the demesne has a Classical temple/summer house, a wildfowl collection, sunken garden and, down by the lough, a bird hide. The Wards continued not seeing eye to eye and later separated.

St Patrick was probably born in Scotland or Wales, the son of a Roman centurion, and was taken to Ulster as a boy slave. He escaped and returned to preach the gospel after years of studying with Martin of Tours in Gaul. The Slaney river where he is said to have landed in the fifth century is now a rivulet near the townland of Ringbane north of Saul. The chieftain of Lecale at that time was Dichu who was apparently quickly converted and gave Patrick a barn (*sabhal* in Gaelic, pronounced 'saul') for holding services. In the 30 years up to 461 when he died in the abbey

Saul Church

at Saul, he preached throughout Ulster and is said to have travel-
led over the whole country, converting the Irish. According to the
eighth-century *Hymn of St Fiacc*, St Patrick received his last communion from St Tassach. The slight ruins of St Tassach's church,
one of Ireland's earliest Christian buildings, are behind an isolated
row of houses at Raholp (townland).

At **Saul** itself, a Celtic-revival-style Anglican church (with a
round tower adjoining the chancel) on the site of an important
twelfth-century monastery is where St Patrick's abbey is thought
to have been. In the churchyard is an early Christian mortuary
house. Built in 1932 by the Church of Ireland to commemorate the
fifteenth centenary of the saint's landfall, the church contains a
thirteenth-century font basin and a small, informative permanent
exhibition. The statue of St Patrick, prominent on a hill across the
valley, was designed by Francis Doyle-Jones for the Roman

THINGS TO SEE NEAR DOWNPATRICK

Castle Ward Demesne
Mid-eighteenth-century stately home of the quarrelsome Wards, half Classical, half Gothic. Victorian laundry. Garden temple and early eighteenth-century canal. (National Trust).

St Patrick's Grave, Down Cathedral
A place of pilgrimage since the fifth century. Historic cathedral on a holy hill.

Inch Abbey
Founded 1180 by John de Courcy on an island site in the Quoile marshes (approached by a causeway).

St Patrick's Wells, Struell
Four holy wells fed by a swift underground stream. Separate-sex bath houses, drinking well, eye well. Ruined eighteenth-century church.

Catholic church. It too was erected in 1932. A 10-minute walk up to the statue to examine the bronze panels round the base has the bonus of a fine view over Strangford's islands.

According to the precious *Book of Armagh* (AD802), now in Trinity College Library, Dublin, Patrick is buried on the great hill at Downpatrick. The reputed grave near the site of an old round tower in the churchyard of Down cathedral is a place of pilgrimage. So much earth was scooped up from the grave and carried away that a granite monolith was placed over the top in 1901 to protect it. Pilgrims strew daffodils on the stone on St Patrick's Day (17 March). John de Courcy claimed to have dug up the remains of Ireland's other two great saints, Columba (died Iona 597) and Brigid (died Kildare 523), and to have put them in St Patrick's grave.

Downpatrick (population 8,250) takes its name from the dun (fort) where a sixth-century monastery, an Augustinian church, a Benedictine church and several versions of Down cathedral, were built — not to be confused with the other great earthworks called the Mound of Down on the edge of the Quoile marshes. The strong association with St Patrick brought many medieval religious orders to Downpatrick and the monasteries established here grew into the regional capital which, by extension, gave its name to County Down.

As was the norm in Ulster, the cathedral was pillaged, burnt and rebuilt on several occasions. An earthquake damaged it in 1245, and in 1538 Lord Deputy Grey used it as stables — a

*Downpatrick Cathedral
from Gallows Hill*

St Patrick's Grave

sacrilege that counted towards his execution not long afterwards.
The chancel was restored 1790–1818 and a tower added in 1829.
The interior has undulating pews and a tall elegant Georgian organ
case. The organ was given to the cathedral in 1802 by George III.
Some of the carved capitals are fourteenth- or fifteenth-century,
others are eighteenth-century restorations. The coats of arms of
the county's leading families, post-plantation, are ranged round
the upper walls. There is a slab in the porch to the governor of
Lecale, Lord Edward Cromwell, and his grandson Oliver Cromwell.
These Cromwells, ennobled to the Earls of Ardglass, were direct

descendants of Thomas Cromwell, secretary to Henry VIII and chief architect of the dissolution of the monasteries. The Lecale Cromwells were Royalists. (Oliver Cromwell, the Lord Protector of England, was distantly related to Secretary Cromwell.)

Outside the cathedral a worn tenth-century high cross faces into English Street which runs down the hill to meet Scotch Street and Irish Street at the bottom. This enclosed and hilly town has some interesting Georgian buildings. In English Street the former county gaol, built 1789–96, houses Down Museum which has a section devoted to St Patrick. It contains a three-storey cell block and the prison governor's house. Troops were billeted here in both World Wars. The United Irishman Thomas Russell was hanged from the sill over the entrance gate. You can see the bricked-up holes which were made to support the gallows. Russell survived the 1798 uprising but was implicated in the Emmet conspiracy in 1803. The inscribed stone over his grave, in the churchyard of the parish church (1737) lower down the street, was put there by Mary Ann McCracken.

Up the side street next to the museum, the 'new' gaol, opened in 1835, has a very imposing gatehouse. It was last used in 1891. The redbrick alms house and school of the Southwell Charity opposite the museum was established in 1733 to support six old men and six old women and to educate ten poor boys and ten poor girls. Now used as flats for elderly people, the buildings are rather spoilt by the high level of the road, raised 15ft in 1790. Denvir's Hotel (1642) at the bottom of English Street had a sanctuary for debtors in the back yard and also in the recess at the front. Creditors had to wait outside. One Georgian building is now used as club rooms by the Downe Hunt, the oldest hunt club in the British Isles. The T-shaped non-subscribing Presbyterian church of 1710, Stream Street, has preserved intact its original pews and high pulpit .

North of Downpatrick the ruins of **Inch Abbey** overlook the Quoile river. There was a monastery here in AD800. It was plundered in 1001 by Vikings, destroyed again in 1149 and founded as a Cistercian abbey by John de Courcy in 1180. The whole of the foundations have been excavated. The most striking feature still standing is the tall triple east window. Traces of a hospital and a bakery, with a well, lie between the church and the river. It is a lovely position, within sight of the cathedral and the Mound of Down. A nature reserve runs along the river banks from Quoile Bridge to the flood-control barrage. Built in 1957 the barrage has

Inch Abbey

artificially converted the saltwater estuary to a slow-moving
freshwater lake which has resulted in some unusually rich
colonisations by insects, fish and vegetation.

Taking the Ardglass road (B1) south from the city, past the
enormous red-and-yellow hospital (1834), **Struell Wells** is signposted. The miraculous healing powers of the water in this rocky
valley, where yellow whin grows in ridges, were first mentioned in
written records of 1306. The wells are built along the course of an
underground stream. The roofed men's bath house has an ante-
room with seats and a sunken bath. The women's house, a bit
smaller and minus its roof, is near a large sycamore tree. There is
a drinking well and, in the centre of the enclosure, an eye well with
a pyramid roof. Pilgrims carry the magic away in bottles. Mass is
said here on midsummer night.

West of Struell on the Ballyhornan road is Bishop's Court air-
force base. The quiet farming and fishing village of **Ballyhornan**
faces **Guns Island**, which you can get to at low tide. Rare seaside and lime-loving plants, including orchids, grow in the nature
reserve at Killard Point north of the village. To the south, on the
A2, the little **Chapeltown** Roman Catholic church of 1791 has a

life-size pre-Reformation stone statue of the Virgin and Child in a niche in the east gable.

Ardglass (population 1300) was once the busiest seaport in Ulster. You can catch codling, pollack and coalfish off the quay at the deep double harbour, and the town is still an important fishing port. What is most striking is the way castles pop up everywhere. Between the fourteenth and sixteenth century a ring of tower houses and fortified warehouses were built to protect the harbour. Jordan's Castle (early fifteenth-century) in the middle of the town was besieged in about 1600 but held out for 3 years. It was bought and repaired in 1911 by a Belfast solicitor, F. J. Bigger, who filled it with antiquities and left it to the government in his will. It is still used as a local museum. A curious row of fortified warehouses, now used as a golf clubhouse, has a tiny tower house (Gowd Castle) at the end. Other well kept fortified buildings include a circular battlemented tower on top of a small tower house (no.7, Green Road) and two early nineteenth-century castellated structures, Isabella's Tower and King's Castle.

Killough (population 500) is a quiet backwater. The main street, unbroken façades of single- and two-storey early Victorian houses, is lined with tall sycamore trees. The village has a pretty parish church on the wall of the silted-up harbour and almshouses built by Lanyon, Lynn & Lanyon in 1868. There is little work here, since the brickworks closed. You could park past the windmill stump near the coastguard station, and walk to **St John's Point** along a rather rough coastal path. Alternatively, drive to the point, where there is a lighthouse and a ruined tenth-century church and then walk towards the beaches of Minerstown and Tyrella Strand along the edge of Dundrum Bay for ever-improving views of the Mournes.

3 THE MOURNES AND MID-DOWN

'Where the Mountains of Mourne sweep down to the sea.'

The melody and words of the popular song have made the **Mournes** the best known mountains in Ireland. In this compact range, 15 miles long and 8 miles wide, only a dozen of the sixty or so individual summits rise above 2,000ft, with Slieve Donard, at 2,796ft, the province's highest peak.

Deciding which way to drive through the Mournes can present something of a dilemma since they are beautiful from every direction. The ancient Kingdom of Mourne, isolated but well populated, is hidden away behind the bare eastern summits which, from the north, appear as an unbroken line of steep and shapely hills. South Down is dominated by these much painted, much walked mountains and whichever route you take south from Belfast, there they are, in front of you.

Saintfield (population 1,400) was the scene of the first of two County Down battles in the 1798 rebellion. The local Presbyterian minister, the Rev. T.L. Birch, was active in the United Irishmen Society (founded in Belfast in 1791 to win religious equality and parliamentary reform) and he established a branch in the town. The rebels managed to hold Saintfield for a few days but were defeated at Ballynahinch soon afterwards. The long grassy graveyard of Mr Birch's church contains the headstones of his slain parishioners and a memorial plaque (First Presbyterian ✳ church, Main Street). Many residents now commute by car to offices in Belfast although the town still has a livestock market. The old railway station (closed 1950) has been preserved. A four-storey flour mill stump stands near the railway bridge in Windmill Road.

A mile south, **Rowallane** is well known for its lovely show of ⚓ rhododendrons and azaleas. The nice old house on the estate, now the National Trust's headquarters in Northern Ireland, was inherited in 1903 by Hugh Armitage Moore, a distinguished plantsman who spent the next half century creating and working in the

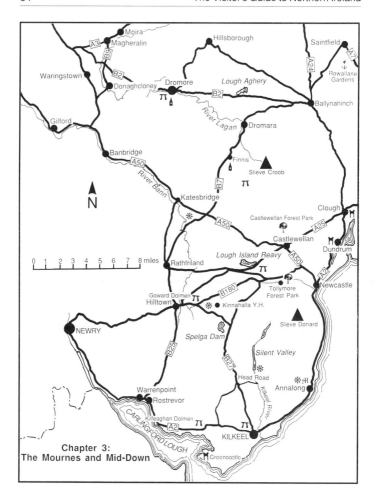

Chapter 3:
The Mournes and Mid-Down

50-acre garden. Two hundred feet above sea level, the garden is
encircled by a windbreak of Australian laurels, hollies, pines and
beech trees growing in the thin layer of soil covering the little
glacial hills — drumlins — of County Down. The spectacular
massed plantings of rhododendrons flourish in the light acid soil,
sharp drainage, gentle rain and even temperature. Plants in the
walled gardens include rare primulas, blue Himalayan poppies
(mecanopsis), plantain lilies (hostas), roses, magnolias and

Trassey Bridge in the Mournes

autumn crocuses (colchinums). There is a big handkerchief tree, many viburnums and chaenomeles, and a natural rock garden fringed with more mecanopsis. The estate has attractive stone farm buildings, with a bell-cote in the entrance archway to the farmyard.

The wide streets of **Ballynahinch** (population 3,700) were laid out in about 1640 by the Earls of Moira, whose former seat, Montalto, is to the south. From the stump on Windmill Hill you can see across the valley to the wooded demesne of Montalto. The last and biggest battle of the United Irishmen's rebellion was fought in this valley. If the rebels had taken Ballynahinch, right in the middle of the country, their strategic advantage would have been considerable. As it turned out, they lost the battle. A handful of the leaders were executed, including Henry Munro, and Henry Joy McCracken who had been defeated at the Battle of Antrim a

PLACES TO VISIT IN MID-DOWN

Rowallane Gardens, Saintfield
Plantsman's garden in a natural setting of whinstone rock. Noted for rhododendrons, azaleas, herbaceous plants, bulbs. Wild flower areas.(National Trust).

Dromore Cathedral
Rebuilt in 1660s on sixth-century monastic site. Resting place of two bishops of literary distinction, Jeremy Taylor (died 1667) and Thomas Percy (died 1811).

Legananny Dolmen
Long-legged tripod 'giant's grave' on Slieve Croob slopes.

Dundrum Castle
Impressive twelfth-century ruins with spiral staircase. Views over Dundrum Bay.

Murlough Sand Dunes
Guided walks through nature reserve. Seabirds, woodland and heath wildlife. Bird hides, information centre, shop. (National Trust).

Castlewellan Arboretum
Started in 1740, the arboretum is the showpiece of Castlewellan Forest Park. One of the greenhouses contains free-flying tropical birds.

few days earlier, but nearly all the rest were pardoned and went home quietly. Lord Kelvin's father, Dr James Thomson who was Professor of Mathematics at Belfast College ('Inst'), was in the rebel camp on the night before the battle. He gave a vivid description of it in the *Belfast Magazine* years later (1825). The Ballynahinch antiquarian booksellers, Davidsons (Broomhill Road), have recently produced a book of eye-witness accounts, *Ulster in '98* — one of numerous venerable works they publish in facsimile editions.

Like Saintfield, this town was badly damaged in 1798 and at various times since. St Patrick's church (Roman Catholic, 1843) has an interesting Classical interior, with a baptistry under the gallery stairs and rich Victorian stained glass. The rear of the nearby parish church of 1772 looks on to the river valley and the Montalto woods. Harris's cornmill near the bridge on the Newcastle road grinds corn and barley for animal feed. The large waterwheel, made in 1816, is powered by the Ballynahinch river. At **Spa** crossroads (on the B175) are the buildings of the once fashionable spa, popular from about 1770. The old assembly rooms, formal gardens (laid out as a maze) and chalybeate water springs went out of style at the outbreak of war in 1914.

Clough Castle, a few yards off the A24/A25 crossroads, is a good example of a motte and bailey castle, built during the early phase of the Anglo-Norman conquest of Ireland. The stone keep on top of the big hill is late thirteenth-century. To appreciate mottes and baileys you have to concentrate on the grassy mounds, even when the stone buildings on top look rather more interesting. The motte, a flat-topped artificial earthwork with a ditch round it, had a lower level enclosure (bailey) as the first line of defence. The bailey at Clough is a kidney-shaped mound. If the castle came under attack, those on the motte could isolate them-selves from the bailey by pulling away the ladder bridging the ditch. A hail of arrows from the wooden palisade on top of the motte would, with luck, discourage unwelcome visitors.

These motte and bailey castles were the first things the Nor-mans built in Ireland. There are about forty in County Down alone, and County Antrim has almost twice as many. The further west you go, the scarcer they are. The Normans never penetrated far west. They made little impact on the Mournes either, though there is a strategic motte at Hilltown, one of the band of County Down mottes ending with the Crown Mound near Newry. On the A1 south of Lisburn **Duneight** motte is signposted, and 6 miles on, at Dro-more, is a very impressive motte with an oblong bailey. Most mottes were only about 60ft across, cramped and uncomfortable places to live, and the Normans soon abandoned them and moved into decent stone castles like Dundrum, 3 miles down the road.

Up a steep turning off the A2 and surrounded by tall trees, ruined **Dundrum Castle** stands on a rock above Dundrum inner bay. King John captured it in 1210, the Magennises occupied it in the fourteenth century, and Cromwell's troops damaged it in 1652. The massive circular keep has a spiral staircase and two latrines are built into the curtain wall. It is one of a line of castles that con-trolled this coast from Greencastle, on Carlingford Lough, to Car-rickfergus. Communications between them were usually by sea. Shelduck nest in old rabbit burrows down around the bay, and there are mallard, mergansers and herons. The birds, and the seals sunning themselves on the point, seem unperturbed by the popping from a nearby army rifle-range across the narrow channel at Ballykinler. About 1^1/2 miles beyond Dundrum village, turn inland at a small carpark and toilets, and over a stone bridge to see the handsome **Slidderyford dolmen** in a field on the left. Returning to the A2 you reach the sand dunes of **Murlough** nature reserve (National Trust) after 200yd. The Normans farmed the dunes as a rabbit warren, and warrening (for meat and skins) was an important local trade for centuries. There is an interesting

Dundrum Castle

interpretative centre near the carpark.

Approached from Dundrum, the resort of **Newcastle** (population 6,250) seems quite spacious, with a curved raised beach. At the south end it squeezes on to a ledge up against the mountain, with room for the road and not much else. The caravan sites are all at the 'fat' end, invisible from the long promenade that stretches from an outsize redbrick Victorian hotel (appropriately named after the province's biggest mountain) round to the harbour bars and yacht club yard. Percy French (1854–1920) celebrated Newcastle 'where the Mountains of Mourne sweep down to the sea' in his popular song and the grateful town built him a memorial fountain in the promenade gardens.

✳   A large inscribed stone in the promenade wall near the warm sea water pool commemorates Harry Ferguson's flight in a home-made monoplane along the beach in 1910. The town gave him £100 as a reward. Ferguson was the inventor of the four-wheel drive system, and he sued the Ford Motor Company for $250 million for infringing patents for his most famous invention, the modern tractor.

The most distinctive building in the town, a 1960s Roman Catholic church with a green copper parasol roof, is visible from far off. At the south end of the promenade an odd Victorian cottage with a drinking fountain in front is the Annesley estate

The Arboretum, Castlewellan Forest Park

office. Donard Park, behind the town, tends to be overshadowed
by the proximity of the forest park of Tollymore but it has nice
walks up the tumbling Glen river. The championship courses of
the Royal County Down golf club are at the north end of the town.
Evening entertainment and plenty of restaurants help make this a
lively place.

Visitors to **Castlewellan** (population 2,100) are mostly heading for one or other of the two forest parks nearby but this
agreeable market town deserves more than a passing glance. It
has two squares, two market houses and two attractive churches. Like other villages in the Mournes, it had been a stronghold
of the Magennis clan dispossessed in 1642. In 1741 it was bought
by William Annesley, descendant of an Elizabethan army captain,
the same Annesley who purchased Newcastle a few years later.

Castlewellan, County Down

He laid out Castlewellan to a spacious street plan on a ridge near his demesne. The market house-cum-courthouse was built in 1764 but its church-like tower with a large clock face was added later. Tall St Malachy's church (Roman Catholic,1884) is close to the other market house. The Annesleys had their own private entrance to St Paul's, the early Victorian Church of Ireland church, and their own large pew out of sight of the congregation.

Many prehistoric and early Christian monuments in the Mournes have vanished in extensive quarrying, but there are still numerous stone-walled cashels in these rocky uplands including, near Lough (lake) Island Reavy at **Drumena**, a well preserved oval-shaped one with a souterrain you can go inside (signposted off the A25 to Rathfriland, 2 miles south-west of Castlewellan). Dressed Mourne granite has been exported since the late eighteenth century, and the granite base of the Albert Memorial in London's Hyde Park came from a quarry west of Castlewellan.

The outstanding feature of **Castlewellan Forest Park** is the national arboretum dating from 1740, and developed in the 1870s by the fifth Earl of Annesley. The present arboretum is ten times the size of the old walled garden but the original south-sloping Annesley garden with two ancient Wellingtonias at the entrance, remains the showpiece. The largest of three greenhouses, about 100ft long, has aquatic plants growing in ponds and a collection of small tropical birds flying around freely inside. There is a spring garden, rhododendron wood, dwarf conifer beds and, along the edge of Castlewellan lake, a wood planted for autumn colour. Visitors using the carpark at the end of an avenue of tall limes (café and shop adjacent) will see a range of early eighteenth-century stable and farm buildings with three courtyards and a dovecote. Trout fishing in the lake is permitted and a popular pony trek is up Slievenaslat mountain.

Tollymore, the province's first forest park (opened 1955) belonged first to a Magennis and passed by inheritance to the Earls of Roden in 1798. The Roden mansion has been demolished but the demesne is celebrated for its follies, gateways and bridges. The main entrance, Barbican Gate, with chunky round castellated turrets and quatrefoil loopholes, and Bryansford Gate (the exit), with a Gothic arch, pinnacles and flying buttresses, are in keeping with the extravagant follies inside. These include a gateway with stone acorns and strange bobbles like buns (or baps) on top, a pair of immense gate pillars with spires and baps, a melancholy grotto or hermitage, and at least eight handsome bridges, some studded with large stone bobbles, over streams and close to waterfalls. An information centre and café are housed in what looks like a Gothic church but is actually a barn. Himalayan cedars, a 100ft Wellingtonia, a Monterey pine, silver firs and beeches are among outstanding trees. Most of the modern timber forests (conifers) are away on the other side of the river. The Mournes mountain rescue team is based in the log-cabined mountain centre on the Hilltown road.

Tollymore is a convenient departure point for walks into the heart of the Mournes, and there are marked paths to follow. The footpath west joins up with the **Hare's Gap**, the path south-west follows the course of the Spinkwee river up to Slievenaglogh and the Diamond Rocks. Up here you can see smoky quartz and black mica crystals in cavities in the granite. You might even come across the occasional topaz, beryl and tourmaline. Silver jewellery set with semi-precious Mourne stones, and ornaments made from polished granite, are sold in Kilkeel.

The coast from Newcastle south to Greencastle was notorious for smuggling and still has many coastguard lookout points. Whenever it paid, especially in the eighteenth and early nineteenth century, wines and spirits, tobacco, tea, silk and soap were brought across from the Isle of Man in small boats, landed at lonely beaches and carried on ponies through the mountains

The Barbican Gate, Tollymore Forest Park

along the **Brandy Pad**, an old smugglers' trail, to Hilltown in the
western foothills, the main distribution centre.

The **Kingdom of Mourne** has very precise limits, clearly
marked on the three main roads through it. It comprises the southern uplands and the coastal plain of south-facing farms with
potato fields enclosed in dry-stone walls, centred on the market
town and fishing port of Kilkeel. One 'welcome' sign is up on the
B27 from Kilkeel towards Hilltown, another is at Cassy Water on
the A2 5 miles west of Kilkeel. A third sign is 2 miles south of Newcastle, before Maggie's Leap, where the A2 turns in slightly. St
Patrick is said not to have ventured beyond a small stream here.
The task of making Christians out of the men of Mourne was left to
St Donard (died 506) who lived inside a stone cell on top of the
mountain now named after him. **Bloody Bridge** carpark, just

*Annalong Harbour
and Cornmill*

inside the kingdom boundary, is a convenient place from which to
climb Slieve Donard, although not the most attractive because of
quarrying. Scene of a massacre by the Magennises in 1641,
Bloody Bridge is where the Brandy Pad begins, running up the
side of the river.

The only access to the high Mournes is on foot or horseback
but the water authority allows vehicle access to the south end of
the **Silent Valley**   reservoir, two artificial lakes which supply ✳
Belfast's water — 30 million gallons of 'soft' water a day (Belfast's

Kilkeel Harbour

kettles never need descaling). Until recently, when erosion damage by thousands of pounding boots forced a halt, the Mourne Wall Walk brought walkers from far afield every June to walk the length of the 22-mile wall surrounding the Silent Valley. This huge wall of rough stone 5ft high runs up and down fifteen mountains and provided work for unemployed men in the Mournes from 1910 to 1922 every spring and summer. While the reservoir was being built (1923–33) a temporary rail link with Annalong brought cement up the mountain.

Several minor scenic roads between Annalong and Kilkeel will take you there. A simple route is up the B27 from Kilkeel — after 4 miles go right, up Head Road (1.7 miles) to the Water Commissioners' big red gates (open 10am-5pm). (Note: the B27 in Kilkeel is not well marked. Entering from the Annalong direction turn right just before the traffic lights.)

The road into the pretty fishing village of **Annalong** (population 1,800) is lined with dull modern houses. Turn down quickly to the marine park and harbour where a cornmill is working away at the river mouth. The panoramic backdrop of craggy **Slieve Binnian** with a patchwork of small fields running up the mountain slopes appears in hundreds of landscape paintings. The main stone-working district was above Annalong and the picturesque harbour was enlarged in the 1880s to cope with increased granite exports. The large stone-coasters that crowded out the fishing boats have gone and there is more than enough room now for the few inshore herring skiffs. A stone-dressing yard, navigation mark with a stone bobble, fishermen's cottages with flowery gardens, friendly pub and fish smokery are all part of the harbour scene. Across the bridge, the cornmill (restored) is powered by a ⚙ waterwheel and a 1920s Marshall 'hot-bulb' engine. Behind the visitor centre is a herb garden. A good way to climb Binnian is to walk up the west side of the Annalong river.

Going south through **Ballymartin** (population 200) it is easy to miss the small beach well below road level. Black Rock at Point Sands is a popular diving spot. Approaching Kilkeel on the east side, there is an 8ft-high dolmen, called the Crawtree Stone (on a 🝙 private road). The harbour at **Kilkeel** (population 6,050), bustling country town with the province's largest fleet, is busiest during landings and at auction time when fish, including herring, is sold on the quay. There are fish-processing factories around the port, pleasure angling off the piers and miles of lobster pots along the coast. The town has winding streets, terraced shops and houses with stepped pavements, and a bend in the middle round the ruins of the Old Church, a fifteenth-century church with a sixth-century ⚱ predecessor from which the town took its name — *cill caol* ('church at the narrows'). The Church of Ireland moved to a new church in 1818 and the Old Church became a Free School (for all denominations). The water in the granite bullaun (hollowed stone) in the churchyard will only cure a wart if you first drop a pin in it.

The megalithic tomb of **Dunnaman**, a court grave with a long 🝙 gallery, is at **Massforth** on the A2 west of Kilkeel, just inside the speed limit, behind St Colman's church. An unobtrusive sign on the parochial house indicates the path between clipped hedges. St Colman's is typical of the huge nineteenth-century Roman Cath- ⚱ olic churches with acres of adjacent concrete carparking which occupy sites on the edge of towns or out in the country miles from anywhere. Designed by O'Neill and Byrne of Belfast, St Colman's serves the people of Upper Mourne. It needed to be big since, when it opened in 1879, it had 5,000 parishioners. From 1540 (when the Catholic priests who controlled the Old Church in Kil- keel were expelled) until the relaxation of the penal code in the 1770s, the Catholic clergy ministered to their flocks in private houses or out in the open at Mass rocks. Even in the mid-nine- teenth century there were so few Catholic churches in Ireland that

Carlingford Lough

an average congregation was 3,000. The Presbyterians and other nonconformists had also been subject to the penal laws though to a lesser extent, and they too had few churches (e.g. one for every 1,500 Presbyterians in 1834). However, they have all made up for lost time since. St Colman's is Gothic squared granite. The pinnacles were added in about 1910. The T-shaped interior has rich stained glass with Stations of the Cross by Mayer of Munich. The church at **Attical** in the mountains is its small sister (1890).

About 3¹/₂ miles west of Kilkeel, **Kilfeaghan dolmen** (clearly signposted off A2) is at the end of a half-mile single track, with parking near a bed-and-breakfast sign. The dolmen has a gigantic capstone weighing 35 tons. (Access beyond the round gate pillars through small gates in the dry-stone walls.)

The ruined royal fortress of **Greencastle**, with a formidable jagged rock-cut ditch, looks across narrows to another Norman

Greencastle

pile guarding the opposite shore of **Carlingford Lough**. After 1495 the same constable (who had to be an Englishman) controlled both castles. Unlike Carlingford, Greencastle village was never much more than a hamlet of scattered farms, though it had a famous Ram Fair until about 1880. The remains of a medieval church are in a field between the massive ruins and a motte behind the coastguard station. The views are worth the short run from Kilkeel (4 miles). There are bird sanctuaries on the islands off **Cranfield Point** which has dunes and a sandy beach where the water is said to be the least cold in Ulster.

Stop for the view at the carpark above the **Spelga Dam**, which supplies water to Banbridge and Craigavon and has good trout fishing. South of the dam, the B27 runs close to Pigeon Rock Mountain, where there is a popular rock climb called The Thing. Tors on Hen Mountain opposite the Kinnahalla youth hostel also attract rock climbers.

One mile west of Kinnahalla, a few yards from the road at **Bush Town**, is the largest fairy thorn in Ulster, an ancient sprawling tree immune from the axe. Farmers are careful to plough round sacred thorns, a familiar feature of the Irish countryside, standing alone in potato fields. To cut one down invariably brings bad luck, and they are a potent image in Irish myth and magic.

INTERESTING PLACES AROUND THE MOURNES

Cornmill, Annalong Harbour
Working cornmill built about 1830, with waterwheel and 'hot-bulb' engine. Grain-drying kiln and millstones. Mills and milling exhibition. Guided tour. Shop.

Tollymore Forest Park
Naturalistic landscape park scattered with extravagant stone follies by the last Earl of Clanbrassil. Picturesque mountain and valley setting. Camping.

Silent Valley
Shapely water reservoir in the high Mournes ringed by 22-mile long wall. Parkland, views.

Fairy Thorn, Bush Town
Largest surviving sacred tree in Ulster. West of Kinnahalla youth hostel.

Greencastle
Ruined medieval fortress. Views across beautiful Carlingford Lough.

The Ulster poet Samuel Ferguson (1810–86) wrote a poem *The Fairy Thorn* about a group of young girls going at twilight to dance round one of these trees. Overcome by the intensity of the experience, they are seduced by the fairy folk:

'Soft o'er their bosoms' beating — the only human sound, They hear the silky footsteps of the silent fairy crowd, Like a river in the air . . .'.

At the T-junction the ruins of **Clonduff** church contain a Magennis gravestone (gate may be locked).

The many pubs of **Hilltown** (population 650) — eight in the high street — are a legacy from eighteenth-century smugglers who shared out their contraband here. The village has a livestock market on alternate Saturdays, a picturesque sheep fair and festival in early July and a large sale of rams in September. The Georgian market house opposite St John's parish church (1766) adjoins the old hostelry, the Downshire Arms (a pub with bed-and-breakfast accommodation). The weathervane on the pretty cupola is a fish, a reminder of the good fishing in the Bann and its tributaries. The forge at Katesbridge 10 miles downstream has a similar vane.

The more recent (1844) of the two Roman Catholic churches, which has Mayer of Munich stained glass, was built on land given by Hilltown's Protestant landlord. Small impoverished Catholic communities were often dependent on such gifts, which were not uncommon after emancipation. To visit the **Goward dolmen**,

Drumballyroney Church

cross Eight Mile Bridge where Redmond O'Hanlon, a famous high-
wayman, was slain in 1681, and take the B8 east. The dolmen is
signposted on the right after 2 miles. The track ends after less
than a mile at a carpark close to the dolmen — called locally Pat
Kearney's Big Stone.

From the square at **Rathfriland** (population 2,250) on top of
a steep hill, five streets with stepped terraces fall away sharply
on all sides. Before the combustion engine, the cheery residents
usually walked home, getting out of their traps and carts to spare
the ponies. The all-round views from such a position are likely to
be good, and so they are. The town has a mid-week variety market in the square and 3 livestock sale days a week. During the
nineteenth-century potato famine, the market house (1770) was
used as a soup kitchen though Rathfriland was spared the worst,
since cereals as well as potatoes were grown locally. Four substantial Presbyterian churches are testimony to past differences
of opinion. The old Quaker meeting house is now a scout hall, and
the small shop with pointed windows on the first floor was origin-
ally the town's Methodist chapel. A very prominent funnel-shaped
water tower occupies the high point in the riverless town, near the
site of a sixteenth-century Magennis castle, now vanished.

This part of County Down has distinguished connections with
pioneer Canada. The intrepid Catherine O'Hare, mother of the first

European child born west of the Rockies (delivered by Indian mid-wives in 1862), was herself born in Rathfriland in 1835. She and her husband, Augustus Schubert, joined 200 Overlanders who went west in search of gold, and blazed the trail for the Canadian Pacific Railway. Rathfriland has not yet erected a memorial to this remarkable woman, though in Kamloops city park British Columbia is named after her, and Armstrong also has a monument.

The scenic Dromara road (B7) from Rathfriland passes **Drumballyroney** parish church and school where Patrick Prunty, father of the novelists Charlotte, Emily and Anne Brontë, was parish schoolmaster before moving to England, becoming a clergyman and 'improving' his name. Several other places connected with him or his family are signposted (Brontë homeland drive). These include ruined Magherally Old Church which, however, is more interesting as the burial place of the scholar and author Helen Waddell (1889–1965). Best known for the phenomenally successful novel *Peter Abelard*, her reputation was built on some passionate renderings in English of secular ninth- to twelfth-century Latin lyrics. The noble many-arched stone bridge at **Katesbridge** village is said to have withstood the weight of several Churchill tanks during World War II. It is a good spot for fishing (salmon, trout, pike). Although he has a new electrified forge, the blacksmith keeps the old forge and handbellows in good repair in case there is a power cut while he is shoeing.

There are various mottes around **Ballyroney** village, an enormous Presbyterian church, a lough with an island in the centre and, signposted on the right, the side road to the **Legananny dolmen.** This elegant tripod is the best known, most photographed of the province's dolmens — partly because of its theatrical setting on the southern slope of Slieve Croob and also for its unusually tall and slender uprights. It has genuine star quality. Continuing along the B7, St Michael's church, at a kink in the road at **Finnis**, is next to a Mass house of 1760 (now an outhouse of the parochial house) which this large Roman Catholic church replaced in the 1830s. The architect, Thomas Duff, also designed Newry cathedral which was started the same year, though St Michael's took a decade to complete. There are many old Mass sites in this area where a small tributary runs into the infant **Lagan**, only 2 miles from its source on Slieve Croob. A mile north is the village of **Dromara** with nice hump bridges over the broadening river. The scenic road from Dromara to Castlewellan gives views across Dundrum Bay to the Mournes.

Katesbridge

Banbridge (population 9,650) is the industrial centre of this district. It was an important stop on the Dublin-Belfast road. The underpass which slices down the middle of the broad, very steep, main street was cut out in 1834 to assist Royal Mail coaches to go through the town centre. Ironically the coach inn had to be demolished to make room for the coach underpass. In Church Square the statue of Captain Francis Crozier RN, who discovered the North-West Passage in 1848, is flanked by four large and friendly looking polar bears. A blue plaque on a large Regency house nearby records that this was his birthplace in 1796. Banbridge's other blue plaque is to hymn writer ('What a friend we have in Jesus') and benefactor of Port Hope, Ontario, Joseph Scriven (1819–86), born in a house on the Dromore road.

At Tullylish, on the road from Banbridge to Gilford, part of the old mill is a restaurant. John Yeats, father of the poet W.B. Yeats, was a native of Tullylish. At **Gilford** (population 1,500) the old mill has only recently ceased to function.

Legananny Dolmen

A dramatic motte and bailey and a modest Anglican cathedral underline the past importance of **Dromore** (population 3,100), a market town on the Lagan where St Colman founded an abbey in the sixth century. Every building of significance was destroyed in 1641. A Celtic cross built into the cathedral graveyard boundary wall and a single stone (St Colman's Pillow) in the south wall of the chancel, are the only relics of early times. Two outstanding bishops of Dromore, both men of great literary distinction, Jeremy Taylor (1613–67) and Thomas Percy (1729–1811), are buried here (for access ask at the rectory). Taylor, author of *Holy Living; Holy Dying*, one of the best of all seventeenth-century prose works, rebuilt the cathedral in the 1660s. Percy, who enlarged it, is best

The Crozier Monument, Banbridge

remembered for his *Reliques* of ancient English poetry — a collection of old ballads that was a main literary influence on the poetic revival signalled by Wordsworth's *Lyrical Ballads* (1798). The stocks outside the town hall are occasionally used — for brides and grooms before their wedding. A huge viaduct south of the town once carried the Banbridge and Lisburn railway. The local running club holds races on the third Saturday in August in memory of Sam Ferris who ran in three Olympic marathons but did not win any. There is a horse fair in Dromore in late September.

Between Dromore and Lough Neagh, the Lagan meanders down through meadowland, under eighteenth-century whinstone bridges and past small country towns founded in the plantation period. A feature of the area is yeoman planter's houses (late seventeenth- to eighteenth-century) and massive round gate pillars with conical tops marking the entrance to farms and fields. Taking the B2 west from Dromore for 5½ miles, a white late eighteenth-century slated farmhouse stands on the B9 cross-roads. From here you are 1½ miles from each of three villages. Go south for Donaghcloney, straight on for Waringstown, north for Magheralin.

The former factory village of **Donaghcloney** (population

650), where kerbs and bridge parapets are lavishly painted red, white and blue, has a solid redbrick parish church with a war memorial in front. It is an odd combination of church and house — net curtains at the windows and a television aerial on the roof.

Half a mile west of the B2/B9 crossroads, the turning to Waringstown is marked by a huge pair of gate pillars at a delightful thatched yeoman's house (built about 1680). A second pair flanks the farmyard. The founder of **Waringstown** (population 1,150) built himself a two-storey Jacobean-style gentleman's house, one of the first unfortified houses in Ireland (1667). A third storey was added later. A handsome flaky pink-painted mansion with tall Tudor-revival chimneys, it looks solid enough but is actually built of mud and rubble. Across the road are seven curious terraces in sets of three and four houses, with scalloped garden walls and railings — some of Waring's seventeenth-century cottages rebuilt in 1930s style. The Waring fortune was founded on linen, and Dutch-style houses were built along the main street for the weavers, most of whom came from Flanders. The present whitewashed houses with flowerbeds, though modern, have a certain harmony. A yeoman's house (built 1698, now a restaurant) stands on a high bend in the road. Waringstown cricket club, founded in 1851, fields a strong team (as does Donaghcloney). The big

Dromore Cross

house and the parish church (1681) had the same designer, James Robb, chief mason of the king's works in Ireland. The church's Jacobean interior is largely of ancient oak — roof, panelling, choir screen and a notable pulpit.

There is fishing at New Forge Bridge near Drumcro House on the B9 near **Magheralin** (population 900). Big trees, meadows, planters' houses and old cornmills make this an attractive approach to this blink-and-miss village. Stained glass in the Victorian parish church includes windows by Irish artists depicting scenes from the lives of Irish saints. The eighteenth-century memorials came from the church of 1657 up the road, in use until 1845, now ruined but well tended. To see the stained glass, ask at the rectory (pointed door in wall opposite, always open). John Macoun, naturalist and explorer of the Rockies, was born in Magheralin in 1831. He was the surveyor for the Canadian Pacific Railway.

Though small (population 950) **Moira** feels like a real town, with a town hall (former courthouse, built about 1800), a wide main street lined with red-berried rowans and eighteenth-century blackstone houses divided by carriage archways. Built mostly by Sir Arthur Rawdon, whose famous formal gardens have vanished, the town has a habit of winning civic flower awards. For most of the year the place is a mass of flowering shrubs, roses, flowerbeds and hanging baskets. On the north side, a long grassy avenue terminates in Moira parish church, a rather top-heavy but most appealing building of 1723 where William Butler Yeats (the poet's grandfather) was curate in the 1830s. The communion rails came from the staircase of the Rawdon mansion. Looking down from the church, the lawns seem to continue, unbroken, into the flowerbeds and trees of the old Rawdon demesne but they are in fact bisected by the busy A3 trunk road. The road opposite Station Road leads to Berwick Hall, a thatched yeoman's house of 1700. Moira was the scene of a victory in AD637 by the king of Tara over Comgall, king of Ulster.

4 COUNTY ARMAGH AND NEWRY

St Patrick made Armagh the centre of his mission in Ireland in the
fifth century. He might have built his church among the ruins of
Eamhain Mhacha (Navan Fort), destroyed in AD332, but he
settled for a high hill 2 miles east. Long before the coming of
Christianity, the House of the Red Branch ruled all Ulster (*Uladh*)
from the stronghold at Navan Fort, a great earthworks off the A28
near Armagh city which appears as *Isamnium* in Ptolemy's
second-century world atlas. Irish vernacular literature, by far the
oldest and richest north of the Alps, had its greatest flowering in
this part of Ireland.

The M1 from Belfast to Dungannon runs along the top of
County Armagh, across the flattish countryside of Lough Neagh's
southern shore. Although not the most picturesque introduction
to this delightfully rural county, it gives fast access to the populated Lurgan/Portadown area — the comparatively industrialised
* north-east corner. Craigavon is very thoroughly signposted from
the M1. Turn off at junction 11 for a look at the province's first
'New Town', designated in 1965, and named after James Craig,
Lord Craigavon (1871–1941), first prime minister of Northern
Ireland.

The plan was for the existing towns of Lurgan and Portadown
to develop towards each other in linear fashion, taking overspill
from Belfast and growing to a population of 180,000. The mayoral
chairs from Lurgan and Portadown, removed to the civic centre,
stand outside the council chamber. However, the town is still
waiting for the people to arrive. Large isolated buildings stand in a
landscape of manmade lakes, dual carriageways, roundabouts
and bridges, at the end of a stumpy little motorway, the M12. The
Belfast-Dublin railway line runs between two 'balancing' lakes
which help drain this part of the Lough Neagh basin. Only about
6ft deep, the lakes are used for boating and other water sports in
summer. Outside Craigavon's bold and uncompromising essay in
town planning, the scenery soon reverts to a pastoral landscape

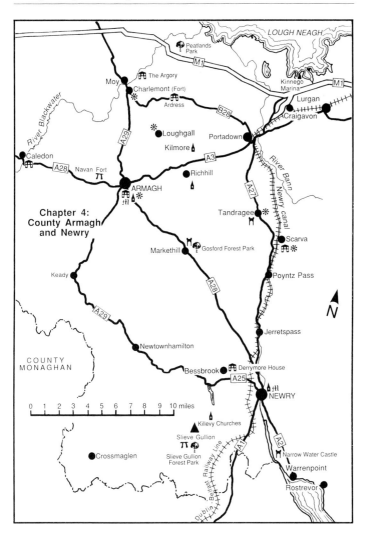

of small dairy farms and winding leafy lanes.

An unpretentious town with an agreeable broad main street, **Lurgan** (population 21,000) was granted to the Brownlows of Nottingham (later Lords Lurgan) after 1607. The place did not really get going until the end of the century when Samuel Waring introduced linen-damask weaving to Ulster. Textile firms and clothing manufacturers are still important here. You can see weavers' cottages, with projecting front parlours built to accommodate the loom, if you go looking for them around Bownes Lane. The old Shankill burial ground and eighteenth-century parish church in the town centre contain interesting memorials, including the Brownlow family monument. The parish's most famous personality is Master McGrath, the coursing greyhound which won the Waterloo Cup three times between 1868 and 1871. Behind the pulpit a stained glass window bears his image. A local bard composed a ballad to him, and the council placed his effigy at the top of the town's coat of arms. His proud master, the second Lord Lurgan, raised an imposing monument outside the Brownlow mansion on the grave of the noble Irish canine.

The precious *Book of Armagh*, oldest of the great illuminated Irish manuscripts (now in Trinity College Library, Dublin), was 'lost' for 200 years among the books of Arthur Brownlow, a seventeenth-century antiquarian. The manuscript somehow found its way into Brownlow's library after being pawned in 1680 for £5.
 Brownlow House is a romantic honey-coloured Tudor-style mansion of 1836 with tall chimney-pots and lanterned tower, designed by the Edinburgh architect William Playfair (1783-1857). It is now the headquarters of the grandly-named Imperial Grand Black Chapter of the British Commonwealth (cognate with the
 Orange Order). The grounds, landscaped in the eighteenth century, are a public park, with a lake and golf course. The mansion's present owners have renovated the interior and occasionally open the house to the public.

Distinguished Lurganites include James Logan (1674–1751), scholar and scientist. Son of a Quaker schoolmaster, he helped found Pennsylvania, becoming president of the infant state's
 council. A plaque in High Street on one of the gate pillars of the Quaker meeting house marks his birthplace. Lurgan had the first meeting house in Ireland (1653). Field Marshal Sir John Dill, who liaised between the British and US governments in World War II, was a Lurganite (died 1947, buried Arlington National Cemetery, Washington), as was Lord Dugan, governor of South Australia until 1939 and of Victoria until 1949. The poet, painter and polemicist George Russell ('Æ') was born in William Street in 1867. He shared with W.B. Yeats an interest in mysticism and the supernatural, was much involved in the Gaelic revival, and edited the influential *Irish Homestead* and *Irish Statesman* for nearly 30 years.

The building of the canal from Newry to Lough Neagh in the

1730s brought prosperity to **Portadown** (population 21,350). Like Lurgan, this busy textile and manufacturing town developed with the linen industry, which gave way to synthetic fibres in about 1950. Today it has factories making carpets, industrial ceramics and jam. Roses appear on the town's old coat of arms, a reminder of the days when Portadown rose grower Sam McGredy carried off all the trophies, starting in 1905 with 'Countess of Gosford', a huge pink rose. In the heyday of rail, Portadown was a major junction with large marshalling yards. There is a big cattle market on Fridays when the farmers' Volvos and Mercedes are parked up towards Colin Turner's art gallery (144 Thomas Street ⌂ — landscapes). A covered market is held on Saturday in the William Street halls.

The wide sloping main street has a triangular 'square' at either end. More than a dozen denominations have built churches and chapels in one small central area. A Baptist church stands adjacent to a convent, nearby is a small Elim Pentecostal chapel and a Presbyterian church, a blackstone Catholic church in William Street looks across at a Methodist church which has an imposing façade but is all blackstone 'potted meat' behind. In front of St Mark's (Anglican), the bronze statue of a nineteenth-century Irish-Unionist Party leader is adorned with an Orange sash in July when Portadown Loyalists commemorate the Battle of the Boyne in 1690. There are plenty of other places of worship too: up near the A4/B28 roundabout, next to an older, ruined church, the grey concrete exterior of the Catholic church of St John Baptist, Drumcree, conceals a harmonious interior.

Sir Robert Hart (1835–1911), who created the Chinese Post Office and founded their lighthouse service, was born in Woodhouse Street. Hart's house has been knocked down to make way for a supermarket but he appears in street and school names and is commemorated in St Mark's vestry. Queen's University, Belfast, has his voluminous diaries of 54 years in China. He also introduced the Chinese to the music of the brass band — one of his less fêted achievements. This was a fitting service from a native of Portadown, since the town goes in for bands in a big way — including silver, flute, pipe and accordion bands — and has a good male voice choir. It is a vigorous kind of place, with courteous people in the banks and shops. Tourist information and a street plan is available from the old Carnegie Library, Edward Street, beyond the police station.

Fishing on the Bann near Portadown

Lough Neagh

The main recreation area for north Armagh is Lough Neagh around **Oxford Island** and Kinnego marina. Anglers come here in hordes to fish the **Bann** up to Portadown. The lough is fished commercially for freshwater herring (pollan), and dollaghan (a kind of huge salmon-trout) is caught around Washing Bay, **Maghery** and in the Main river flowing into the lough near Shane's Castle. But Lough Neagh, which covers 153 sq. miles, is most famous for eels. Millions of elvers (young eels) swim up the Bann from the north coast but about 20 million lucky ones are saved the trouble. They are trapped at Coleraine and transported by tanker south to the lough to grow to maturity. In the spring and early summer there are as many as 200 boats line-fishing for eels.

The shores of this inland sea and its handful of islands have large bird populations, especially at the southern end. Swans breed on Croaghan Island, a colony of great crested grebe nest in the reed beds of Oxford Island, with a heronry on Raughlan peninsula opposite. Tours of the nature reserve start from Oxford Island information centre. The ruined keep and holy well on wooded **Coney Island**, a bird sanctuary at the Blackwater estuary, can be reached by boat from the small marina at Maghery or from Kinnego. A hand-operated car ferry across the Upper Bann was a convenient way to explore the marshy land round here but now there is no one to work it and you have to go round the long way.

The level of the lough was lowered in 1846 and twice since, the last time in 1959, but drainage round the edge is still not adequate for arable farming. US troops used the area as a training and assembly ground in preparation for the invasion of Europe (1942–5) and there are still some old airfield remains. Pieces of petrified wood, altered by silica salts, are sometimes washed up on the shore. Belfast street hawkers used to sell them as knife sharpeners with the cry

'Lough Neagh hones! Lough Neagh hones!
You put them in sticks, and you take them out stones!'

Be prepared for the nuisance of the Lough Neagh fly (chiron-omid midge) which has a spectacular emergence at certain times in spring and summer. These harmless non-biting midges des-cend in clouds on windless days and get into everything.

Sand and gravel extraction from the lough is long established, and lignite is becoming big business. An estimated 200 million recoverable tons of this brown coal, half the price of imported coal, has been identified at **Coagh** on the west shore, twice that amount at **Crumlin** near the airport, and an even thicker seam directly underneath **Ballymoney** town. The only natural energy source discovered in significant quantities in the province, lignite is a focus of future energy development (intensified since a plan to pipe natural gas from the Irish Republic's Kinsale field receded in 1984).

For unusual peaty landscapes visit **Peatlands Park** where wooded drumlins stick up through the flat bog of cut-over peat (M1 exit 13). The Department of the Environment has a narrow gauge railway here with locomotives formerly used for peat extraction. The Birches, 4 miles due east (or take M1 exit 12), was the ancestral home of 'Stonewall' Jackson, the great Confederate general killed in 1863 at Chancellorsville in the American Civil War. A blue plaque in the pretty courtyard of Waugh's farm records the connection.

The Armagh/Down county border south of Portadown follows the line of the Upper Bann/Newry canal. Down settlements benefiting from the construction in the 1730s of the 18-mile canal included Scarva, Poyntz Pass and Jerrettspass. These sleepy places are heavy with history. Anyone attending the 'Sham Fight' pageant at **Scarva** (population 250) on 13 July (see page 23) will tell you

Plaque at Waugh's Farm, The Birches

about the seventeenth-century significance of the three passes
of Scarva, Poyntz and Jerrett. However, the importance of
Scarva as a strategic point along the line of the huge defensive
earthworks and ditch, variously called the Black Pig's Dyke and
the Dane's Cast, is of much greater antiquity. A section of this
earthworks, built in the fourth century BC by the Ulster kings after
their retreat east from Navan Fort (*Eamhain Mhacha*), is clearly
visible in the grounds of Scarva House, a two-storey house of
about 1717 with a charming courtyard. The large raths, or forts, of
Lisnagade (1¼ miles east of Scarva village) and Lisnavaragh (½
mile west of Lisnagade on a bend in the road) are believed to mark
the north end of the Dane's Cast.

The cathedral town of **Newry** (population 19,400) is well
placed at the head of the 'Gap of the North'. Through this pass
between two ranges of hills the men of Ulster sallied forth to harry
the tribes of Leinster in the days of the Fianna legends. Because
of its strategic position, the town was repeatedly destroyed in the
wars for the control of the North. Newry is named from a yew tree
said to have been planted by St Patrick himself. An abbey on the
east bank of the Clanrye river was colonised by Cistercians in
1153. In the sixteenth century Sir Nicholas Bagenal, marshal of
Ireland and founder of the town, used it as his residence. All trace
of the abbey has vanished except for a slab of granite inscribed
with a plain Celtic cross inside McCann's Bakery. One stone
castle after another was built near the abbey. The third and last
one was destroyed in 1566 by Shane (the Proud) O'Neill. In 1578,
Bagenal built the first post-Reformation (i.e. Protestant) church in
Ireland on top of the steep hill 500yd due east of the town hall.
The church has kept its original tower, despite a battering in 1641,
and Bagenal's coat of arms is on a tablet in the porch.

There is a good view of Bagenal's church from the garden of
the Poor Clares' tall pink convent in High Street. The convent
garden almost encircles the burial ground of the town's first Presbyterian (Unitarian) congregation, established in 1650. John
Mitchel (1815–75), the celebrated republican and author, is buried
here. (If the graveyard is locked, ask at the convent about
access). Mitchel's best known book is the famous *Jail Journal*, a
classic of anglophobia but quite readable. His statue stands in
the pedestrianised shopping centre.

The A1 dual carriageway slices through the east side of Newry
over the site of the abbey and divides this old quarter from the
rest of the town. Newry's considerable prosperity in the eight-

Newry Town Hall

John Mitchel Statue

eenth century stemmed largely from its ingenious waterway, the earliest inland canal in the British Isles. It was built in 1730–42 and extended down to **Carlingford Lough** as a ship canal in 1761. The town's mercantile past is reflected in names such as Buttercrane Quay, Sugar Island and Sugarhouse Quay, close to the six-storey redbrick Sands's Mill (1876) with rounded windows. Tall eighteenth-century warehouses line the quays. The main downstream (export) traffic was linen, Tyrone coal, Mourne granite, farm produce — and early emigrants who bought passage on American flaxseed ships returning to New York and Philadelphia with Irish linen. By the 1840s, however, canal trade had declined.

PLACES TO VISIT IN AND AROUND NEWRY

Newry Canal (town stretch)
Earliest inland canal in the British
Isles, started 1730, with associated warehouses, quays and
swing bridge.

**Newry Museum & Arts
Centre**
Prehistory and history of the 'Gap
of the North' area. Temporary
exhibitions in arts centre.

Bessbrook Model Village
Unspoilt linen mill village, founded
1845, once linked by 3-mile
tramway to Newry. Model for
Cadbury village of Bournville.

Slieve Gullion Forest Park
(5 miles south-west)
Neolithic passage grave and wild
goats on the south summit, panoramic views of rugged ring dyke.

Killevy Churches
Two churches joined together on
site of important fifth-century
nunnery, occupied until 1542.

The last vessel passed through the fourteen locks in the 1930s
and, except for one at the bottom of Monaghan Street, the swing
bridges have gone. Even so, the idea of re-opening the canal for
tourism is one that won't go away.

The characterful town hall, half in Down, half in Armagh, strad-
dles the river which runs in parallel with the canal. A marble bust
of Charles Russell, Lord Russell of Killowen, stands in the foyer.
Born in 1832 at 50 Queen Street (now Dominic Street), Russell
was leading counsel for Parnell in 1888 and Lord Chief Justice of
England (1894–1900). The bust was a gift from the English Law
Society. The museum and an arts centre are across the road. The
autumn arts festival attracts international names.

Since about 1750 Newry has been the cathedral town of the
Catholic diocese of Dromore, and the Tudor-Gothic cathedral (St
Patrick and St Colman) occupies a prominent position. Thomas
Duff was the architect (1825) though the tower and transepts
were added in 1888, and the cathedral's rich stained glass and
mosaics more recently still. Duff designed the Classical courthouse with glass dome (1841), and had a hand in the Anglican
church of St Mary's. The Unitarian church of 1853 is the work of
his pupil, W.J. Barre, also of Newry.

No. 1 Trevor Hill, a five-bay granite house, is the oldest (1775)
in a row of handsome late Georgian houses built for the gentry
and their clergy. They include a fine mansion occupied by the
Bank of Ireland for the past century, designed in about 1826, pos-

Narrow Water Castle, near Newry

sibly by Francis Johnston. Atmospheric crumbly corners of old Newry include River Street (south of John Mitchel Place) — a row of tiny houses with eagles over the doors, and Ballybot ('poor town') beyond the former cattle market. At one time the universal roofing material was slate from the North Wales quarries, and many Newry houses are still roofed with 'Bangor blues'. The town is a main shopping centre, with a general market on Thursday and Saturday. An open-air market on Sunday, a few miles south at **Jonesborough**, draws big crowds from both sides of the border.

Four miles from Newry, along the fast A2 towards Warrenpoint, the picturesque ruin of **Narrow Water Castle** stands on a rock, jutting into the estuary. It was built in about 1560 to guard the entrance to the Clanrye river which flows into Carlingford Lough a mile south. King John's army crossed the lough by pontoon bridge in 1210, close to the mound of a late twelfth-century castle, about 400yd further on.

Warrenpoint and Rostrevor are small resorts, 3 miles apart, on the lough's sheltered north shore. The port at **Warrenpoint** (population 4,800) handles container traffic and substantial coal,

Warrenpoint, County Down

timber, paper and grain tonnages, with a regular service to Rotter-
dam. When Newry port closed in the 1970s, this harbour was enlarged, and the town has an animated waterfront, long promenade, and a spacious square used mostly as a carpark but also
for fêtes and occasional markets.

The road into **Rostrevor** (population 2,100) winds past a tall
granite obelisk erected in memory of Major General Robert Ross   ✳
(1766–1814). He was commander of a small British force which
captured Washington in 1814 after unexpectedly defeating the
Americans at Bladensburg. He and his officers burned the White
House after eating a hearty dinner in President Madison's abandoned dining room. Ross was killed at Baltimore soon afterwards.
Palm trees and mimosa flourish in the mild climate of Rostrevor.
There are oak trees in the square, nice old houses, and a long seafront. Natural oakwoods make a fine show in autumn when the
leaves turn. Behind the town, on the wooded slopes of Slieve-
martin, the Cloghmore ('great stone') is a geological curiosity. To
see this enormous glacial erratic block weighing 40 tons, follow
the forest drive to the carpark, then walk to the viewpoint ($^1/_2$ mile)

Ring of Gullion, near Newry

beyond the pines and on up to the stone. Camping in **Kilbroney Park** and Rostrevor Forest is popular.

The bronze bell of Rostrevor's Catholic church was rescued from the ruins of Kilbroney church a mile up the mountain road (B25) where St Bronach, patron saint of seafarers, founded a monastery in the sixth century. A granite cross survives from the early foundation.

From the top of Slieve Gullion the whole of the **Ring of Gullion** is laid out below — a ring dyke of wild and rugged hills about 7 miles in diameter, rising to over 1,000ft. Often shrouded in mist, the mountain dominates the 'Gap of the North' and is rich in myth and legend. Like Navan Fort, it features in the fourth-century prose epic *Taín Bó Cualnge* ('The cattle raid of Cooley'), a famous cycle of stories dating from the Iron Age, in which the chief hero of the men of Ulster is Cuchulainn, who lived around Slieve Gullion. The central story is how he fights off invaders from Connaught who have come to claim a brown bull belonging to Conor, King of Ulster (ruling at Navan Fort). Writing was introduced to Ireland in St Patrick's time, when the *Taín* and other sagas were written down. The region's vanishing folklore is also well documented. Just in time, it found a popular chronicler,

Michael J. Murphy (born 1913), who collected enough Irish folk stories and superstitions ('pisthogues') to fill 300 volumes.

The southern end of Slieve Gullion is a forest park, with a steep drive up to the top. Wild goats move along the ridges and a Neolithic passage grave, known as the House of Calliagh ('old 𝜋 witch') Birra, crowns the south summit (1,894ft). The water of a lake on the bare north summit, close to a round cairn, is said to turn hair grey and cure toothache.

The **Killevy churches**, on Gullion's south-east slope (sign- ♦ posted from A1 and B113), are the back-to-back ruins of two rectangular churches, one tenth-century, the other probably thirteenth-century, joined together but with no way through from one to the other. The most striking feature is the massive lintelled door of the earlier church (west side). The pointed window of the other (east) church dates from the fifteenth century. Killevy is the site of an important fifth-century nunnery founded by St Monenna (also called St Blinne who, like St Bronach, was a patron saint of seafarers). A granite slab in the graveyard is traditionally this female saint's grave, and a holy well associated with her is further up the mountain. The Vikings raided the nunnery in 923 but it was in use as a convent of Augustinian nuns up until the dissolution (1542).

Other spiritual testaments to the ancient denizens of the region include: Ballymacdermot cairn, near Bernish viewpoint 𝜋 (1¹/2 miles from Killevy, back towards Newry); Ballykeel dolmen, between Slieve Gullion and Camlough; and the eighth-century pillar stone of Kilnasaggart, with thirteen crosses and a long Irish inscription carved on it, 1¹/4 miles south of Jonesborough. The ruined tower near the pillar stone was part of Moyry Castle, built by the English in 1601 to control the pass below.

The A25 runs between two waters at the north end of Camlough, a ribbony lake which supplies the taps of Newry and is a good angling spot. The south Armagh hills peter out at the border in small rock-strewn, stone-ditched fields fringed with yellow whin, beyond the Dorsey (a pre-Christian defensive earthworks contemporary with Navan Fort), down towards **Crossmaglen** (population 1,300). This remote village has an exceptionally large market square, an army base and a reputation for, among other things, horse breeding and handmade lace.

One of the earliest of the model villages associated with the Industrial Revolution, the mill village of **Bessbrook** (population 2,750) was founded in 1845 by John Grubb Richardson, a Quaker

Derrymore House, near Bessbrook

linen manufacturer, to house workers at his huge flax mill. Solidly built houses with slate roofs are ranged in terraces round two squares linked by a broad road. Both squares have a green in the middle. The Richardsons built schools, a butcher's shop, dairy, dispensary, savings bank, village hall and several churches but no pub, pawnshop or police house, these last three being deemed undesirable and/or unnecessary. Everything was built of granite quarried nearby, and flax for the mill was grown locally in large quantities. An eighteen-arch viaduct, built in 1851, still carries the Belfast-Dublin railway (trains stop at the small station between here and Newry). Later, in 1885, a narrow gauge electric tram (maximum speed 12mph) brought workers in from Newry 3 miles away. The linens of the Bessbrook Spinning Company were world famous. After World War II, the industry declined and the tramway closed. The big mill (which operated until 1972), its pond, weirs and sluices, and smaller mills along the line of the old tram, are an interesting part of Ulster's industrial archaeology. Earlier than Saltaire in Yorkshire (1852) and Port Sunlight in Cheshire (1888), Bessbrook was the inspiration for the Cadbury garden village of Bournville near Birmingham.

Derrymore House, a delightful eighteenth-century thatched
cottage orné-style manor house just outside the village, was built
by Isaac Corry (1755–1813), MP for Newry and last chancellor of
the Irish Exchequer. As chancellor, he imposed the window tax,
was involved in a number of duels (with pistols), and supported
union between Ireland and Britain. He was a friend of Lord Castlereagh, and the Act of Union was drafted in the pretty drawing room
in 1800. The house is in National Trust care .

Livestock markets 3 days a week bring bustle to aptly named
Markethill village (population 1,250). But the main attraction is
nearby **Gosford Forest Park** with a large mock-Norman castle
in the middle. The first Norman-revival castle in the British Isles,
Gosford (1819) was designed for the Achesons, Earls of Gosford,
by Thomas Hopper who later built Penrhyn Castle in Wales. It is a
huge sprawling building with a square keep, round tower with a circular drawing room, and extremely thick walls. The fourth earl sold
the furniture in 1921 to pay his debts. In World War II the castle
was in military use (writer Anthony Powell was billeted here) and at
one time it housed a circus, including the lions.

The castle replaced a manor house (burnt in about 1805) where
Jonathan Swift spent many months as a guest of the Achesons,
his friends, between 1728 and 1730. Several of the nature walks

Gosford Castle, Markethill

round the estate were devised by him. Dean Swift's Chair, a half-moon seat hedged with yew in the arboretum, is where Swift sat in fine weather composing poems, some of them about Markethill. The Achesons were indulgent hosts but Sir Arthur Acheson was greatly offended when Swift instructed staff, in Sir Arthur's absence, to cut down a fairy tree outside the main gate. Swift's poem, 'On cutting down the old thorn at Markethill', explains why he did it. Close to the ruined house are the original farm buildings, waterwheel and laundry. Below a pretty bridge with waterfall is Swift's Well. A miniature round tower, with a distinctly Teutonic look about it, was built by German prisoners-of-war. The forest park is used by caravanners and campers all year round. It has some fine old walnut trees and a walled cherry garden.

The main street at **Tandragee** (population 2,200), on the Cusher river, curves up the steep hill to a baronial-style castle built in about 1837 by the sixth Duke of Manchester. In the 1950s it became a potato crisp factory. A tour of the factory provides an opportunity to see the inner courtyards — and to learn something about the potato, Ireland's staple food from the mid-seventeenth century. An earlier O'Hanlon castle on the site was confiscated at the plantation of Ulster, but the O'Hanlons recaptured and destroyed it in 1641. Outlawed Redmond O'Hanlon, killed at Hilltown in 1681, is buried at Relicarn (2 miles south-east). The ninth-century Bell of Armagh (now in the National Museum, Dublin) was discovered near his grave in the eighteenth century.

The City of Armagh and Surrounding Area

Spiritual capital of Ireland for 1,500 years, **Armagh** (population 12,700) has preserved an air of quiet dignity and refinement against considerable odds. The city is the seat of both the Anglican and the Roman Catholic archbishops of Ireland. The twin-spired Catholic cathedral is on a hill north-west of the city. Two marble archbishops standing on plinths outside the entrance look mildly across to the Anglican cathedral which crowns the ancient rath where St Patrick built his stone church in AD445. Steep streets, climbing and intersecting, follow the curve of the ditches and banks which ringed the rath and its church. Parking around the Anglican cathedral is not feasible but down the hill there is usually space on the **Mall**, a pleasant, green, tree-lined prom-enade where cricket is played in the summer.

The Mall used to be the city's racecourse, and many of the

Georgian doorway, The Mall, Armagh City

Georgian townhouses along its length have large balconied first-floor reception rooms which would have given a good view of the starting and finishing posts. Archbishop Richard Robinson (1709–94) ejected the punters and turned the course into a mall. The moving spirit behind the city's fine eighteenth-century architecture, Archbishop Robinson was patron of the celebrated Francis Johnston (1761–1829), who left his mark on his native Armagh and, later, on Georgian Dublin.

The dignified gaol (disused) at the south end of the Mall had gallows outside until 1866. The fine Classical **courthouse** closing the north end is by Francis Johnston (1809). On the east side the **Armagh County Museum**, in an Ionic schoolhouse of 1833 with a small lawn of its own, is a most rewarding visit. Its art gallery, natural history and folk collections and library are especially notable. Self-portraits and other works by 'Æ' (George Russell — died 1935) and James Sleator (born Armagh 1889) are on display. At the north-east corner, the **Sovereign's House** contains the museum of the Royal Irish Fusiliers. It was built in 1810 of stone left over from the courthouse. On the west side, an extravagant small church with a campanile is a gospel hall of 1884.

The local building stone, used to good effect, is warm-coloured Carboniferous limestone. The buildings in Charlemont Place, the

The Planetarium, Armagh City

courthouse and the house called Patrick's Fold (36 Scotch Street) are good examples. The colour varies from grey to pink, yellow and red. The brighter stone, from quarries south of the city and called 'Armagh marble', was polished and used for pavements, doorsteps and mantelpieces.

✳   The **planetarium**, in the grounds of an eighteenth-century observatory, has 'star shows' in a domed theatre, a full-scale mock-up of a Gemini spacecraft and original equipment used by American astronauts. Opened in 1968 — its first director was Patrick ('Sky at Night') Moore — the planetarium grew out of the **observatory** which was founded in 1790 by Archbishop Robinson as part of his plan for a university. The building, by Johnston, was not finished until 1825. It has astronomical books and instruments of great interest. Some of these are on public display in the planetarium and include a Herschel Newtonian mirror and Gregorian telescope by Adams, and a 20-inch radius quadrant belonging to George III which were presented to the observatory by Queen Victoria in 1840. Across the road (A3) from the planetarium are the red castellations of the **Royal School**, founded by James I in 1608 and rebuilt by Robinson in 1774.

In AD447 St Patrick ordained that his church in Armagh should have pre-eminence over all the churches of Ireland. Since then, about eighteen successive churches have occupied the hill top.

The **Anglican cathedral** of St Patrick has a medieval core,
and was restored in 1765 by Archbishop Robinson. However, its
present sandstone exterior is later. The cathedral was brand new
when Thackeray visited it in 1842 and admired the eighteenth-
century monuments inside. These include a statue of Sir Thomas
Molyneux by Roubiliac, one of Dean Drelincourt by the Flemish
sculptor Rysbrack, and a bust of Archbishop Robinson by
Nollekens. Notice a fine kneeling figure of Primate William Stuart
by Chantrey, a brass tablet to the archaeologist and historian
Bishop Reeves (who retrieved the lost *Book of Armagh*), a broken
eleventh-century market cross, and a collection of pagan stone
figures in the north transept (chapterhouse) where seventeenth-
century memorials to the Earls of Charlemont are set in the west
wall. The Royal Irish Fusiliers' chapel is in the south transept.

Outside, a small door at the east end leads to Archbishop Patrick O'Scanail's thirteenth-century crypt. Note grotesque medieval stone heads high up round the exterior walls and a sundial of
1706. A slab in the north transept west wall marks the position of
the grave of Brian Boru, high king of Ireland, who defeated the
Norsemen at Clontarf in 1014. Brian, aged 73, and his son Mur-
chard were killed in the battle and their bodies brought to this
place for burial. Here, in 1004, Brian had formally acknowledged
the primacy of Armagh. A scion of the Munster house of O'Brien,
Brian Boru was considered a usurper of the Irish throne. Because
of this, no northern contingents helped him at Clontarf but he still
won, thus ending two centuries of Viking supremacy in Ireland.

The **cathedral library** (1771) was the first public library in
Ireland outside Dublin. It contains a copy of *Gulliver's Travels*
corrected in Swift's hand and the *Claims of the Innocents* (pleas
to Oliver Cromwell). The registers of archbishops of Armagh from
1361 are in the Public Record Office, Belfast. One of these archbishops, the learned James Ussher, primate from 1624, is remembered for a statement in his 1650 diary that the world was created
on 23 October in 4004BC. An adjacent infirmary (like the library,
founded by the generous Robinson) is still in out-patient use.
Stones from an early twelfth-century Augustinian abbey (St Peter
and St Paul) on this site were used for the Presbyterian church
(1722) lower down Abbey Street. Dean Swift passed the church
(now disused) during construction and observed stone masons
'chipping the popery out of the stones'. Vicar's Row, opposite the
cathedral's west door, is a terrace of small houses for clergy
widows. Nos. 1–4, the earliest in the row, started in about 1720,

✳ have tiny windows. The end house, no. 11, is the birthplace of Charles Wood (1866–1926), composer of organ music, string quartets and anthems. Early eighteenth-century terraced houses in Castle Street have recently been demolished by the Housing Executive, the province's public housing authority, and replaced by some agreeable modern terraces which curve round the south-east side of the rath.

⌀ The **Catholic cathedral**, also dedicated to St Patrick, was begun in 1840. Building stopped during the great famine and for years afterwards. The walls were only about 15ft high when J.J. McCarthy resumed construction, changing the style from Duff's comparatively modest Perpendicular Gothic design to lofty Decorated Gothic. The outside was finished in 1873. The finest view of the twin spires is from the city's west and north-west approaches. The pope and many of Europe's royal families helped with the builders' bills but mostly the cash was raised through collections, bazaars and raffles. A grandfather clock, a prize in the 1865 bazaar, is still waiting in the sacristy for the lucky winner to collect it. The two archbishops, whose statues flank a long flight of steps up to the grand entrance, were the incumbents under whom building began (Primate Crolly) and ended (Primate McGettigan). Cardinal Logue later beautified the interior, a dazzle of mosaic, painting, stained glass, Italian marbles and red 'Armagh marble'.

The old Irish game of road bowls is popular in Armagh. Competitions are held regularly on the road below the Catholic cathedral. Players hurl heavy metal bowls along the road, cutting corners and flying over hedges to complete the course in as few throws as possible. Armagh's main rivals are Corkmen, and betting is brisk.

🏠 The fine house at **36 Scotch Street** (until recently a bank, now flats), set back from the present building line, was designed for the Dobbin family by Johnston in 1812. It is reputed to be the site of a church built by St Patrick in AD444, the year before he obtained the prime site up on the hill. To visit the remains of the ⌀ longest friary church in Ireland (163ft), you have to cross the (busy) A28. The ruins are just beyond the gates of the former bishop's palace demesne and are all that survives of a **Franciscan friary** established in 1263 by Archbishop O'Scanail. From here, you can see a large obelisk raised by Archbishop Robinson, and looking back towards the city, the bawn-like modern St Malachy's church (Roman Catholic). St Malachy was born in Armagh and was archbishop in 1129–48.

Armagh , from the Catholic Cathedral

The Anglican **archbishop's palace** (at present used as council offices) was built in 1770 by Cooley. Johnston added a third storey in 1786 and also designed the beautiful, delicate interior of the primate's chapel, a detached Ionic temple to the

PLACES OF INTEREST IN AND AROUND ARMAGH CITY

Armagh County Museum
Historical relics, social and
natural history, costume, lace,
toys. Art gallery, map paintings.
Outstanding library.

**Anglican Cathedral &
Library**
 Historic cathedral on site of St
Patrick's original church, burying
place (1014) of high king Brian
Boru, thirteenth-century crypt,
fine marble memorials. Nearby
library contains copy of *Gulliver's
Travels* \annotated by Swift.

Planetarium
Star shows, exhibits from American space programme, weather
satellite station, bookshop.
Displays of astronomical
instruments.

Roman Catholic Cathedral
Impressive twin-spired hilltop
cathedral. Started a decade after
Catholic emancipation.

Armagh Friary
Ruins of Ireland's longest (163ft)
friary church, founded 1263 for
the Grey Friars (Franciscans). In
grounds of archbishop's palace.

Navan Fort (2 miles west)
Chief stronghold of kings of Ulster
for 1,000 years.

Gosford Forest Park
(6 miles south-east)
Associations (1728-30) with Dean
Swift. He devised walks through
park now surrounding enormous
Norman-revival castle. Walled
cherry garden, arboretum,
walnuts, wildfowl. Camping.

right of the main entrance. Among interesting paintings in the
palace's grand chandeliered entrance hall are portraits of George
III and Queen Charlotte.

π   **Navan Fort** is signposted off the Caledon-Killylea road (A28)
1¹/₂ miles west of Armagh. This was the chief stronghold of the
Celtic kings of Ulster from about 700BC until its destruction in
AD332. Queen Macha's palace (*Eamhain Mhacha*) crowned the
summit, and her hospital ('house of sorrow') sheltered the sick;
Deirdre of the Sorrows first encountered her lover, Noisi, on the
ramparts; Cuchulainn practised feats of arms below the palace,
and the deeds of the Red Branch knights were celebrated in song.
Later a huge Celtic temple, 120ft wide and 40ft high, was erected
on the top. Described on the Department of the Environment's
notice board merely as an 'Iron Age hill enclosure', all that
remains of this fabulous kingdom is a grassy 16-acre circular
mound surrounded by a ditch inside an earthen bank. From the
breezy top, beyond a limestone quarry, is a wonderful view of the

PLACES TO VISIT IN NORTH ARMAGH

Oxford Island Nature Reserve, Lough Neagh.
Nature trails around 'island'(a peninsula since 1846 when the lough level was lowered). Birds include nesting great crested grebe, heronry, breeding corncrake, whooper and Bewick's swans. Bird hides. Boat hire.

Ardress House
Elegant plasterwork by Stapleton. Good furniture and paintings. Working eighteenth-century farmyard. Woodland walks. Picnicking. (National Trust).

The Argory
Early nineteenth-century house still lit by gas plant installed 1906 by Sunbeam Acetylene Gas Company, Belfast. Original furniture. Garden pavilions, coach house. Shop, tea room. (National Trust).

cathedrals of Armagh. The rise of Christian Armagh came soon after the fall of *Eamhain Mhacha*.

The big house with curvilinear Dutch gables at **Richhill** (population 1,700) was built after 1664. Its magnificent wrought-iron gates, made in 1745 by the Thornberry brothers of Armagh, were moved to Hillsborough Castle in 1936. A mile south-east at **Aghory** (take B131) the Presbyterian church commemorates the father-and-son founders of the Disciples of Christ, a huge indigenous American fundamentalist church which now has over

Apple blossom time at Kilmore

The Drawing Room, Ardress House

1¹/₂ million adherents. Thomas Campbell had a small farm and bible teaching school here. He emigrated from Richhill to the Pennsylvanian backwoods, followed shortly (1809) by his son Alexander, known as the 'Sage of Bethany'. The tower and memorial window at Aghory were a gift from American church members. Another interesting church near here is at **Kilmore** where a medieval spiral staircase is built into a massive square tower.

This area, north-east of Armagh, is Ireland's apple orchard country. The bulk of the crop is the tangy Bramley Seedling cooker, harvested in October and sold on the fresh market in Belfast and Dublin. (The apple pies of Ireland have lost out lately to pavlovas, black forest gâteaux and other cold comforts of the sweet trolley. If it is available, a well made Bramley apple pie, hot from the oven, should be your choice.) The seventeenth-century settlers came here from Worcestershire and their orchards were laid out on the same pattern as in the Vale of Evesham. Round-roofed houses dotted about are mushroom production units. Soft fruit growing has declined though Armagh strawberries are still sold at the roadside in summer.

Loughgall (population 250) is surrounded by 5,000 acres of

The Argory, near Moy

apple orchards, prettiest at blossom time (May/June). Loughgall
Manor, at the end of an avenue of mature lime trees, is a picturesque gabled mansion with a lake. It is now a government horticultural centre, visitable on open days and by appointment. Work on
the estate includes livestock husbandry (mostly sheep) and plant
breeding as well as fruit and vegetable research. An ancient yew
walk near the manor house was planted over 300 years ago by the
Cope family who settled here in 1610.

The Orange Order was founded by Protestant farmers in 1795
at Sloane's Bar (now kept as a museum) in Loughgall after a fight
between Peep o' Day boys (Protestant) and Defenders (Catholic)
at the Diamond, outside the village. Ask the custodian next door
to see the museum's collection of early Orange sashes, flags and
documents.

Ardress House and the Argory are two National Trust properties barely 3 miles apart, and it is easy to see both houses in an
afternoon (if you check opening days). **Ardress House** has a
long imposing front, with urns on the parapets and a pedimented
porch. It was a modest seventeenth-century farmhouse until its
witty architect-owner, George Ensor, enlarged it in about 1770,
adding a wing at one end and, to balance it, a wall with dummy windows at the other. The beautiful Neo-Classical decoration of the
drawing room, with exquisite plaques representing the Four Sea-

sons, is by Michael Stapleton, the Dublin stuccodore who was the leading Irish plasterer of the time. Behind the house is an eighteenth-century working cobbled farmyard with piggery, smithy, chicken houses, and a well in the middle.

The Argory, a large Neo-Classical house of about 1820, overlooks the Blackwater river. Its owners, the McGeough-Bonds, were much preoccupied with heating and lighting. A handsome cast-iron stove in the front hall heated the central part of the house, and in 1906 the family installed an acetylene gas plant for lighting. On the first floor is an unusual cabinet barrel organ (1824). The house has a cheerful lived-in feeling, full of furniture, pictures and bric-à-brac. The gas plant, one of very few surviving in the British Isles, can be inspected in the laundry yard. Piped to the light fixtures, the gas gives a warm yellow light. A herd of Moilies, a rare native Irish breed of red-and-white cattle, is kept on the estate.

At the B28/A29 junction outside **Moy**, 2^1/2 miles south of the Argory, is ruined **Charlemont Fort**, built in 1602 by Lord Deputy Mountjoy (not signposted). Right on the Armagh/Tyrone border, the star-shaped fort faced across the Blackwater into the territory of Hugh O'Neill. In 1598 he had resoundingly beaten the English at Yellow Ford, a few miles from Charlemont, and his power had increased. A campaign by the Earl of Essex had been a miserable failure and Elizabeth I now sent Charles Blount, Lord Mountjoy, to crush O'Neill once and for all. The fort was an important part of the English strategy.

The gatehouse entrance is visible from the road (B28) at the end of a short avenue of trees. Go through the adjacent farm gate (close it properly) to see the ramparts, in the shape of a star, stretching down towards the river. (Another approach is via stone steps on Moy bridge.) The main accommodation inside was thatched cottages. One wonders how well the garrison slept in this isolated and dangerous place, so close to Tyrone territory. The people across the river had good reason to hate and fear Mountjoy, Elizabeth's toughest and most effective general. The Lord Deputy campaigned all year round. He swept off the cattle, burnt crops, destroyed the peasants' looms and distaffs, and starved O'Neill into submission in 1603. The fort was finally burnt down in 1922.

5 FERMANAGH LAKELAND
AND THE CLOGHER VALLEY

It is only in the last 20 years or so that Fermanagh's beautiful lakeland has been developed as a holiday area. The limestone cave system at Marble Arch, in the south-west of the county, was opened to the public as recently as 1985. In fact the whole of this watery, forested region is still agreeably empty of crowds. Certainly for cruising there is nowhere in Europe with so much water for so few boats as Lough Erne.

A long sinuous waterway, 50 miles from end to end, **Lough Erne** is divided in two by a constriction in the middle where the small county town of Enniskillen stands. The highway between the ancient provinces of Ulster in the north and Connaught in the south went across the narrows at this point, and the area is exceptionally rich in Celtic and early Christian antiquities. The lower lake, navigable down as far as Belleek, is 5 miles wide in places, with quite big waves when the wind gets up. The shallow upper lake is a jigsaw of heavily wooded islands and has few open stretches. Even good map readers, armed with the navigation guides of the Ordnance Survey, can get happily confused by the maze of look-alike islands and headlands.

In the Middle Ages there was a chain of island monasteries down the lake — convenient stopping places for the endless stream of pilgrims on their way to St Patrick's Purgatory, an important shrine on Lough Derg, County Donegal. Water transport was the main way of travelling around. Bishop Chiericati, a papal nuncio who passed through Fermanagh in 1517, found the county 'full of robbers, woods, lakes and marshes'. The lakeside is high and rocky in parts, and overland travel was hard going. The Maguire clan, chieftains of Fermanagh, policed the lake with a private navy of 1,500 boats which were stationed at Enniskillen Castle and Hare Island. Many of the ecclesiastical sites around the lake can be visited by car, and Fermanagh's ruined castles and historic houses open to the public are conveniently close to main roads. Sooner or later, however, you will find yourself on a

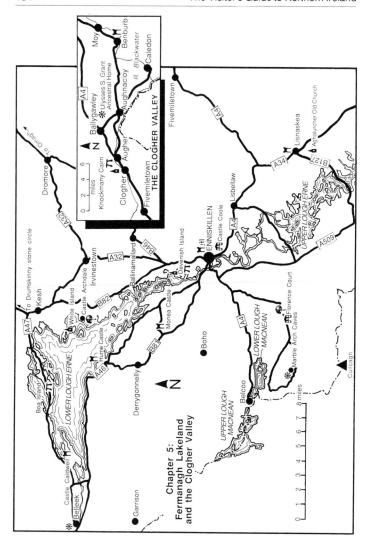

boat heading out to see the island monasteries and high crosses.

Access to Fermanagh, once so remote from the rest of the
province, is easy. The quickest route is via the M1 motorway and
then through south Tyrone and the **Clogher Valley**. The quiet
villages of this part of County Tyrone, along the meandering

course of the Blackwater river, deserve more than a cursory in-
spection.

Moy (population 850) was laid out in the 1760s for the Volunteer Earl — the patriot and aesthete James Caulfield, Earl of
Charlemont (1728–99) — opposite Charlemont Fort across the
Blackwater. The formal rectangular market place, with lawns and
horse-chestnut trees, was inspired by the square at Marengo in
Lombardy, admired by the arty young earl during his grand tour of
Europe. Houses round the sides are mostly eighteenth-century
though all the four churches are later. St John's parish church
(1819) used to open on to the market place but after one of the
Charlemont ladies objected to the draught in her pew, the front
door was walled up and the church has a peculiar blind look about
it. In the nineteenth century the Charlemont seat was at Roxbor-
ough Castle. Though the house was burnt in 1921, two heavy,   ✳
white-painted gates and a fine screen surmounted by red
dragons, still mark the castle entrance near the river.

A local riding school is the last vestige of the days of the great
Moy horse fair, held once a month and lasting a whole week. For
over 100 years, Moy supplied the best cavalry and carriage
horses in the British Isles. The village had stabling for 2,500
horses. World War I records of one Moy dealer are an indication of
the scale of the operation: a standing weekly order from the Army
for 100 troopers and chargers, plus a horse which had to weigh an
imperial ton. These noble beasts were destined to pull the gun
carriages across the battlefields of Europe. In the 1920s the fair
dwindled to a 2-day event and ceased altogether by 1950. The
Ulster poet Paul Muldoon, who grew up here, has written memorably about the fair at 'The Moy'.

The centre of **Benburb** (population 200) is dominated by a
cheerful redbrick mansion which was dedicated as a Servite   ♠
priory in 1948 — the first community of this monastic order to be
established in Ireland. The Victorian ballroom is now a chapel and
the stable block contains an art gallery. The Brothers have constructed a turbine on the Blackwater which generates their electricity. The fast rapids attract canoeists, and fishing is good.There
is a fine view from the priory lawns down the gorge to the Blackwater where a ruined castle stands on a rock 120ft above the
water. Sir Richard Wingfield built Benburb Castle in 1615, on the   ⚔
site of an O'Neill fort. Inside the massive bawn walls it is a sur-
prise to come on a small house with a tv aerial and burglar alarm
on the chimney. In the village street, tiny cottages used for years

as apple peeling sheds have been repaired. They date from the seventeenth century.

Clonfeacle parish church (1618), outside the priory gates, is one of the oldest churches in regular use in the province. Basically a hall (the belfry tower was added in 1892), the church has a seventeenth-century font and bell, and a monument to Captain James Hamilton. Hamilton was one of 3,000 Scots killed at the battle of Benburb in 1646. Led by Major General Robert Monroe, the Scots were routed in a disastrous encounter with Owen Roe O'Neill, charismatic nephew of the great Hugh O'Neill. The Irish are said to have lost only forty men.

The tidy village of **Caledon** (population 450) takes its name from the Earls of Caledon. Their mansion, designed by Thomas Cooley (1779) and enlarged by John Nash (1810), is the fourth great house to be built here. It has a beautiful Regency drawing room and library, and the fourth earl kept black bears in the park. His third son, born in 1891, was Field Marshal Earl Alexander of Tunis. On the estate is the ruin of a strange folly made out of the knuckle bones of cattle. It was built in the eighteenth century by Lord Orrery who hoped, he said, to 'strike the Caledonians with wonder and amazement'. The butchers and tanners of Tyrone supplied the bones, though their opinions of the 'bone house' do not appear to have been recorded. The village street has some appealing nineteenth-century buildings. Archbishop Robinson built the eighteenth-century Anglican church and the needle spire was added by Nash.

Caledon was one of thirty-six villages and halts which were joined by the Clogher Valley Railway. This line, 37 miles long, ran from Tynan in County Armagh to Maguiresbridge in County Fermanagh. It closed in 1941. The picturesque well-built redbrick stations are now private houses and some have been turned into shops and offices.

The station house at **Aughnacloy** (population 650) is now a masonic hall and carefully maintained. This is more than can be said for many of the tall houses, old hotels and faded shop fronts — 'Medical Hall', 'Georgian Hall of Antiques' — lining the main street. It is unusual to see such obvious neglect in an Ulster village. Despite its generally derelict air, however, Aughnacloy has some attractive houses, a spruce bed-and-breakfast guesthouse, a bicycle shop (where Mr Speers will loan you a bike) and two eighteenth-century churches (St James's built 1736, and a Presbyterian church of 1774). A Dublin doctor, Alexander Jack-

PLACES TO VISIT IN THE CLOGHER VALLEY

Benburb Castle and Priory
Ruined plantation castle, overlooking Blackwater, in grounds of
Servite priory. Art gallery in
priory. The Brothers have built
their own turbine.

**Ulysses S. Grant
Ancestral Home**
Thatched cottage of US President Grant's ancestors. Adjoining
farm is worked in nineteenth-
century style. Interpretative
centre, shop.

son, gave a £10,000 endowment to build the still charming gabled
almshouses, now badly in need of repair. The village runs along a
high ridge, with good views of **Slieve Beagh**. An elaborate num-
bering system marked out along the wide main street is for the
benefit of stall holders at the big street market held here twice a
month (first and third Wednesday). Here you are only half a mile
from the Republic, and the border customs post is more or less in
the village. Four miles east is Rehaghey House, a restored Georgian mansion in pleasant gardens. It is open to visitors and has a
restaurant.

The **ancestral home** of American president **Ulysses** ✳
Simpson Grant has been rebuilt and is open all year round. His
place in history was won as commander of the victorious Federal
armies in the American Civil War. Robert E. Lee surrendered the
Confederate forces to Grant on the Appomattox river, Virginia, in
1865. The house is signposted off the A4 east of Ballygawley.
John Simpson, Grant's maternal great-grandfather, was one of
many young County Tyrone men who left for America in the
eighteenth century. He was born in the thatched cottage in 1738.
A small adjoining farm is worked in nineteenth-century style and   ⚏
the interpretative centre includes a souvenir shop. Grant came to
Ulster on a visit in 1878 at the end of his two terms as president
(1869–77).

Antiquities near **Ballygawley** (population,   500) are a pas-   𝛑
sage grave at **Sess Kilgreen** (a mile north-west), and a
fifteenth-century ruined church dedicated to St Kieran over-   🜍
looking the Clogher Valley at **Errigal Keerogue** (3 miles west).
The romantic castle of Spur Royal across the lake at **Augher**   🎪
(population 400) incorporates part of an early seventeenth-
century bawn. Tourists can stay here in style. Near the railway
station house (now a tea shop/craft centre) is a cheese factory.

A preserved cottage at Springtown, a mile south of Augher,

Carleton's Cottage, near Augher

 was the childhood home of William Carleton (1794–1869), author of many stories of Irish peasant life, some sad, some humorous. *Traits and Stories of the Irish Peasantry* was followed by numerous popular novels, including a bleak tale of the potato famine *Black Prophet* (1847). Youngest son of a Roman Catholic Gaelic-speaking tenant farmer, Carleton was largely self-educated. The cottage where he and his thirteen brothers and sisters grew up is down a winding track shaded by trees (ample turning space at the house). His parents are buried in the graveyard of **St MacCartan's church** in Ballynagurragh townland a short distance away.

Inside the church, a stained glass window commemorates Archbishop John Joseph Hughes, first archbishop of New York, baptised here in 1797. Hughes worked as a gardener on Favour Royal estate nearby before emigrating in 1817. An authoritarian figure, he was an energetic pamphleteer and politician who championed the cause of the immigrant Irish in America and built St Patrick's cathedral on Fifth Avenue. Carleton's Cottage and St MacCartan's church are both signposted from the A4. A path from the river in **Favour Royal forest** leads to St Patrick's Well and Chair at Altnadaven (signposted from A28), an atmospheric mossy little place which is the venue for Bilberry Sunday, a local festival in late July.

Carved stones, Knockmany Chambered Cairn, Augher

Knockmany Hill, 2 miles north-west of Augher, is topped by
a large passage grave with stones incised with swirling patterns. 𝚷
The spiral motives are similar to those at Newgrange in County
Meath. A cairn was built over the top in 1959 to protect the

Clogher Cathedral

Knockmany grave, which appears above ground in old photographs. To get inside the tomb, ask at the ranger's house at the
forest entrance (Race Road), though there is a general view of the
stones through an iron grid. The mythological mother goddess,
Ainé, loved by the warrior Finn McCool, is traditionally buried on
top of this hill.

   Clogher (population 550) was the fifth-century seat of the
diocese of Clogher, the oldest bishopric in Ireland, and gives its
name to two dioceses, Protestant and Catholic. The diocese
corresponds roughly with Fermanagh, south Tyrone, and County
Monaghan in the Republic. The first bishop here was St Mac-
Cartan (died 506), a disciple of St Patrick. In medieval times
there were endless power struggles between the bishops of
Clogher and the vicars general of the deanery of Lough Erne.
Pope Sixtus IV made several appointments to the see but the
bishop was rarely able to take possession. When the Blessed
Oliver Plunket, primate of Armagh, visited Clogher in 1671 he inspected the old diocesan register which catalogued all the
bishops. These included Bishop Eoghan (died 1515) who lost a finger on his left hand 'in defence of his church'. The first Protestant
bishop, Myler MacGrath, was appointed in 1570.

   The little Anglican cathedral, rebuilt in purply blue stone in

1744, preserves a fine early sculptured slab cross, a gallery of portraits of sixteenth- to eighteenth-century bishops, and some good stained glass. The tower gives a view right down the Clogher Valley. Ask at the deanery for access.

In the churchyard are seventeenth-century monuments and two high crosses as well as some mournful memorials of Ulster's more recent past. This is the older of two Anglican cathedrals in the diocese. The other, at Enniskillen, was raised from parish church status in 1924. Both are dedicated to St MacCartan (though the Enniskilleners insist on spelling theirs 'Macartin'). An impressive earthworks in the park behind Clogher cathedral was the seat of the old kings of Oriel, ancestors of the Maguires. Driving south from the village, you cannot avoid seeing, on the left, a tall nineteenth-century hilltop tower known as **Brackenridge's** **Folly**. The local squirearchy of the time steadfastly refused to admit Mr George Brackenridge to their midst. He remedied this injustice by building the tower as his own mausoleum, thus obliging the county bigwigs who looked down on the living Mr Brackenridge to look up to him when dead. The locals are still amiably rude about him. Sepulchral humour of this kind is not untypical of Northern Ireland.

Blessingbourne House, outside Fivemiletown, is an unusually nice Elizabethan-style manor looking on to a small round lake. It was built in the 1870s. The stable yard is divided into holiday flats popular with pike fishermen, and a small carriage and costumes museum can be visited by appointment (ask at the library in the village). **Fivemiletown** (population 1,000) is so called because it is 5 Irish miles from the villages of Clogher, **Brookeborough** and **Tempo** (1 Irish mile = 2,240yd). Its simple parish church was built in the same year as St James's in Aughnacloy (1736). Old photographs showing the railway running down the middle of the main street are displayed in the library. Ask here for directions to houses where lace is made — a local cottage industry.

After Fivemiletown, the road enters Fermanagh, passing Colebrooke Park. This was the ancestral home of Field Marshal Lord Alanbrooke (1883–1963), chief of the British Imperial General Staff during World War II, and also the home of Lord Brookeborough, prime minister of Northern Ireland 1943–63. The second Viscount Brookeborough, who died in 1987, was ADC to Field Marshal Alexander and had a distinguished war record. The two houses in the grounds are Colebrooke, a large Classical mansion of pinkish sandstone, and Ashbrooke, a dower house. There is a

Lough Erne from Knockninny Hill

riding school and a herd of deer on the estate, and several self-catering holiday cottages. **Aghalurcher** church (Anglican, 1762), prominent on an adjoining hill, contains Alanbrooke's banners of the Orders of the Bath and Garter and monuments to many other battling Brookes, including a young dragoon killed at Waterloo.

A distinctive long, flat mountain about 20 miles directly ahead is the ridge of the **Cuilcagh mountains** rising to 2,188ft and marking the south-west extremity of Fermanagh. An indirect approach to the lakes is by minor roads south off the A4 through an attractive area of forest and little lakes. The main road runs into Enniskillen, passing the bell tower of **Lisbellaw** parish church and Castle Coole stately home.

A glance at the map shows virtually all major roads in Fermanagh converging on **Enniskillen** (population 10,450) on its island between Upper and Lower Lough Erne. The result is considerable congestion around the town. The loop roads and improved bridges of the traffic engineers, and housing estates on neighbouring hillsides, have effectively deprived the casual visitor of any sense of being on an island. However, as a good

The Water Gate, Enniskillen

shopping centre, with first-rate angling facilities, a lively cultural scene (including a large lakeside theatre) and friendly people, Enniskillen makes a convenient base for exploring this lovely watery part of the province.

The long main street changes its name half a dozen times as it curves and wiggles from East Bridge to West Bridge, up and down two slight hills. Enniskillen Castle at the west end was in turn a Maguire fort, plantation castle and, from the late eighteenth-century, artillery barracks. The English first captured it in 1594. The Maguires got it back briefly but were expelled again in 1607, after which the whole of Enniskillen was granted to Sir William

Cole. As constable, and captain of the king's long boats, Cole enlarged the castle, built the fairy-tale Water Gate and created the plantation town. The Water Gate, which is really just a short length of wall flanked by two towers with nothing behind it, is best seen by boat, approaching from the upper lough. There are always a few anglers under its romantic towers, pole fishing for eels, roach and bream from the river bank.

Enniskillen was the only stronghold in Fermanagh to escape destruction in the seventeenth century. Cole's garrison successfully defended it against Roderick Maguire during the 1641 rising, and again resisted in 1688 when the town rallied to William of Orange. The Enniskilleners were able to stop Jacobite troops at Belleek and prevented a large Irish force from joining the attack on Londonderry, and they formed William's personal guard at the Battle of the Boyne. Two famous regiments, the Royal Inniskilling Fusiliers and the Inniskilling Dragoons, originated from this time (the town later changed the I for an E). Napoleonic battle trophies and other militaria of the Inniskilling regiments, both long since merged with other regiments, are in a small museum in the castle keep. Most rooms in the keep, which has an incongruous slate roof but dates from the castle of Hugh the Hospitable (died 1428), are occupied by the county museum. Exhibits of local antiquities include splendidly grotesque stone idols.

At the east end of the town is a delightful Victorian town park of humpy hillocks squeezed on to the slopes of Fort Hill. In the middle is a fine cast-iron bandstand with a clock tower and cupola. Nearby a statue to Sir Galbraith Lowry Cole (1772–1842), one of Wellington's generals in the Peninsular War, stands on top of a Doric column. The spiral staircase to the top is closed off so it is not possible to share his panoramic view of the lakes — nor, for that matter, to examine too closely Sir Galbraith who is holding a fearsome-looking cavalry sabre in his left hand.

The Anglican cathedral on the main street contains a full-length martial portrait of this same general, still brandishing his sabre. The cathedral tower, which survives from a seventeenth-century church on the site, contains a bell cast from cannon used in the Battle of the Boyne. Colours of the Inniskilling regiments hang in the light and airy late Georgian interior. Notable features are the seventeenth-century font and a stone tablet to William Pokrich (died, 1628) with half the inscription upside down. Across the narrow street is an immensely tall and thin nineteenth-century Catholic church, St Michael's, with a long nave and steep roof. A

Round Tower, Devenish Island

window in the south aisle portrays St Molaise, the abbot founder of Devenish monastery, holding the Devenish Gospel Shrine. Down the street the atmospheric William Blake Bar (1887) has a characterful Victorian shop-front and pine-boarded snugs. Further along, upon the town hall tower are niche statues of a fusilier and a dragoon. Go into the lobby to see a brass plate commemorating brave Captain Oates of the 6th Inniskilling Dragoons, who walked out into a blizzard on Scott's tragic return journey from the South Pole in March 1912. The chapel in the convent below Fort Hill contains good stained glass by Irish artists (in the nave).

Enniskillen was the most important of a ring of castles — Crom, Portora, Tully, Archdale, Crevenish and Caldwell — which the planters built round the lough shore to control this huge waterway. Ruined Portora Castle (built about 1613), which commanded the entrance to the lower lough, is now in the grounds of Portora Royal School, founded by James 1 in 1608 and moved to this site above the river in 1777. (The castle's ruinous state is partly the result of an experiment by the chemistry class of 1859.) A large oil painting of Oscar Wilde (1854–1900), the school's most famous old boy, adorns the entrance hall. Other pupils included Henry Francis Lyte (1793–1847), the divine who wrote the hymn 'Abide with me', and the dramatist Samuel Beckett (born 1905). Nurse Edith Cavell, the English patriot, was a friend of the headmaster's wife and occasionally ministered to boarders in the school sanatorium. A matron in Brussels during World War I, she was shot by the Germans in 1915 for helping Allied soldiers escape over the Dutch frontier.

Islands of Lower Lough Erne

Devenish Island, 2 miles downstream from the town, is the site of a sixth-century monastery founded by St Molaise (died 563), one of the 'twelve apostles of Ireland'. Arbitrator in the quarrels of the Ulster chieftains, and mentor of St Columba, Molaise had 1,500 students attached to Devenish. The monastery was raided by Vikings in the ninth century and burned in 1157 but then remained an important religious centre until the early seventeenth century. The island's greatest treasure, the *Soiscél Molaise*, an early eleventh-century book shrine, is in the National Museum, Dublin. Follow the path up from the east jetty, and you will pass a remarkable succession of ecclesiastical remains.

1. Ruined *Teampull Mór*, the lower church, dates from about 1225 and has a fine south window of that period. It was greatly extended in about 1300 and was in turn a Culdee monastery and the parish church of Devenish. The Culdees (*Céli-Dé* — Companions of God) were a strict Celtic anchorite order founded at the end of the eighth century. Killadeas, a small angling and boating resort down the lough (east shore), is named after the Culdees. The arms of the Maguires of Tempo appear in two places outside their

sixteenth-century burial chamber here, and the graveyard below the church contains some interesting stones, including an eleventh-century cross-carved slab.

2. St Molaise's House is a tiny twelfth-century church with thick walls which once had a stone roof. Though much ruined, it still has a sturdy look about it.

3. The perfect round tower (also twelfth-century) has a site as beautiful as any in Ireland. Over 80ft high, with a decorated cornice round the conical cap, it has five floors which are ascended by interior ladders. The four windows at the top gave the sentry an all-round view of strangers approaching over the water, and time for him to sound his bell in warning. The door of the tower, 9ft off the ground, faces the entrance to St Molaise's House and so the monks — having snatched up books and relics from the church — could hurry to the safety of the tower, pull up the outside ladder and hope for the best. An earlier round tower (foundations a few yards away) may have been destroyed by Vikings who arrived on Lough Erne in 837 and established a base at Belleek. Their long boats had no difficulty in reaching the island monasteries.

4. Beyond the round tower are the ruins of St Mary's, an Augustinian priory, built by the master mason Matthew O'Dubigan in 1449 when, according to an inscription on the south wall, Bartholomew O'Flanagan was prior. The O'Flanagan sept supplied the last prior of St Mary's too, and also many of the priests for Inishmacsaint. The most notable feature is the north door to the chancel which has elaborate carvings. The east window was taken to the Anglican parish church at Monea (B81/C443 junction, 1 mile southwest of Monea Castle) where it was reset in 1890. The site museum preserves a female head from the west door into the nave. Note the unusual design of a pretty fifteenth-century cross in the graveyard. The Augustinian priory and the Culdee monastery down the hill co-existed in apparent harmony until both were abandoned in 1603 at the dissolution of monasteries in Fermanagh.

Inishmacsaint Island also had a sixth-century monastery — one of the thousands that sprang up all over Ireland in the generation after St Patrick's death. This one was founded in about 523 by St Ninnid who, like St Molaise, studied under St Finian at Clonard. The island has an ancient rath (prehistoric hillfort), a

Stone figures, White Island

⚑ ruined twelfth-century church, and a striking 14ft-high cross
(tenth-century) with splayed arms and a broad shaft. It lacks the
usual Celtic circle and looks as though the stone carver was
called away before he could finish it.

⚑ **White Island** has seven stone figures, lined up on the far wall
of a roofless twelfth-century church, and they are first glimpsed

ISLANDS OF LOUGH ERNE

There are nearly 100 islands, big and small, on the lower lake, and about sixty on the upper lake. Apart from Galloon, those listed here are on the lower lake.

Devenish
Perfect round tower and St Molaise's House — both twelfth-century; thirteenth-century church ruins with eleventh-century gravestones; Augustinian priory, fine fifteenth-century cross; site museum. Ferry from Trory (signposted at B82/A32 junction).

White Island
Seven mysterious stone figures (from AD900), twelfth-century Romanesque church on site of early monastery. Ferry from Castle Archdale Country Park (north-west of Enniskillen on B82).

Inishmacsaint
Tall tenth-century cross with splayed arms, church ruins. Public jetty.

Boa Island
Pagan Janus figure and 'Lusty Man' Celtic idols in Christian graveyard of Caldragh. Access by road (small signpost off A47 at west end of island).

Lustybeg
Bird sanctuary, pretty harbour, holiday chalets, restaurant. Small private ferry (summoned by jetty telephone at carpark).

Galloon
Two tenth-century crosses at opposite ends of graveyard. Worn sculpture includes (on taller cross) the Fall, Daniel in the lions' den, sacrifice of Isaac; smaller cross: Last Judgment, Adoration of the Magi, Christ's baptism.

through a Romanesque doorway as you walk through trees from the jetty. Dating from the ninth or tenth century, these Christian statues have a distinctly pagan mien and their significance has been much debated. The builders of a later church used them as ordinary masonry stones but sockets on the heads indicate they were intended as supports. From left to right: a female fertility figure (*sheelnagig*) with a wide suggestive grin; a seated man holding a book; an abbot or abbess with bell and crozier; another priestly figure scratching his chin; a man with a kiss-curl fringe holding two griffins by the scruff of their necks; a second curly-haired man with sword, shield and a big brooch; the seventh figure is unfinished. (An eighth stone, a medieval sour-faced mask, is unconnected with the others.) Look out for an eleventh-century gravestone in the church. A large earthworks round the outside remains from an early monastery.

Interesting sites which can be reached by car are at **Killadeas** and on Boa Island. The Bishop's Stone in Killadeas churchyard, near an old Irish yew, depicts on one side a little cleric walking briskly, and on another side a grotesque moon face with slack mouth — a ninth-century Charles Laughton. Note an even earlier cross-ornamented slab nearby. Older than these, and unparalleled in Ireland is the two-faced Celtic idol in overgrown Caldragh cemetery on **Boa**, a long narrow island joined to the mainland by bridges. Between the heads is a deep libation stoup. Both faces have staring eyes, pointed chins and arms crossed over their chests. Just behind the Janus is the 'Lusty Man', a smaller idol, with an outsize head and shapely, womanly arms. (He, or she, was brought here from nearby **Lustymore Island** — hence the name.) Heavily wooded **Lustybeg**, an adjacent holiday island with chalets, restaurant and bird sanctuary, was the home of Ned Allingham, reclusive brother of the Ulster-born poet William Allingham (1824–89) whose best known poem recreates the spirit world of superstitious old Ireland:

'Up the airy mountain,
Down the rushy glen,
We daren't go a-hunting
For fear of little men.'

Upper Lough Sites

The maze of islands in the shallow, reedy upper lake are better known for their natural beauty and wild birds than for their ecclesiastical sites. Most of them are uninhabited, some with ruined mansions and abandoned cottages, others with heronries, or wild goats who run up and steal your picnic sandwiches. However, a few islands still retain traces of the religious communities that flourished here in early Christian times. Three which can be reached by either car or boat are Inishkeen, Cleenish and Galloon.

Inishkeen (accessible by causeway 3 miles south-east of Enniskillen off A4) has a rath at either end, and strange carved stones in old St Fergus' cemetery — a god's head with antlers and an angel sitting in a boat, or it could be a devil boiling in a cauldron. The *Annals of Ulster* report that, in 1421, Hugh Maguire slew the three sons of Art Maguire on Inishkeen. Opposite the northern tip of the island, across the picturesque reach used by the

Florence Court

rowing club, is the site of Lisgoole Abbey. A battlemented tower, now incorporated into a Georgian house, dates from the twelfth-century monastery which passed from Augustinians to Franciscans in the sixteenth century. At Lisgoole, in 1631, Brother Michael O'Clery and other learned friars compiled the *Book of Invasions*, an ingenious synthesis of pagan myths and Christian beliefs.

Cleenish (reached across a metal bridge south-east of **Bellanaleck**) had a celebrated abbot, St Sinell, tutor to St Columbanus, the austere Irish missionary who went to Europe in 589 and founded famous Celtic monasteries in France (Luxeuil) and at Bobbio near Milan. The island has some distinctive carved gravestones. The father of Field Marshal Sir Claude Auchinleck (died 1981) was a native of Cleenish. On Inishrath, a small island further upstream, Hare Krishna devotees have turned an 1840s mansion into a Hindu shrine. The wooded demesne of Crom Castle, home of the Earls of Erne, occupies a long headland west of Galloon. The romantic ruin of a plantation castle (1611) is down by the shore (jetty) close to a big yew tree. The family's present home, New Crom Castle, is a nineteenth-century castellated mansion half a mile away (private).

Lower Lough Erne

Galloon (3 miles south-west of Newtownbutler) supports a small farming community. Whooper swans are common round here, and corncrakes breed in the fields that stretch down to the water's edge. The churchyard contains fragmentary remains of two very weathered tenth-century crosses and some fine eight-eenth-century grave slabs carved with skull and crossbones, coffins, bell and sand timer. The Adam and Eve cross in Lisnaskea market place is thought to have come from Galloon, and similar grave slabs are at **Aghalurcher Old Church** (south of Lisnaskea), many of them in a covered vault. The church itself was abandoned in 1484, the year a Maguire slew a kinsman on the altar.

Marble Arch Caves

Castle Coole

The rivers and small lakes around **Lisnaskea** (population 1,550) are rich fishing waters. The town's main street is crowded with pubs, and the library preserves a local publican's folk collection. A carved market cross and ruined Castle Balfour (built about 1618) are noteworthy. The **Share Centre**, to the south, is a remarkable lakeside activity holiday centre for both disabled and able-bodied people. The centre's specially-designed chalets, and supervised activities like canoeing, sailing, indoor riding and camping on the islands have an international reputation. From the Share Centre, a good road (B127) crosses Upper Lough Erne via bridges at either end of Trasna Island, joining the main Enniskillen road at **Derrylin** hamlet. Look out for Derrylin's weird black-and-white stone man, with a pudding-basin hairdo, bow tie and dinner jacket (next to Blake's public house). The craggy outline of **Knockninny Hill** is a striking feature on the upper lake. The hill is a well known beauty spot and, although only 600ft high, there is a fine view of the islands from the top (3 miles north of Derrylin).

Florence Court and Castle Coole are two fine properties owned by the National Trust near Enniskillen. The magnificent Neo-Classical mansion at Castle Coole, the most palatial of Ireland's

late eighteenth-century houses, is the more famous but the setting of **Florence Court** is memorably dramatic. The house
stands in a natural amphitheatre of mountains — the hump of Ben-
aughlin to the south, Cuilcagh and the Leitrim hills to the west,
and Mount Belmore on the north side. Former seat of the Earls of
Enniskillen (descendants of planter-constable William Cole),
Florence Court is a three-storey early eighteenth-century house
joined by long arcades to small pavilions (added in about 1770 by
Davis Ducart). Sumptuous rococo plasterwork (about 1755) by
the Dublin stuccodore, Robert West, is the most notable feature
of the interior.

The surrounding woodlands, now a forest park, shelter the
original Irish Yew, progenitor of the columnar tree now found
throughout the world (*taxus baccata fastigiata*). Discovered as a
seedling on the rocky slopes of Cuilcagh in the mid-eighteenth
century, the tree can be propagated only by cuttings. A great
number of cuttings have been taken from the old mother tree
which stands, exhausted and gaunt, at the edge of a clearing.
Cuilcagh (2,188ft) can be climbed from Florence Court, if you
have 7 hours or so to spare, and the right boots. The top is very
steep and rugged.

The first big house at **Castle Coole** was a plantation castle
which was destroyed in 1641. Two more houses, each bigger and
better than the last, came and went before the present master-
piece was completed in 1798. Designed by James Wyatt for the
Lowry-Corry family, Earls of Belmore, it has a beautiful Palladian
main front, 275ft long, with pillared colonnades and elegant pavilions at each end. Silver-coloured Portland stone, imported at
great expense by boat and hauled here by ox-cart, was used for
the façade. The splendid interior of the house, which art histor-
ians describe in tremulous tones of emotion, should soon be on
show again following a major programme of stonework restoration.
The garden front overlooks a lake, where a large breeding colony
of greylag geese has lived since 1700, and the park has some
noble beeches and a four-row avenue of ancient oaks. The
stables and the head gardener's house were built in the 1820s by
Richard Morrison. A young French emigré, the Chevalier de Latoc-
naye, who visited Castle Coole in 1796, ventured the opinion that
Lord Belmore's palace was rather too grand for a private
individual. 'The temples should be left to the gods,' he said.

During his visit to Fermanagh the Chevalier went into the underground caves at **Marble Arch** and got lost when his candle blew

Lough Macnean

out. Until structural engineering work was completed in 1985, only geologists, cavers and a few adventurous individuals went down into the caves. Now they are a big public attraction. The entrance is signposted up the **Marlbank Loop** road, immediately west of Florence Court. Apart from the things one expects to see in caves, like stalagmites, there are subterranean lakes and rivers fed by surface streams rising in the Cuilcagh mountains. A boat trip across the lower lake is a highlight of the guided tour. The 'marble arch' — a detached limestone arch 30ft high — is above ground, at the lower entrance to the caves in a flowery glen where the Cladagh river rushes out from underground and flows beneath the arch.

These show caves are only a fraction of the extensive cave systems of County Fermanagh. Caves on the moors around **Boho** hamlet (due north of Marble Arch) include **Noon's Hole**, the deepest pothole in Ireland (nearly 300ft). **Knockmore Cliff**, an 800ft-high sheer reef of limestone with a fine view, has several visitable caves (north-west of Boho). Generally speaking, however, it is not advisable to go exploring round here without a guide. When leaving the Marble Arch carpark, turn right to complete the scenic run along the wild Cuilcagh plateau, passing first a small bridge where the Sruh Croppa river suddenly vanishes into a crevice called the Cat's Hole. After 2 miles the loop rejoins the lower road (turn right, back to Florence Court). Two nearby lakes, the **Macneans**, are full of heavyweight pike which anglers come to do battle with — in particular German and Swiss anglers, who are partial to poached pike.

Guesthouses and bed-and-breakfast places with views over the lake punctuate the shore route from Enniskillen to Belleek (A46). The road runs through Ely Lodge forest, especially pretty in autumn when the leaves turn. Ely Lodge, the Irish seat of the Duke of Westminster, is on a promontory beyond (visible from the lake). An earlier house on the site was blown up by its owner, the

Belleek Pottery

PLACES OF INTEREST IN FERMANAGH

Marble Arch Caves
Underground limestone caves, recently opened. Stalactites, stalagmites, flowstones. Guided tour includes boat trip across subterranean lake.

Enniskillen Castle and Museums
Romantic seventeenth-century Water Gate.
The fifteenth-century castle keep houses Inniskilling Regimental Museum and Fermanagh County Museum.

Florence Court
Georgian home of the Earls of Enniskillen. Notable plasterwork. Shop, café (National Trust). Parent of all Irish yews in forest park. Walks, views.

Castle Coole
Palatial eighteenth-century house of the Earls of Belmore. Outstanding woodwork, fireplaces, furniture. Lake, breeding greylag geese. Golf course. House closed for stonework restoration at time of writing. (National Trust).

Lough Navar Forest Viewpoint
Panoramic view of Lough Erne.

Monea Castle
Impressive ruined planter's castle with striking Scottish corbelling.

Belleek Pottery Tour
See craftsmen 'weaving' elaborately decorated porcelain. Interesting exhibition of collectors' pieces. Shop.

---

fourth Marquis of Ely, to celebrate his 21st birthday (and, it is said, to prevent Queen Victoria from coming to stay).

Turn inland to see **Monea Castle**, a superb ruined castle surrounded by bog, overlooking a lake. Built in 1618 by Malcolm Hamilton, Rector of Devenish, later Archbishop of Cashel, Monea has an impressive entrance front — two glowering circular towers with square turrets supported on Scottish-type corbels at the top. The 1641 insurgents captured it (one wonders how) but the Hamiltons soon got it back. The governor of Enniskillen, Gustavus Hamilton, who was one of William III's generals at the Boyne, lived in the castle. After the battle, and now raised to the peerage, the new Viscount Boyne moved out of Monea and built a grand country residence not so far from the battleground (in County Meath) and called it after himself — Boyne House.

Derrygonnelly (population 600) is an 1830s village with a harmonious main street lined with two-storey houses, shops and bars, one of which has a remarkable collection of over 100 antique clocks all ticking and striking away (The Bond Store).

Just north of the village is a small ruined church that combines medieval and Renaissance features, built in 1627 by Sir John Dunbar. His arms are over the doorway. The B81 from Derrygonnelly runs north to **Tully Bay** where the ruin of a small castle overlooks Lower Lough Erne. Built in 1613 by Sir John Hume, it was burnt by the ousted Maguires in 1641. The Maguires were in a particularly vengeful mood. Though they spared the Humes they killed everyone else in the castle and, since the garrison was away, these were mostly women and children.

The most interesting, certainly the most virtuous route, to one of the best panoramas in Ireland is a steep zigzag path from the A46 (waymarked, Ulster Way) up 1,000ft to Lough Navar Forest Viewpoint. If you insist on driving, the forest entrance is opposite Correl Glen nature reserve on the C446 road, and you can drive right up to the map table. All Lower Lough Erne lies below, with the cone of Errigal (2,467ft) in County Donegal north-north-west, and Ben Bulben (1,730ft) due west.

Belleek (population 350) is on the border with the Republic (a little bit of the village is actually in the South) and also marks the end of the Erne navigation. The current at the low bridge opposite the famous pottery reaches 6 knots on occasion, and a sluice here controls the level of Lough Erne. Half a mile beyond are the dams of the Erne hydro-electric scheme, after which the river plunges down to the Atlantic at Ballyshannon. There are nice waterside holiday chalets in Belleek and the village hosts an annual fiddle festival when fiddlers from all over Ireland arrive for a weekend of traditional Irish music-making. There is more accommodation 5 miles away in **Garrison** (population 250) at the head of **Lough Melvin**, notable for early salmon and two curious species of trout (gillaroo and sonaghan) .

The pottery was started when local deposits of felspar were discovered at Castle Caldwell in 1857. The porcelain is especially coveted by Americans, and some of the exquisitely glazed early pieces change hands for large sums. Cream-coloured lattice-worked baskets, decorated with pink and yellow rosebuds, blue cornflowers or daisies, are characteristic of the Belleek style. These 'woven' baskets are definitely not for putting things in but the pottery also makes a wide range of tableware and less fragile ornaments. A tour of the works is of great interest. Elaborate showpieces are displayed in the visitor centre where there is a shop. The felspar is now imported from Norway.

Castle Caldwell estate, in the fork of a double-pronged

peninsula east of Belleek, is a nature reserve with good facilities (reception centre, hides, etc). The two prongs are managed as state timber forest, and the deep bay between them is fringed with rare fen and reed-swamp vegetation. Nature trails run down each prong. Crossbills nest here and sparrowhawks breed nearby. Wooded offshore islands are the main breeding ground in the British Isles of the common scoter, a diving sea duck. The drake is all black, with a large knob and an orange patch on his bill. Old Castle Caldwell, first built in 1612, passed in 1662 to the Caldwell family. It is now very ruined and covered in ivy. In front of the gate lodge (on A47) is a giant stone fiddle, 5ft high, inscribed with an obituary poem to Denis McCabe, an inebriated fiddler who was drowned when he fell off the Caldwells' barge in 1770. To see the Bronze Age stone circle at **Drumskinny**, take the Castlederg road north from the fishing village of **Kesh** (population 600) for about 4$^{1}/_{2}$ miles.

Further west past Kesh, **Castle Archdale Country Park** has a youth hostel, camping and caravan sites, and a modern marina where you can take the public ferry to White Island. The exceedingly ruined old castle in the forest was built by John Archdale, an English planter from Norfolk, in 1615 and destroyed during the Williamite wars. 'New' Castle Archdale (1773) was used by the RAF from 1941 when Sunderlands and Catalinas were based on the lake. The outhouses of this eighteenth-century house, which is now derelict, contain a small exhibition featuring the Battle of the Atlantic. More concrete reminders of those days are the huge ramps at the yacht club at Goblusk Bay and, nearby, **St Angelo airfield** which was opened in 1941 and used by Dakotas.

Irvinestown (population 1,800) is enlivened in summer by a 10-day carnival. A clock tower with pinnacled battlements is all that is left of the 1734 church of Dr Patrick Delany, then rector at Irvinestown, later dean of Down. His wife, Mrs Mary Delany (1700–88, *née* Granville), was a brilliant London literary and society hostess, confidante of Pope, Burke and Horace Walpole, and a favourite at court. Delany met her through his friend, Swift. After their marriage in 1743, Mrs Delany accompanied her husband all over Ireland, meeting everyone, staying in all the great Anglo-Irish houses, and writing it all down. Her voluminous autobiography and correspondence, published in 1861–2, include spirited portraits of eighteenth-century Irish society.

6 THE SPERRINS
AND THE NORTH WEST

When the Four Citizens of London came to the north-west of Ulster in 1609, their guide was under instructions from the Lord Deputy of Ireland not to show them the Sperrin mountains. As agents for the City of London merchant companies, the visitors were looking at the region's investment potential, and the fear was that these rugged peaty hills would create a bad impression. Nowadays, the **Sperrins** are the haunt of trout fishermen, turf-cutters, and people panning for gold in the Foyle headwaters above the beautiful Owenkillew river. You may come across a lone walker 'doing' the Ulster Way, or small parties on archae-ological tramps. There are thousands of standing stones and chambered graves across the moors, mysterious testaments to the prehistoric Irish who lived up here.

Threaded by streams and small roads, the main expanse of the Sperrins is bounded by the towns of Strabane, Dungiven, Drapers-town and Newtownstewart. A section of the range spills south towards **Omagh** over the Owenkillew, and the north-east fringe is bisected by the **Glenshane pass** — the most direct route to Londonderry from Belfast.

There are more hills further north, running along the east side of the fertile **Roe valley**, with craggy **Binevenagh** rearing 1,271ft over **Lough Foyle**. The highest peak, **Sawel**, is only 2,240ft but the range and its extensions are sprawling, and ac-cess to the landlocked settlements of Tyrone and County London-derry was difficult until modern times. For the same reason, over-land attacks on Derry (called Londonderry after 1613 because of its associations with London), were rarely successful. Built on a hill on the banks of the Foyle estuary, the city is close to the open sea, and enemies and allies alike found it easier to approach by water. The Vikings arrived this way, starting in 812 when they destroyed St Columba's monastery on the hill, and the Jacobite siege of 1688–9 was lifted after 105 days when English ships forced their way down the estuary to relieve the city.

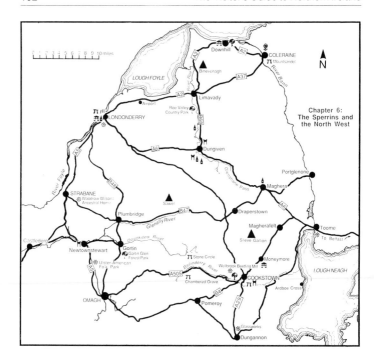

Ireland's last Gaelic stronghold was the densely forested country of Tyrone. Here the Earls of Tyrone and Tyrconnell, O'Neill and O'Donnell, held out against the government in the later sixteenth century. The price of this defiance was confiscation of their lands and property, though some local Irish Catholic land-owners managed to keep their estates following the Flight of the Earls in 1607. However, these too were forfeit after the 1641 rebellion. The beginning of this bloody and prolonged rebellion, which spread all over Ireland, was signalled by Sir Phelim O'Neill's seizure of Charlemont and Dungannon in Tyrone. The Irish wanted restitution of their lands. Their slaughter of Scots and English set-tlers was remembered at Drogheda 8 years later when Oliver Crom-well put the people of Drogheda to the sword.

South of the Sperrins the main centres of population are Dungannon, Cookstown and Omagh. The M1 from Belfast ends around **Dungannon** (population 8,300), a market and textile manufacturing town where the focus of interest for visitors is the glassware works of Tyrone Crystal (year-round tours). Dungan-

The Sperrins

non was the chief seat of the O'Neills from the fourteenth century until the plantation, and the first bible in Irish characters was produced here on a printing press established by Shane O'Neill in about 1567. All trace of the O'Neill castle on the hill has gone. The Royal School in Northland Row dates from the early seventeenth century. Its first headmaster died in the 1641 rebellion but the school reopened in 1662. The bronze statue in front of the present eighteenth-century building is ex-pupil General John Nicholson, killed storming Delhi during the Indian Mutiny (1857). The statue stood at the Kashmir Gate in Delhi until 1960. This same general pops up again in the market place in his home town of Lisburn, though the Dungannon bronze is nicer.

The development of the Tyrone coalfields in the nineteenth century was not a success story. The coal is still there, waiting for someone to work out a way to extract it profitably. The countryside around **Coalisland** (population 3,300) where brick-making is a local industry, is disfigured by large-scale sand, gravel and clay extraction and the detritus of old coal mines. Industrial archaeologists enthuse about the beehive kilns, old brickworks chimneys and the derelict canal basin. The town was briefly the inland port for the coalfields. Off the B161 from Coalisland, **Mountjoy Castle** is a ruined fort with four rectangular corner towers not far from **Washing Bay**. It was built in 1605 and was garrisoned during the Williamite wars.

Parkanaur, west of Dungannon, is a pretty forest park with an arboretum and a herd of white deer. Much history attaches to the fortified mansion and the church (of Donaghmore parish) at nearby **Castlecaulfield** (population 350). Sir Toby Caulfield, ancestor of the Earls of Charlemont, was an Oxfordshire knight who commanded Charlemont Fort during Mountjoy's 1602 campaign. He built the Castlecaulfield mansion in 1619 on the site of a Donnelly fort. After being burnt in 1641, it was repaired and lived in by the Caulfield/Charlemont family until about 1670. The tolerant first Viscount Charlemont allowed the Catholic primate, Oliver Plunket, to use the courtyard for ordinations in 1670, and John Wesley preached here on at least four occasions. Now in ruins, and incongruously surrounded by a housing estate, the mansion retains a gatehouse with murder-holes, gunloops and the Caulfield arms over the top.

Outside the graveyard of the seventeenth-century parish church, a blue plaque commemorates the poet Charles Wolfe (1791–1823) who was curate of Donaghmore 1818–21. His famous lines on 'The Burial of Sir John Moore' were published in the *Newry Telegraph* in 1817. Rector of Donaghmore from 1674 was the Rev. George Walker, better known as governor of Londonderry during the great siege. He was killed at the Boyne in 1690 and is buried in the south transept. The gabled porch is carved with cherubs holding a bible open at psalm 24. Various pieces inside the church, including the windows in the south nave, were brought from a vanished medieval church 2 miles north in **Donaghmore** (population 500), a village with a tenth-century high cross at the top of the main street. The cross, now rather worn, is 15ft tall and carved with biblical scenes. Close to the site of an early monastery associated with St Patrick, it was damaged in the seventeenth century. The obvious join midway up the shaft suggests that when it was reassembled in 1776, bits from two separate crosses were used. A pillar in the graveyard behind the cross is a modern memorial to Hugh O'Neill.

The chief crowning place of the O'Neills, from the early twelfth to the seventeenth century, was 2 miles outside **Cookstown** at **Tullaghoge**, headquarters of the O'Hagans, chief justices of Tyrone. There is a fine view of the old kingdom of Tyrone from the top of this tree-ringed hill. The circular graveyard nearby, with a wall round it, was the O'Hagan burial place. During the ceremony

---

┌───┐
│   **THINGS TO SEE WEST OF LOUGH NEAGH**   │
└───┘

Tenth-century carved High Crosses

Ardboe — very tall impressive cross at lakeside near ruined seventeenth-century church. Donaghmore —15ft cross in village street near O'Neill memorial pillar.

Tyrone Crystal, Dungannon

Glass blowing and cutting. Works tour lasts an hour. Shop.

Wellbrook Beetling Mill, Cookstown

Two-storey water-driven mill for beetling — hammering linen cloth to produce smooth finish. Working machinery. Mill race walk. (National Trust).

Moneymore and Springhill House

Sophisticated plantation village largely rebuilt in about 1820 by the Drapers' Company for £30,000. Springhill is a seventeenth-century manor (with additions) which was home of Conyngham family for 300 years. Family furniture. Costume collection. (NationalTrust).

---

the king-elect sat on a stone inauguration chair, new sandals were placed on his feet, the assembled chiefs chanted his name in unison 'amid the clang of bucklers and the music of a hundred harps', and he was then anointed and crowned by the primate of Armagh. The last king to sit on the chair was the great Hugh O'Neill in 1593. The O'Hagan role as prominent law officers continued into modern times, and the first Lord O'Hagan (1812–85) was chancellor of Ireland.

The rebel leader, Phelim O'Neill, had himself inaugurated at Tullaghoge in 1641. He had to manage without the chair — Lord Mounjoy smashed it in 1602. Sir Phelim epitomised the political turmoil and shaky allegiances of the day: he was simultaneously a knight of the realm, premier prince of Ulster (as recognised by the pope), member of parliament for Dungannon and executioner of many of his English and Scottish constituents. He remained at large until 1653, when he was captured near Newmills, north-east of Dungannon, hiding on the crannog in **Roughan Lough** (now popular with water-skiers), taken to Dublin and hanged for treason. Ruined Roughan Castle, a fortress with stubby round towers near the lake, was built by Sir Andrew Stewart in 1618.

The main street in **Cookstown** (population 7,650) is perfectly straight, 1¼ miles long with a hump in the middle, and 130ft wide. It was part of an ambitious town plan by William Stewart of

Wellbrook Beetling Mill, near Cookstown

Killymoon, an eighteenth-century Tyrone landlord. However, neither he nor his descendants ever got round to developing the town beyond this remarkable central avenue. Its great advantage, from the visitor's point of view, is convenient parking. The life and bustle of Cookstown, at the centre of good farming country, focuses wholly on the main street which, for some reason, changes its name no fewer than eight times. Although the shops and houses are rather ordinary, the broad avenue has a certain theatrical appeal, with the bleak outline of **Slieve Gallion** (1,737ft) looming up 8 miles directly north. Biggest building by far is Holy Trinity, a Catholic church halfway down the west side. Built in 1855 by J.J. McCarthy, it has a massive tower and spire, visible from far off.

The linen industry was important here. The father of the botanist Augustine Henry (born Cookstown 1857) was a Cookstown flax buyer, and there are old mills along the nearby Ballinderry river. The modern town is known for its sausages, made in the large bacon factory. There are livestock markets and a flourishing Saturday street market. A golf course occupies the parkland of **Killymoon Castle**, a Norman-revival castle designed for the

Ardboe Cross

Stewarts in 1802 by John Nash, the celebrated English architect (1752–1835). Its present owner allows visitors to look round during 'reasonable hours'. South of the town is Loughry Manor (now an agricultural college), a plantation mansion which has associations with Dean Jonathan Swift. He stayed here as a guest of the Lindsay family, while writing *Gulliver's Travels* (published 1726). Portraits of 'Stella' (Esther Johnson, died 1728) and ✳ 'Vanessa' (Esther Vanhomrigh, died 1723) still hang in the Old Library. The Dean loved them both, and made them both miserable.

Ardboe high cross, over 18ft tall, stands inside a small railing on an early monastic site along a bleak stretch of Lough Neagh's western shore. Though much eroded, the tenth-century cross is impressive and has twenty-two carved panels. Old Testament scenes on the east side start at the bottom with Adam and Eve, with New Testament scenes up the west side. Nearby is the ruin of a seventeenth-century church. Lughnasa (Lammas) used to be celebrated at Ardboe, with praying at the cross and much washing in the lake. It is reckoned that eel fishing has gone on here for 5,000 years. The monks of the sixth-century monastery at Ardboe used eel oil in their lamps. The small farms around Ardboe are mostly owned by eel fishermen. From May onwards you can see them setting lines in sections up to 2 miles long. The catch is worth several millions of pounds a year.

West of Cookstown, past **Drum Manor Forest Park** on the A505, a lane runs down to **Wellbrook** beetling mill in a pretty setting on the fast-flowing river. It started work in 1768 and was one of six beetling mills serving a local bleachworks. Beetling was the noisy process that gave sheen and smoothness to the linen cloth by pounding it with heavy wooden hammers, or beetles. The two-storey mill, big waterwheel and picturesque mill race have been restored by the National Trust. The seven large engines inside are in working order and there is an exhibition on linen-making in the loft. If your idea of how a mill race works is vague, a walk along the path at the back is instructive.

There are many ancient monuments around here. Be sceptical of signposting. As in other parts of Tyrone, direction signs are frequently vandalised, though local people will go out of their way to help if you ask. The striking prehistoric stones at **Beaghmore** on the fringe of the Sperrins were discovered in the 1930s. Seven stone circles, three pairs and an odd one, and a dozen or so stone alignments and round cairns, have been cleared of peat. Most of the circle stones are small — no more than 2 or 3ft feet high. Many are barely a foot tall, and the tallest is only about 4ft. The site dates from the middle of the Bronze Age. Other similar sets of circles and alignments have been found in the Sperrins, including Moymore near Lough Bracken, 2 miles from Pomeroy. The heathery windswept moors around Beaghmore are littered with the remains of other monuments which have been turned up by turf cutting.

Cregganconroe court grave, overlooking Cam Lough, is signposted off the main Cookstown-Omagh road (A505). It is

Beaghmore Stone Circles

typical of some 300 similar North Irish megalithic graves, where the narrow burial chamber is entered through a wider forecourt. A similar grave, on the west side of Lough Mallon at **Creggand-** π **evesky**, was excavated a few years ago. To be up here at twilight is an eery experience, even on a summer day.

A secondary road (B4) from Cookstown to Omagh runs through the upland village of **Pomeroy** (population 700), with a modern forestry school on the estate of the Rev. James Lowry, eighteenth-century planner of the village. The Anglican church (1841) in the neat market square later acquired a belfry and spire which, according to an inscription, were added by John and Armar Lowry 'as a tribute of attachment to their birthplace'.

American connections in the area are interesting. The grandfather of James B. Irwin, the Apollo 15 astronaut who drove round the moon in a buggy in 1971, was born in Pomeroy. Irwins still live in the house. James Shields, one of Lincoln's generals in the American Civil War, was born in 1806 near **Cappagh**, south of Pomeroy. A now derelict building in Cappagh village was the Shields' family bank, the Altmore Loan Fund, which flourished from 1852 to 1903. James Shields, who emigrated at the age of twenty, defeated the great Confederate general, Stonewall Jackson, at Kernstown, Virginia. Jackson's own ancestral home, **The Birches**, is just across the Tyrone/Armagh border. President James Buchanan's father emigrated from **Deroran**,

The Mellon Home, Ulster-American Folk Park, near Omagh

south-east of Omagh, to Pennsylvania where the future president was born in 1791. Buchanan, president from 1857 to 1861, was one of the only three first-generation Americans ever to occupy the White House. All three of them were sons of Ulster emigrants.

Omagh

Eclectic snippets like this, and the broader picture of Ulster emigrations to the North American continent, can be discovered in the exhibition galleries of the **Ulster-American Folk Park** ⌂ outside Omagh. Opened in 1976 and attracting about 70,000 visitors a year, the folk park has been developed round the cottage where Judge Thomas Mellon, founder of the fabulously rich Mellon dynasty, was born in 1813. His son, Andrew, built the steel town of Pittsburgh. Mellon money helped build the Waldorf Astoria, San Francisco's Golden Gate bridge and the gates of the

Panama canal. Thomas was aged five when the family emigrated.
Another Tyrone native, John Joseph Hughes, later archbishop of
New York, left at the same time as the Mellons. His boyhood
home, rebuilt stone by stone, has been moved into the park which
also contains replicas of American log cabins and early farmsteads.

Omagh (population 14,650), a market town with a large agricultural hinterland, grew at the place where two rivers (Camowen
and Drumragh) meet to form the wide, shallow Strule. The town
centre is a hilly, architectural muddle of nineteenth-century and
twentieth-century buildings away from the pretty rivers down
below. Despite this, and the frequent batterings which have made
Omagh a security-conscious place, the town has character and a
cheerfulness stemming, perhaps, from its 200 years as county
town of Tyrone until local government reorganisation in 1973. The
most prominent landmark is the Sacred Heart Catholic church
(1893–9), with twin spires, unequal in height, dominating the somewhat earlier Anglican church, and the Classical courthouse (1814,
by John Hargrave) at the top of the steep main street. The Black
Bell of Drumragh, said to be ninth-century, is preserved inside —
to see it ask at the sacristy (or call at 33 George's Street, right of
the taller spire).

Local trout and salmon fishing, and pike and roach in the
Strule and Fairy Water, bring anglers into town for bait and tackle.
Omagh is also a centre for wildfowling and for fishing the remote
lakes to the west, beyond **Drumquin** (population 600). The Black
Bog, a very old, deep bog, north-west of the A505/B46 crossroads, supplies refined peat for the local craft industry of
ornaments made from compressed peat. Playwright Brian Friel,
author of *Philadelphia here I come* and *Translations*, was born in
Omagh (1930) and so was Jimmy Kennedy (1903–84) who wrote
'The teddy bears' picnic' and 'South of the border' and many other
popular songs. Ulster poet John Montague (born 1929) grew up in
nearby **Fintona** (population 1,350), an attractive little town well
equipped with public houses, including the Poet's Pub, once
owned by Montague's mother. Outside Fintona, Seskinore Game
Farm rears pheasants and partridges, and woodcock and rough
game bring field sportsmen to this part of the Sperrins.

Up towards the great gorge of **Gortin Glen Forest Park**,
there are scenic drives around Mullaghcarn mountain (1,778ft),
Gortin, and Plumbridge on the Glenelly river. A history park is
being developed at **Gortin** (population 300), a pleasant village

Gortin Forest

with a youth hostel. **Plumbridge** (population 250), hemmed in by crags at the bottom of a narrow valley, has a quaint cattle market. There has been periodic gold-rush fever hereabouts, and recent commercial prospecting in the area has revived the rumours. Locals will tell you that it takes weeks of laborious panning in the headwaters of the Foyle system to extract minuscule amounts of the stuff.

An attractive drive is east from Gortin, then north through the very scenic **Barnes Gap** to join up with the Plumbridge-Draperstown road (B47), running east along the **Glenelly valley** to **Sperrin hamlet** (at 570ft) at the foot of **Sawel** (2,240ft). If you have time and energy, for a really wide panorama, park at the pub in Sperrin and stride out north. After 2 miles, leave the road and make for Sawel summit (an hour's tramp) for superlative views of Lough Neagh, the Foyle estuary and the Mournes. Dart mountain (2,040ft) is half an hour's walk west along the ridge. Turning south to Cranagh hamlet (45 minutes), you are back to the B47 and only 45 minutes from Sperrin — and a pot of tea, or a pint, in the tiny pub. (Allow 4 hours for this walk.)

From the Ulster-American Folk Park, the A5 passes between two small hills called Bessie Bell (west side) and Mary Gray (east)

PLACES OF INTEREST AROUND THE SPERRINS

Beaghmore Stone Circles
Prehistoric circles, alignments
and cairns. Information panels at
protected site in rugged scenery.
Take A505 from Cookstown for
8¹/2 miles, then turn north, 3
miles.

**Ulster-American Folk Park,
Omagh**
Preserves Ulster's links with pioneer America. Original and recon-
structed Irish and American buildings in open-air museum. Large

modern exhibition galleries. Bookshop.

Sion Mills
Model linen village. Interesting
architectural mix.

**Woodrow Wilson Ancestral
Home, near Strabane**
President Wilson's grandfather,
James Wilson, emigrated from
this farmhouse in 1807. Original
furniture, photographs. Wilsons
still work the farm.

---

following the course of the Strule into **Newtownstewart**
(population 1,450). James II spent the night here in 1689 on his
way back from the unsuccessful assault on Londonderry. He got
up next morning in a bad mood and ordered the Stewart castle,
and the town, to be burnt down. In the main street a piece of the
castle wall still stands. The Northern Bank building on the corner
was the scene of a famous murder in 1871 when bank cashier
William Glass was done to death and robbed of £1,600. District
Inspector Montgomery, of the Royal Irish Constabulary, who was
in charge of the case, turned out to be the murderer. Half a mile
south-west, on a hill, is ruined **Harry Avery's Castle**, a
fourteenth-century Gaelic stone castle — most unusual in Ulster.
Only the massive D-shaped twin towers of the keep, built by
Henry Aimbreidh O'Neill (died 1392), are left.

The great house of **Baronscourt**, country seat of the Hamilton family, the Dukes of Abercorn, is set in a landscaped park
with terraced Italian-style gardens, and three lakes, one with a
crannog in it. The mansion dates from about 1780. The park is
private, although tourists staying in the holiday cottages near the
golf course can arrange pike fishing and water-skiing on the
lakes. Visitors to the estate garden centre, which has a café and
craft shop, will notice the elegant Agent's House, built in 1741 by
James Martin, architect of the cathedral at Clogher.

There is good angling in the Mourne around **Victoria Bridge**
and **Douglas Bridge**. These are blink-and-miss hamlets on
opposite banks of the river, but Douglas Bridge features in a

Gray's Printing Shop,
Strabane

ballad by the Irish-American poet, Francis Carlin:

> 'On Douglas Bridge I met a man
> Who lived adjacent to Strabane,
> Before the English hung him high
> For riding with O'Hanlon.'

The outlaw, 'Count' Redmond O'Hanlon, who was killed at Hilltown in 1681, was the political heir of Sir Phelim O'Neill. At one time a narrow gauge railway ran from Victoria Bridge to the lively little market town of **Castlederg** (population 1,750), now the remotest town in the province. The plantation castle built in Castlederg by Sir John Davies (1619) was besieged in 1641 by Sir Phelim who, despite not being able to capture it, damaged it so badly that it was never repaired. The Anglican church, with a good Classical doorway, dates from 1731.

Sion Mills (population 1,750) was laid out as a model linen village by the god-fearing Herdman brothers, James, John and George. In 1835 they converted an old flour mill on the Mourne into a flax-spinning mill, and erected a bigger mill behind it in the 1850s. Their factory is still working. The village is an exotic mix of polychrome brick, black-and-white half-timbered buildings, and terraced millworkers' cottages, all set off by wide grassy verges, horse-chestnut trees and, on the Strabane road, some nice beeches. Nearly everything in Sion Mills except St Teresa's church was designed by James Herdman's son-in-law, the English architect William Unsworth. Sion House, a half-timbered Elizabethan-style mansion with pepperpot chimneys, was planned by Unsworth at the same time as he was designing the first Shakespeare memorial theatre in Stratford-on-Avon (opened in 1879, destroyed by a fire in 1926).

More modest half-timbered buildings include the pretty gatehouse, the recreation hall and Old St Saviour's church. Unsworth based his design for the polychrome Anglican church (1909) on a church in Pistoia in Tuscany. It has tall campanili and huge semicircular windows. By contrast the modern Catholic church of St Teresa (1963, by Patrick Haughey) is admirable for its severely plain lines — a long rectangle with a striking representation of the Last Supper on the slate façade. Oisin Kelly was the artist.

The border town of **Strabane** (population 10,750) looks northwest across the Foyle to Lifford, a mile downstream in County Donegal. James II made his base here in 1688–9 for the attack on Londonderry. Unlikely though it seems now, Strabane was an important printing and book publishing centre in the eighteenth century. The only relic of that humanistic tradition is a little shop with a Georgian front in Main Street — Gray's Printing Shop, rescued by the National Trust. Meetinghouse Street was the birthplace of John Dunlap (1747–1812) who printed the broadsheets of the American Declaration of Independence which were sent round the world in July 1776. Dunlap published the Declaration a few days later on the front page of his little *Pennsylvania Packet* which grew into a daily newspaper — America's first daily (1784).James Wilson, grandfather of President Woodrow Wilson (1913-21), was also a printer, and editor of a Philadelphia newspaper. He served his apprenticeship in Strabane and emigrated in 1807. He married a girl from Sion Mills, Annie Adams, whom he

President Wilson Ancestral Home, near Strabane

met on the ship. The **Wilson ancestral home**, a thatched farm- ❋
house at Dergalt, 2 miles down the Plumbridge road, is open all
year. Some of the furniture is original. Wilsons live in the modern
house next door and still work the farm.

Other notable emigrants from Strabane included William Knox
who founded the Alabama Central Bank. He lost all his money in
the American Civil War after loaning half a million pounds to the
short-lived Confederate government. Alexander Porter, who became a supreme court judge in the state of Louisiana, was educated in the town. He was the eldest son of a United Irishman, the
Rev. James Porter of Ballindrait, hanged after the 1798 rebellion.
Alexander's brother, James, became attorney general of Louisiana. Even during the booming linen years there were plenty who
had no stake in the town's prosperity — for example, the children
of the Strabane workhouse, who were sent off to America in about
1840 — and there was a steady stream of emigrants from
Strabane long before the great exodus at the time of the potato
famine.

Londonderry and the Surrounding Area

Londonderry (population 62,750) is the province's second
largest city and has an important shirt-making trade which started
in the 1820s. In World War II it was both naval base and airbase.
Some 20,000 American sailors were stationed here, Al Jolson and
Bob Hope came to entertain the troops, and the UK's largest con-
voy escorts across the Atlantic were centred on the port.

The city stands on a hill on the Foyle estuary and, for most of
its history, has been an important seaport. St Columba founded
the first monastery on the hill in AD546 which, at that time, was
covered in trees and entirely surrounded by water. The city's
popular name, Derry, derives from the Gaelic *doire* which means
'a place of oaks'. Columba went to Iona in 563 and began the con-
version of Scotland and Northumbria by the Celtic Church. Mean-
while the Derry monastery thrived and, despite attacks of various
kinds, successive communities of Augustinians, Cistercians,
Dominicans and Franciscans flourished here throughout the
Middle Ages.

The royal charter of 1613, which gave Derry a mayor and corporation and added London to its name, saw it as suitable as 'both
a town of war and a town of merchandise', and that is how it turned
out. There are no visible remains of the pre-plantation town but

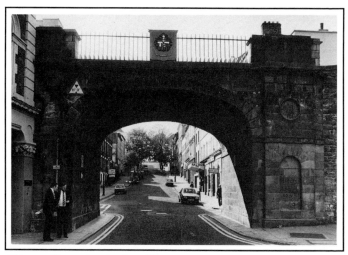

Shipquay Street , Londonderry City

PLACES OF INTEREST IN LONDONDERRY

Walls of Derry
One-mile circuit along ramparts enclosing historic city centre. Many seventeenth-century cannon. Roaring Meg, an 18-pounder dating from 1642 and used in the great siege, is mounted at Double Bastion. Easy access from Shipquay Gate. Guided tours start from tourist office near Guildhall.

Guildhall
The city's history in stained glass. Sir Cahir O'Doherty's two-headed double-edged sword. Concerts, theatre.

St Columb's Cathedral
Anglican cathedral built 1633. Memorials, plaques and monuments reiterate the London connection. Portraits, engravings, manuscripts in chapter-house.

Long Tower Church
Built in 1786, it first had only a mud floor. Rococo interior has stepped galleries. Churchyard bronzes, double bullaun stone.

St Eugene's Cathedral
Roman Catholic cathedral completed 1873. The 256ft spire was added in 1903.

Heritage Library, 12 Bishop Street.
Reference library and reading room, private manuscript and map collection. Exhibitions, lectures.

the city has a wealth of eighteenth-century buildings, and there are vivid memorials to its long, tumultuous past. These, together with the soft-spoken, wry and friendly people, well aware of Londonderry's reputation as a Northern Ireland trouble spot, give the place an interesting extra dimension which visitors will not encounter anywhere else in the province.

The English first came here in 1566 after a revolt by Shane O'Neill. They installed a garrison which was wiped out the following year after the arsenal — installed inside the medieval cathedral — exploded accidentally. There was another revolt in 1600, and in 1608 the fortifications were over-run by the O'Dohertys, chiefs of Inishowen. To prevent future rebellions, James I gave the City of London responsibility for settling this whole region of Ulster. Accustomed to stumping up vast sums for the crown, the City was on this occasion cajoled and bullied into an intimate and permanent involvement — the plantation of Londonderry, rebuilding and fortifying the ruined medieval town, planning and building dozens of smaller towns and villages, and supplying craftsmen to do the work. The financial commitment was to last for hundreds of years.

A new county, called Londonderry, was created by combining Derry town with the lands of the troublesome O'Cahans in the old county of Coleraine and adding various tracts of Tyrone and Antrim. The City of London set up a special body, The Honourable The Irish Society, to manage their lands, keeping direct control over three strategic main towns — Derry, Coleraine and Limavady — and parcelling out the rest of County Londonderry between the twelve ancient London livery companies.

Until 1984 there was only ever one bridge over the Foyle to link Londonderry City with the county it administered. The wooden bridge of 1790 was replaced in 1863, and then again in 1931 by the present double-deck Craigavon Bridge. A second bridge, opened a little downstream in 1984, has relieved traffic congestion and, for visitors to Donegal, bypasses the city.

❋   The great seventeenth-century walls which encircle the historic centre are 20-25ft high, 30ft wide in places and a mile round. Inside, four main streets radiate out from the Diamond, or square, to the four original gates, **Bishop's Gate**, **Butcher's Gate**, **Shipquay Gate** and **Ferryquay Gate**. Three more gates were let into the walls later. Completed by 1618 and still entire, with old cannon pointing over the ramparts, the walls are a most striking feature. Their first test came with a siege in 1641, and again in 1648, when supplies were brought in by sea, and lastly and most memorably, in the siege of 1688–9.

You can make a complete circuit along the top of the walls apart from a short section above St Columb's cathedral where there is a (modern) military lookout plonked on top of the Neo-Classical Bishop's Gate, which was rebuilt in 1789. One of the ❋ cannon over Shipquay Gate was a gift from Elizabeth I in 1590. Four others were given to the city in 1642 by the Mercers, Grocers, Vintners and Merchant Taylors of London. The walls are punctuated at intervals with bastions and picturesque stone watch towers, and dozens of gunloops — small ones for muskets and large ones open at the top for cannon.

The great siege began after thirteen apprentice boys seized the keys of the town and locked the gates against an approaching Jacobite regiment. The citizens expelled the vacillating governor, Colonel Lundy (who is still burnt in effigy every year in a sort of Guy Fawkes ritual) and civil administration was taken over by George Walker, a formidable clergyman from Donaghmore. The city thus declared for William of Orange and against King James II. James landed in Ireland in March 1689 and hurried north to

Fountain, Foyle Street, Londonderry City

restore his authority, arriving outside Bishop's Gate on 18 April. Since his engineers were too few to scale the walls, he set up guns opposite Shipquay Gate and waited.

For the people inside, help was slow in coming. About 7,000 of them died of starvation and disease. Near the end cats and dogs were being sold in butchers' shops and even a rat cost a shilling. The besiegers had the foresight to build a wooden boom across the river (at the place where Boom Hall, a Georgian villa, now stands) to stop supply ships reaching the town. On 28 July a ship commanded by Captain Michael Browning, a native of Londonderry, sailed up the Foyle in the face of artillery fire, broke through the boom and relieved the city.

The siege had wide repercussions in Europe. It gave William a crucial breathing space to organise his army, paving the way to his decisive victory in 1690 at the Boyne — the battle which secured William as king of England and damaged the prestige of Louis XIV in Europe. This European dimension led Macaulay to call the siege 'the most memorable in the annals of the British Isles'. For Ireland it meant two things: a Protestant ascendancy throughout the eighteenth century, and a long period of peace and stability that, so far, has not been repeated.

There is parking at the **Guildhall** in Foyle Street close to Shipquay Gate, convenient for getting up on to the walls. A plaque
below the pretty fountain in Foyle Street marks the quay where
hundreds of thousands of emigrants embarked for America.
Guided tours leave from the tourist information centre across the
carpark. The Guildhall has dozens of stained glass windows illus-
trating almost every episode of note in the city's history. The
story flows up the staircase and floods all the chambers with light.
The building was burnt out in 1908 and bombed in 1972. The City
of London finished restoring the glass in 1984 — the year the city
council, now with a nationalist majority, renamed itself Derry City
Council.

A medieval-looking exhibition tower peering over the walls at
Shipquay Gate is an agreeable fake on the site of Sir Cahir O'Doherty's long-vanished castle. The tower is at the centre of a new
'heritage village' and is a focal point for O'Doherty clan gather-
ings. From the river the main thoroughfare rises steeply 200ft,
past a modern shopping centre to the war memorial in the Diamond, and on up Bishop's Street, passing basement pubs and
shops, a heritage library and an excellent adjoining bookshop,
and fine Georgian buildings in varying states of repair. The **Irish
Society House** (1764) is well preserved and so is the Classical
courthouse (1813) across the road from the Regency-style
former **bishop's palace**. Narrow side-streets and smaller roads
in the shadow of the walls give some dramatic architectural
perspectives.

The most interesting church inside the walls, and the chief
repository of the city's turbulent seventeenth-century memories,
is **St Columb's Anglican cathedral** built in 1633. The London link is proclaimed on the famous date stone preserved in the
porch:

'If stones could speake then London's prayse should sound
Who built this church and cittie from the grounde.'

Among scores of plaques and memorials ranged round the walls is
a marble monument shared by Colonel Henry Baker, a city
governor who died on the 74th day of the siege, and Captain
Browning, killed by a shot after his ship broke the boom a month
later. One window depicts St Columba's sixth-century mission to
Britain; another illustrates hymns written by Mrs C.F. Alexander
(1818–95), wife of a bishop of Derry. Her *Hymns for Little
Children*, published in 1848, went into sixty-nine editions during

The Guildhall, Londonderry City

her life. The three represented here are 'There is a green hill far
away', 'Once in royal David's city', and 'The golden gates are
lifted up'. An organ case over the west door is by the celebrated
wood carver, Grinling Gibbons, whose commissions included

Londonderry City

Hampton Court and the choir of St Paul's Cathedral in London. Two groynes near the organ are likenesses of George Walker, governor of Derry to the end of the siege, and George Berkeley (1685–1753), the metaphysical philosopher, who was appointed Dean of Derry in 1724.

Among treasures in the **chapterhouse** are the seventeenth-century locks and keys of the city gates, Lord Macaulay's manuscript account of the siege, interesting paintings, and a pair of duelling pistols belonging to Frederick Hervey, fourth Earl of Bristol and Bishop of Derry (1730–1803). This Byronic nobleman, a flamboyant character whose name is preserved in all the Bristol Hotels in Europe, acquired the rich bishopric of Derry in 1768 and immediately began building churches and improving old ones. He spent £1,000 on putting an enormous stone spire on St Columb's but it was much too heavy and had to be dismantled. Active in the Volunteer movement and a supporter of emancipation, the Earl Bishop is also remembered for his support for Roman Catholic and nonconformist church building, including Long Tower Church a few yards outside the walls. Go through Bishop's Gate to see it.

Long Tower Church is the city's oldest Catholic church (1784–6). Its name recalls the great medieval cathedral, the Templemore, which was built by the Augustinian abbot O'Broclain in 1164 when Derry was an important monastic centre. After the cathedral was flattened by the explosion of 1567, a tenth-century round tower — the Long Tower — survived nearby for another 100 years or so. The present Long Tower Church has steeply stepped galleries and double-gabled transepts and, in the church-yard, bronzes by Mayer of Munich.

Returning through Bishop's Gate, turn left to get back on to the walls. Spread out down below the ramparts are the unlovely acres of the Bogside housing estate. Beyond it, towards the north-west, rises the large Catholic cathedral, **St Eugene's**. It was com-pleted in 1873 to designs by J.J. McCarthy, though it had to wait 30 years more for the spire. The east window, a memorial to the cathedral's builder, Bishop Francis Kelly, depicts the crucifixion and seven Irish saints. St Eugene's is best reached from Strand Road (A2) which is also the route for the University of Ulster campus at Magee. The oldest pub in Derry, Andy Cole's, is at 135 Strand Road. Half a dozen pubs have regular Irish music sessions — check which nights with the tourist office. The music shop in Carlisle Road sells Irish musical instruments like *bodhrans* and tin whistles, and no. 71 Carlisle Road has a large collection of hand-made fiddles. Three miles beyond Magee College, at **Ballyarnet Field**, a cottage exhibition centre com- memorates the transatlantic flight in 1932 by Amelia Earhart, the first woman to fly the Atlantic solo. She landed in this field.

The 'polder' appearance of the coastal strip between London-derry and the mouth of the **Roe** is an unusual landscape to find in Ireland. Drivers along the A2 east from the city will not see it except by turning down side roads, but it is most striking from the train. Reclaimed from the sea in the nineteenth century for flax growing, these fertile polders — called 'levels' locally — are actually below sea level and are drained by pumping stations. The crops now are grain and vegetables, mostly potatoes. In between the polders are mudflats and deserted runways of old wartime aerodromes. The lovely estuary of the Roe is a national nature reserve.

The aerodrome at **Eglinton** (population 1,250), 4 miles east of Londonderry, is now a civilian airport, with regular scheduled services linking north-west Ulster with Glasgow and Dublin. The village was created by the Grocers' Company in 1823–5 and has an elegant courthouse in the main street. At the same time the Fishmongers were developing their model farm at **Ballykelly** (population 900). The famhouse has a paddock at the front and a

Ballykelly Model Farm

walled farmyard. Other appealing plantation buildings in Ballykelly include the Presbyterian church, a school, and a dispensary (now Bridge House). The Earl Bishop built the Anglican parish church (1795), with three-stage tower, needle spire and interesting funerary monuments. North of Ballykelly bridge **Waworth House** is an eighteenth-century five-bay house with three still-intact flankers from the Fishmongers' early seventeenth-century bawn. The ruins of the Company's church of 1629 are opposite the house. At the roadside on the edge of Farlow Wood a mile before Limavady, **Sampson's Tower** was erected in memory of an early nineteenth-century agent for the Fishmongers' estates. The large tree-fringed earthwork a few yards further on, on the other side of the road, is Rough Fort rath. At Broighter, north of here, a priceless collection of prehistoric gold ornaments known as the Broighter Treasure (now in the National Museum, Dublin) was discovered by a ploughman in the 1890s.

   Limavady (population 8,000) is a pretty market town on the Roe river, with some surviving Georgian features. It was created by an energetic Welshman, Sir Thomas Phillips, the City of London's chief agent in Ulster from 1609. W.M. Thackeray stopped for ale at the inn (demolished) in the main street in 1842 and wrote some verses about the barmaid, 'Sweet Peg of Limavady'. No. 51

INTERESTING PLACES NEAR LIMAVADY

Mussenden Temple,
Downhill
Cliff-top rotunda in eighteenth-
century demesne of flamboyant
Earl Bishop of Derry near his
ruined palace. Panoramic views
of Ireland's north coast. Notable
Neo-Classical gateways, gate
lodge, walled garden, dovecote,
ice house.

Bishop's View
Viewpoint on Bishop's Road
across Binevenagh mountain.
Picnic tables.

Roe Valley Country Park
Restored hydro-electric plant,
water mills. Museum in weaving
shed. Unusually interesting
walks. Industrial archaeology
includes ruined beetling mill, flax
retting tanks, bleach greens,
watch towers, tannery, distillery.
Fishing, camping.

Dungiven Priory and
O'Cahan's Tomb
Augustinian priory preserves
Ulster's finest medieval tomb.
Ruins of seventeenth-century
house and bawn in precincts.

Main Street was the home of Jane Ross (1810–79) who noted down the famous 'Londonderry Air' ('Danny Boy') from an itinerant fiddler in 1851. She lived here with her three younger sisters, all unmarried, and a plaque commemorates her single great service in preserving the best known of all Irish melodies. The Ross sisters are buried across the road at the eighteenth-century parish church, which has a collection of several hundred tapestry kneelers, each one different. William Massey, prime minister of New Zealand (1912–25), was born in Irish Green Street in 1856 (plaque). The local hospital occupies a trim Victorian workhouse with all its 1841 buildings intact.

In the gorges of the **Roe Valley Country Park**, a mile south of Limavady, a hydro-electric plant, water mills and a weaving shed are among a tremendous collection of restored rural industrial buildings on the banks of the peaty red river. The park is popular for canoeing, camping and especially game fishing.

The primeval forest of Glenconkeyne north-west of Lough Neagh was chopped down early in the seventeenth century, a raw material for the plantation towns and villages in County Londonderry. The oaks and elms were floated down the Bann to build houses in Limavady and Coleraine, or used as firewood, in particular for smelting the iron ore deposits found around **Slieve Gallion**. By about 1640 most of the forest had gone. There are still reminders of the green gaiety of the ancient wood around

Roe Valley Country Park, Limavady

 **Springhill House**, a National Trust property a mile from Money-more towards Coagh (B18). A thicket of old yews has survived in the grounds of this fortified seventeenth-century house, which is surely the prettiest house in Ulster.

Moneymore (population 1,250) is an unusually harmonious plantation town with many nice buildings along the wide main street. This was the Drapers' first settlement, and the first town in Ulster to have piped water (1615). Like so many such settle-ments, it was destroyed in 1641 and the present buildings, which

include two market houses, two Presbyterian churches, a school
and a dispensary, date from the Georgian period. The centre of
interest shifted eventually from Moneymore to Draperstown which
grew round a big livestock and linen market. The triangular green
at **Draperstown** (population 1,300) is still a lively place on
market days. A small private linen museum at **Upperlands**,
north-east of Draperstown, contains original weaving and bleaching machinery. The market town of **Magherafelt** (population
5,050) was part of the Salters' estates and has a large central
square with wide roads leading off.

Maghera (population 1,950) at the foot of the **Glenshane
pass** was church property before the plantation and, quite unlike
the settlers' towns, the streets are narrow. Its main interest is
Maghera Old Church on the site of a sixth-century monastery
founded by St Lurach. In the Middle Ages Maghera was the seat
of a bishop. The fine twelfth-century west door has sculpted sloping jambs, decorated with animal and floral motifs, and a massive
lintel carved with a crucifixion scene. The door has a square head
on the outside and a semicircular head on the inside. The seventeenth-century tower had a residence for the priest on the first
floor. South of the church is an imposing rectory built in 1825.

Dungiven (population 2,250) was an O'Cahan stronghold
until the plantation when it was granted to the Skinners' Company.
The remains of their bawn are incorporated into a battlemented
nineteenth-century castle which now lies derelict and overgrown,
visible from the A6 on the east side of town. The ruined Augustinian priory of St Mary's, signposted on the same road, preserves
the tomb of Cooey na Gall O'Cahan who died in 1385. The sculptured effigy, wearing Irish armour, lies under a traceried canopy in
the thirteenth-century chancel. Six bare-legged warriors in kilts,
standing in niches below the prone chieftain, were his foreign mer-
cenaries, probably Scots, from whom he derived his nickname 'na
Gall' meaning 'of foreigners'. It is the finest medieval tomb in
Ulster. The priory church dates from about 1150 and was remodelled in the seventeenth century when a house and bawn were
added. Park at the top of the lane and walk down to the ruins. A
thicket of thorn bushes hung with rags, on the right, conceals a
bullaun stone, visited for wart cures.

Ruined **Banagher** church, on a hill 2 miles south-west of Dungiven — take the minor Turmeel road from Dungiven town centre
— was founded in about 1100 by St Muiredach O'Heney. The
nave is the oldest part. It has an impressive square-headed lintel-

O'Cahan's Tomb, Dungiven Priory

led west door, like Maghera but without the carvings. The nave
window closely resembles the one at Dungiven Priory. On a sand-
hill close by is the saint's appealing little mortuary house (built
about 1100) with a carved abbot on the gable end. 'Banagher
sand' scraped from under the tomb is said to bring luck to all

O'Heney's Mortuary House, Banagher

O'Heneys. The most famous bearer of that name hereabouts is the poet Seamus Heaney, born in 1939 on a farm near **Toomebridge**. A similar mortuary house, though more ruined, is at **Bovevagh** off the B192 6 miles north of Dungiven. It seems that the Dungiven, Maghera and Banagher churches all had the same twelfth-century architect.

The scenic Bishop's Road across Binevenagh mountain is joined from the A2 north of Limavady by taking the B201 for a mile and then turning left. The Earl Bishop built the road to improve access to Limavady from his palace at Downhill. After 5 miles stop at the **Bishop's View** for the panorama over the plain. A lovely 7-mile golden strand sweeps round to **Magilligan Point** where a martello tower, built in Napoleonic days, commands the approach to Lough Foyle. Swirling air currents around the point can waft gliders as high as 20,000ft and the Ulster Gliding Club is based at **Bellarena** nearby. A fish smokery in the big house at Bellarena specialises in smoked salmon and sea trout. After the Bishop's View, the road swoops down to rejoin the A2 at **Downhill**. At the roadside a Neo-Classical gateway marks the entrance to Downhill demesne and the start of a lovely glen walk up to a windswept headland.

The Earl Bishop's favourite architect, Michael Shanahan, worked on Downhill Palace on and off from the early 1770s until about 1785, designing a magnificent library and a two-storey picture

Mussenden Temple, Downhill

gallery to accommodate the art treasures which the bishop brought back from his European travels. Much of the collection was lost in a disastrous fire in 1851. The palace itself is now a roofless shell. But the **Mussenden Temple**, a domed rotunda which the bishop used as his summer library, is maintained in perfect condition by the National Trust. Perched precariously on the cliff edge, it shudders a little whenever a train rushes past on the narrow ledge below the cliff. In the bishop's day, the vaulted basement was given over to Roman Catholic worship. A Lucretian inscription on the frieze round the dome translates, rather

Coleraine Town Hall

disconcertingly: 'It is agreeable to watch, from land, some one else involved in a great struggle while winds whip up the waves out at sea.' Inspired by the Temple of Vesta at Tivoli, the temple was built in honour of Mrs Frideswide Mussenden, the bishop's young cousin, though she died before it was completed in 1785. He bequeathed the Downhill estate to her brother.

Downhill strand, where the bishop was accustomed to hold horseback races between his clergy, is popular for surf fishing, especially bass. The view east from the Mussenden Temple embraces the fine beach and sandhills at the resort of **Castlerock** (population 1,000) and the first of a string of fine golf links that stretch eastwards along the coast. On the A2 at Liffock crossroads a mile south of Castlerock, **Hezlett House** is a long, low, thatched rectory with a cruck/truss roof. In this interesting seventeenth-century example, the building method involved balancing curved timbers, or crucks, in pairs to form a series of arches and building the house round this frame which stood on the bare rock. The house was damaged by fire in 1986.

Coleraine (population 16,050), a sedate market town and boating centre above the Bann estuary, is linked to Belfast and Londonderry by rail and has a modern university campus on the outskirts. It was a flourishing settlement in the early seventeenth century and held out against the Irish in 1641, though the

The Cutts, Coleraine

fortifications never amounted to much more than earthen ramparts. A number of functional office blocks and factories are evidence of the town's administrative and manufacturing interests. Apart from a handsome town hall, the centre is unexceptional. However, the river aspect is lively. It has a pretty weir and locks upstream at The Cutts, a nice old town bridge, a quay where coasters load potatoes in exchange for coal, trains swooping across the river on a railway viaduct, a large boating marina downstream and, out at the estuary, waders and wildfowl busy in the reed beds.

At the Guy L. Wilson memorial garden at the University of Ulster, hundreds of daffodil varieties are in bloom in spring. They perpetuate the name of a celebrated Ulster daffodil breeder who died in 1961. Bulbs directly descended from Wilson's stock can be bought in his home town of **Broughshane**, County Antrim, from late August.

Mountsandel, on the east bank of the river a mile south of Coleraine, is the earliest known inhabited place in Ireland. This oval mound, 200ft high, overlooking the Bann, has post holes and hearths of wooden dwellings which are estimated to be 9,000 years old. The site is signposted from the road.

7 THE CAUSEWAY COAST
AND THE GLENS OF ANTRIM

The north Antrim coast became an instant tourist attraction after a description of the **Giant's Causeway** was published in 1693 by the Royal Society. Ever since, people have flocked to look at and sit on and clamber over this amazing geological phenomenon, and have their photograph taken against its tall colonnades. The dramatic beauty of this whole stretch of coast, where craggy headlands give way to sandy bays and small harbours, is much more than a bonus for visitors to the Causeway. The coastal drive from Portrush round to Larne is 60 miles of exceptionally magnificent scenery.

The artist Susanna Drury, who was painting from about 1733 to 1770, helped make the Causeway famous in Europe. Her work may be seen in the Ulster Museum, Belfast. A pair of her pictures, one showing the east, and the other the west prospect, painted on vellum in about 1740, were engraved and circulated widely on the continent. The origins of the columnar structures excited great speculation, particularly among two rival groups of eighteenth-century British and French scientists. The Neptunists said the columns were sedimentary rocks, formed by chemical precipitation in the water. The Vulcanists said they were igneous — the result of volcanic action. By the nineteenth century everyone acknowledged that the Vulcanists were right. The cliffs all the way along the north Antrim coast are still of interest to scientists and geologists. Flows of molten lava buried a whole series of older rocks and protected them from atmospheric destruction. These old rocks now jut out as many-coloured cliffs along the edge of the plateau — red sandstone, chalk, coal, blue clay, iron ore, black basalt. **Fair Head**, a 626ft cliff at the extreme east end, has sixteen different strata.

The Causeway proper is a mass of basalt columns packed tightly together, formed by volcanic rock contracting as it cooled. The tops of the columns form stepping stones leading from the cliff foot and disappearing under the sea. Altogether there are

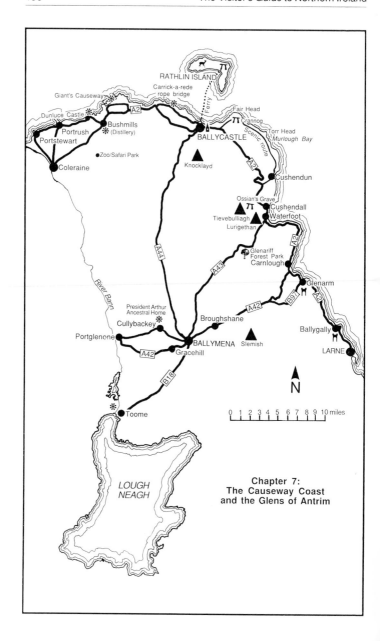

RATHLIN ISLAND

Carrick-a-rede rope bridge

Giant's Causeway

Fair Head

Dunluce Castle   A2

Crannog

Bushmills
(Distillery)

BALLYCASTLE

Portrush
Portstewart

Torr Head
Murlough Bay

Scenic route

Zoo/Safari Park

Coleraine

Knocklayd

A2

Cushendun

Ossian's Grave

Cushendall

Tievebulliagh
Lurigethan

Waterfoot

A44

A43

Glenariff
Forest Park
Carnlough

River Bann

Glenarm

B97

President Arthur
Ancestral Home

Broughshane

A42

Ballygally

Cullybackey

Portglenone

BALLYMENA   Slemish

LARNE

A42   Gracehill

B18

N

0 1 2 3 4 5 6 7 8 9 10 miles

Toome

LOUGH
NEAGH

Chapter 7:
The Causeway Coast
and the Glens of Antrim

about 40,000 of these strangely symmetrical columns, mostly hexagonal but some with four or five, and others with seven or eight sides. The tallest are 40ft high, and the solidified lava in the cliffs is 90ft thick in places.

The ancient Irish must have wondered at the Causeway and inevitably there are many fables. Basically, though, this was giants' work and, more particularly, the work of the giant Finn McCool, the Ulster warrior and commander of the king of Ireland's armies. When he fell in love with a female giant on Staffa, the island of Fingal's cave off the Scottish coast, Finn built this commodious highway to bring her across to Ulster. Fingal is Finn, of course, and there are similar rock formations on Staffa. Like Mrs Drury's paintings, the celebrated description by W.M. Thackeray in his *Irish Sketch Book* (1842) conveys a sense of the fantastic, a fabulous lunar landscape: 'When the world was moulded and fashioned out of formless chaos, this must have been the bit over — a remnant of chaos . . . '. In 1930 H.V. Morton described it as resembling 'an over-photographed actress' and by 1986 it was time for UNESCO to declare that the Giant's Causeway met certain UNESCO criteria and would be going on their 'World Heritage List'.

It is easy to linger long in the visitor centre where the Causeway's geology, flora and fauna, social history and so on, are very well presented. Early visitors got here on horseback or by boat. Then the train from Belfast brought people to **Portrush** where they transferred to jaunting car or horse charabanc. In 1883 the Giant's Causeway Tramway opened — the first hydro-electric tram in Europe. It ran on a narrow gauge railway from Portrush to the Causeway until 1949. One of its 'toast-rack' carriages is on display. But do not allow the visitor centre to detain you. Hurry on down to see the real thing.

A 5-mile circular walk starting from the centre goes down to the **Grand Causeway** and along a narrow path past majestic amphitheatres and rock formations, with names like the Organ and the Harp, past Port na Spaniagh and Lacada Point where gold treasure from the wrecked Spanish Armada galleass, *Girona*, was recovered by divers in 1968, and up a wooden staircase to Benbane Head, returning along the cliff top. A 2-mile circular walk is via the Shepherd's Path. A minibus shuttles between the visitor centre and the Grand Causeway.

Returning to the carpark, you may notice an incongruous whitewashed Austrian Tyrolean church — a 1915 conceit by Clough

The Giant's Causeway

Williams-Ellis, architect of Portmeirion in Wales. A bronze relief of
a girl asleep by a pitcher, at the top of the entrance steps, is by
Rosamund Praeger. The louvred bell tower is not the only eccentric rooftop round here: the profile of the visitor centre mimics the
malt-house roofs of the whiskey distillery at Bushmills 2 miles
south of the Causeway.

The White Rocks, near Portrush

The resort of **Portstewart** (population 5,300), with its small sheltered harbour, substantial houses along the promenade, and 3-mile strand stretching to the Bann mouth, always had more pretensions than neighbouring Portrush. A railway station, for example, was not permitted in Portstewart for fear of bringing vulgar people to the town. The railway company had to build the station a decent but inconvenient distance away, and visitors came the last mile by steam tram. The big motor cycle race now held here every May, with bikes roaring along the roads around Portstewart, would surely have appalled that genteel nineteenth-century society. The motorcar, on the other hand, was tolerated, and drivers still enjoy the traditional practice of taking their cars down to the sea and driving along the firm sands of Portstewart Strand. The seafront buildings are unexceptional. Dominican nuns have built a large convent round an early nineteenth-century stucco castle on a cliff at the west end of the town. A squat house with two drum towers near the beach was the birthplace of Sir George White VC (born 1834) who led the relief of Ladysmith in the Boer War. Cruises to the Causeway operate in summer from both Portstewart and Portrush.

Portrush (population 5,100) has a beautiful position on **Ramore Head** peninsula jutting out into the Atlantic, with sandy beaches running east and west, and picture-postcard seaside terraces above the harbour. The grassy clifftop at the end of the promontory is haunted by ornithologists, in autumn especially, who have humped their tripods and telescopes up here to watch a ceaseless flypast of geese and gulls. The resort has the usual seaside amenities, including an indoor holiday centre with flumes and aquarium, and summer theatre shows in the redbrick town hall, a bulbous and jolly Victorian pile. Spiral patterns of fossil ammonites have been preserved on flat rocks on the shore below Lansdowne Crescent, and the geological significance of these tiny sea creatures is explained in a small exhibition centre nearby.

Two-mile-long East Strand is backed by the sand dunes of the celebrated Royal Portrush Golf Club, scene of many Irish golf championships. The British Open has also been held here. The strand ends at the White Rocks, limestone cliffs weirdly weathered into caves and arches, most notably the Cathedral Cave which is reached by a steep path from the road. This cave is 180ft deep with two enormous limestone columns supporting the roof at the seaward entrance. The picnic site at the carpark near here is a good place to stop for lunch. The view is splendid. **The Skerries**, a chain of small grassy islands a couple of miles offshore, can be inspected at close quarters by excursion boats from Portrush. The islands resound to the gruff yapping of barnacle geese.

The romantic ruin of **Dunluce Castle** teeters on the edge of an isolated crag. Some of it actually fell off during a storm in 1639, carrying away the kitchens, the cooks and all the pots. In the thirteenth century Richard de Burgh built a Norman castle on this desirable site. Defenders could come and go through the large sea cave that slopes up into the castle precincts, and a drawbridge lay across the deep chasm now spanned by a wooden footbridge. In the late sixteenth century the MacDonnells, Lords of the Isles, ruled all this north-east corner of Ulster from their stronghold at Dunluce. Sir John Perrott came up from Dublin in

---

THINGS TO SEE AROUND THE GIANT'S CAUSEWAY

Grand, Middle and Little Causeways
Centrepiece of the Giant's Causeway —a low promontory of symmetrical basalt columns eroded by the sea into three distinct parts. Twenty-minute walk from visitor centre or take minibus shuttle. Visitor centre amenities include informative 25-minute film, souvenir shop with good book section, tea room (National Trust).

Dunluce Castle
Picturesque ruins of Sorley Boy MacDonnell's sixteenth-century castle on rocky headland. Guided tours. Views. Sea cave can be visited by boat in calm weather.

Bushmills Distillery
Tours of the oldest (legal) whiskey distillery in the world (1608 charter). Visitor centre, souvenirs, sampling.

Carrick-a-Rede Rope Bridge (access from Larrybane) Swinging rope bridge across to island salmon fishery. Approach is along half-mile cliff path from the National Trust's Larrybane information centre which has a tea shop and aquarium.

1584 and ejected Sorley Boy MacDonnell after pounding the castle with artillery. As soon as Perrott returned south, having left an English garrison in charge, Sorley Boy regained possession after one of his men, employed in the castle, hauled various MacDonnells up the crag in a basket. The garrison was wiped out and the constable hanged over the wall.

Sorley's antecedents are clear from his name: *Somhairle* is from the Norse for 'summer soldier' or Viking, *Buidhe* is 'yellow' in Gaelic. The Scots were in the habit of leading raiding parties against both the Irish and English and many, like the MacDonnells, stayed on. This yellow-haired summer soldier was soon able to repair the damaged castle with proceeds from the wreck of the Spanish treasure ship *Girona* which sank off the Causeway in October 1588. The pitifully few survivors — only five out of 1,300 men — were put up at Dunluce.

The castle fell into decay after Sorley's descendants, the Earls of Antrim, moved to more comfortable accommodation at Glenarm, in the Glens of Antrim, in the mid-seventeenth century. The extensive ruins include two thirteenth-century towers, a Scottish style gatehouse (about 1600), and the remains of a great hall, part of a seventeenth-century house built inside the defences. From the windows there is a fine view through the limestone arches of the White Rocks. The cave underneath Dunluce can be

Dunluce Castle

visited by boat or dinghy in calm weather. It is one of many narrow sea caves along this coast.

The little port and beach resort of **Portballintrae** (population 600) is reached by a loop road off the A2. It has nice hotels and a half-moon bay. Beyond is Bushfoot Strand and the western end of the Causeway cliffs. The Bush is a great salmon and trout river, with good stretches from Bushmills village up to Ballymoney. **Bushmills** (population 1,400) was traditionally the last stop from Belfast before the final push to the Causeway when travellers restored themselves with a few glasses of whiskey from the Old Bushmills Distillery, in business since 1608. It is the world's oldest legal whiskey distillery. The village has an attractive square with solidly built houses and a Victorian clock tower vaguely resembling an Irish round tower. Many tourists make a beeline

Kinbane Castle

for the distinctive malt-houses of the distillery where the product can be sampled, in moderation, during a tour of the works.

South of here, at **Dervock**, is a small safari park with lions roaming about. In general, however, the interest of north Antrim is confined to the coastal strip. Apart from the Glens, and the prosperous farming region around Ballymena in the Main and Braid river valleys, there is little temptation to turn inland. The hinterland is a rather featureless plateau of peat diggings and blocks of conifer forest.

Anyone walking from the Giant's Causeway to **Benbane Head** can continue along the cliff path to the pear-shaped crag of **Dunseverick Castle** where the path almost converges with the road (B146). It must be said that the very fragmentary ruin of a sixteenth-century gatehouse is a poor thing. Nonetheless, the human history of this impressive crag is long and interesting. Dunseverick, the capital of the ancient kingdom of Dalriada, was the terminal of one of Ireland's five great highways from Tara, near Drogheda, and a main jumping-off point for Scotland. Irishmen from Dalriada had established a colony on the Argyll coast by the fifth century — the colony which St Columba joined and from which he established Iona. Dunseverick is also featured in Ireland's oldest love story, the ninth-century *Longas mac n-Usnig* ('The fate of the children of Uisneach'), as the legendary landing place of Deirdre of the Sorrows and the sons of Uisneach. Deirdre, the intended bride of King Conor, falls in love with his bodyguard, Noisi. To escape the king's wrath they flee to Scotland, together with Noisi's two brothers. Fergus, another of Conor's warriors, in good faith persuades them that the king has forgiven them and that it is safe to return. They land at Dunseverick (some accounts say east of Ballycastle) and take the road south to Conor's court at *Eamhain Mhacha* at Armagh. But the vengeful king kills the brothers and takes Deirdre for himself, whereupon she dashes her head against a stone and dies. Outraged by Conor's treachery, the noble Fergus destroys the palace.

Another ruined sixteenth-century gatehouse with a spectacular position is **Kinbane Castle**, built by Colla Dubh, Sorley Boy MacDonnell's brother, on a long white promontory which is signposted off the B15 2 miles east of Carrick-a-rede. There is a carpark on top of the cliff. Watch out for erosion and steep drops. The cave that goes right through the promontory is only accessible by boat.

Crescent-shaped **Whitepark Bay**, in National Trust care, with a youth hostel and a mile of golden sand backed by grassy dunes, is flanked at the west end by the picturesque hamlet of **Portbraddan**. An odd slate-roofed church squeezed in next to a private house measures only 12ft by 6$\frac{1}{2}$ft, the smallest church in Ireland. There are caves at the raised beach at the other end of the bay, and Neolithic flints have been found here. A footpath leads round to **Ballintoy** harbour, a sturdy limestone harbour set among rocks, lively with small boats and dinghies, and people having tea in the café. The local boatmen will readily take visitors fishing or for trips along the coast. **Sheep Island**, a perpendicular stack with a flat grassy top half a mile offshore, has an enormous cormorant colony. The rats that killed off the island's colony of puffins have themselves been routed and some puffins

Carrick-a-rede Rope Bridge

have come back recently.

The switchback road down to the harbour passes a pretty white church in a meadow. Its tapered square tower has little pinnacles at the corners and very small windows. In 1641 the Earl of Antrim came to the rescue of local Protestants who had taken refuge inside the original church on the site and were being besieged. An eighteenth-century landlord of the village was Downing Fullerton, founder of Downing College, Cambridge. When the castle at Ballintoy was dismantled, the staircase and oak panelling was taken to Cambridge and installed in the college.

The rope bridge at **Carrick-a-rede** is a great tourist attraction and quite frightening. Swinging 80ft above the sea and made of planks strung between wires, it starts bouncing up and down as soon as you step on it. There is no safety netting on the sides and a large notice warns of the risks of crossing. Despite this, or perhaps because of it, there is a steady stream of visitors keen to cross the perilous 60ft-wide chasm to the small rocky island on the other side. The bridge gives access to the commercial salmon fishery on the south-east side of the island. It is removed in

Carrick-a-rede Island

September at the end of the fishing season and put up again in April.

Carrick-a-rede means 'rock in the road' — the road taken by Atlantic salmon returning to spawn in the rivers. The tidal conditions and the deep water are ideal for salmon netting and the fishery has been here for at least 350 years. An engraving of 1790 shows a rope bridge at the rock. A cunning system of nets intercepts the fish as they move westwards, keeping close to the shore searching for their ancestral waters. Until recently a steep path from the main road ran down to the bridge across a field. Now the approach is via a made-up path along half a mile of cliff top from Larrybane carpark where there is a National Trust information centre, aquarium and teashop; campers can pitch a tent for the night here. A lime kiln on chalky **Larrybane Head** is a remnant of past quarrying operations.

Whitepark Bay

Between the Causeway and the Glens of Antrim, **Ballycastle** (population 3,300) is a lively little resort with a variety of diversions and things to see. In June the town hosts a 3-day Irish music and dance festival, the *Fleadh Amhran agus Rince*, and in late August the Ould Lammas Fair, Ireland's oldest popular fair, held here since the MacDonnells obtained a charter in 1606. In its heyday the fair lasted a week, Now a 2-day event, it has sheep and pony sales and several hundred street stalls crammed into the Diamond and down Fairhill Street. The Diamond is lined with some agreeable houses, with Holy Trinity church on one side. An attractive Classical parish church with an octagonal spire, it was built in 1756. The very big clock face, big enough to read from a long way off, is out of all proportion to the square tower. Inside is a star-spangled blue ceiling and memorials to the Boyd family who built up the town in the eighteenth century. The red sandstone memorial with pink marble columns in front of the church was erected to a local nineteenth-century benefactor. A plaque over a newsagent's shop at 21 Ann Street recalls that here John McAuley, a Ballycastle woodcarver, wrote the ever-popular song which asks:

> 'Did you treat your Mary Ann
> To dulse and yellow man
> At the Ould Lammas Fair in Ballycastle-O?'

Dulse is an edible seaweed. Yellow man is a rock-like bright yellow toffee so hard that it has to be broken with a hammer.

An early seventeenth-century MacDonnell castle at the Diamond has vanished completely but the bones of Sorley Boy, who died in 1590 aged 85, are preserved in a vault at the ruined friary of **Bonamargy**, half a mile outside Ballycastle on the A2 to Cushendall. Sorley's descendants, the first Earls of Antrim, are also buried here. Inscriptions on the tomb of Randal MacDonnell, second earl, (died 1682) are in Gaelic as well as the more usual Latin and English. The Gaelic inscription translates with typical Celtic gloom: 'Every seventh year a calamity befalls the Irish. Now that the Marquis has departed, it will occur every year'. Founded for the Franciscans by Rory MacQuillan in about 1500, the friary's survival for 150 years after the dissolution of the monasteries (1537) is something of a puzzle. A flat stone incised with a cross just inside the main entrance to the church marks the grave of Julia MacQuillan, a seventeenth-century recluse known as the Black Nun. Her choice of burial place ensured that worshippers would walk on her when entering the church, thus perpetuating her perfect humility. Sailors lost at sea in the two World Wars and washed on to this treacherous coast are buried in a plot with a large cross in the graveyard corner. They include crewmen from *HMS Drake* torpedoed off Rathlin in 1915.

The rounded mountain of Knocklayd, rising 1,695ft to the south-west, featured in an elaborate geologists' hoax in 1788 when, according to Dublin newspapers, it erupted and engulfed the neighbourhood in boiling lava.

A modernistic memorial near Ballycastle harbour recalls the experimental wireless link which Marconi and his assistant, George Kemp, established in 1898 between Ballycastle and Rathlin Island. Signals were transmitted over a distance of 6 miles between a mast erected near the island's east lighthouse and a house on top of the cliff at Ballycastle. Other transmissions to

Ould Lammas Fair at Ballycastle

Rathlin were made from the spire of the Catholic church in Moyle Street.

Rathlin Island (population 100) is a 50-minute boat trip across the sound from Ballycastle, and only a dozen or so miles from the Mull of Kintyre in Scotland. Shaped like a boomerang with one arm about 4 miles long and the other about 2^1/2, the island has three lighthouses and high white cliffs round most of the coast. The tip of the shorter arm is just 3 miles from Fair Head, a nearly right-angled headland that marks off Ulster's north-east corner. In the angle of the boomerang, the sheltered modern harbour at Church Bay is a useful staging post for yachts heading for the Hebrides. Rathlin boatmen are pleased to point out *Slough-na-More*, 'the swallow of the sea', a whirlpool at the southern tip of Rathlin where St Columba is said to have narrowly escaped drowning on a voyage from Ireland to Iona in the sixth century. The first recorded shipping disaster in Rathlin Sound was in about AD440 when Brecain, son of Niall of the Nine Hostages, and his fleet of fifty curraghs were lost in a great tide rip.

From Easter to September there are daily excursions from

Ballycastle. At other times you may need to negotiate privately with local boatmen. In addition you can get a very cheap passage with the mail boat which leaves at about 10.30am on Monday, Wednesday and Friday year round, weather permitting. If you intend returning the same day, check with the mail man that he is coming back. For the visitor, the island's delightful primitiveness is more apparent than real. A guesthouse, a licensed restaurant, a pub and two shops remove any imperative to do the round trip in a day. You can however visit every corner of the island on foot in 2 days.

Ownership of Rathlin, definitely Irish since a famous seventeenth-century court case, was disputed between Ireland and Scotland on a number of occasions, and the island's history has been regularly punctuated by battles and massacres. It was the first place in Ireland to be raided by Vikings (AD795). Sir Francis Drake landed guns on Rathlin in 1575 when his commander, the Earl of Essex, massacred the MacDonnell population while Sorley Boy MacDonnell looked on helplessly from the mainland. The MacDonnells were again massacred in 1642, this time on the orders of Archibald Campbell, eighth Earl of Argyll. It should be said that the MacDonnells were themselves not averse to perpetrating massacres from time to time.

Fishing, farming and a little tourism are the islanders' chief sources of income. Herring, mackerel and flatfish are plentiful around the shore. Lobster fishing is one of the more profitable occupations. Boats from Ballycastle, Portrush and Portstewart come to take cod, haddock, skate and other large fish. Cattle sold at auction on the island have to be ferried to the mainland in small boats since Ballycastle harbour cannot cope with anything larger. Rathlin has as good a telephone service and television reception as anywhere else, though there is no mains electricity. The supply comes humming and chugging out of generators.

Salty winds rake the island all year round and stop trees from growing more than a few feet; the landscape is virtually treeless. There are many dry stone walls and scattered ruined cottages with pairs of big gate pillars, inhabited when the population was much larger. The water supply is still pumped along miles of plastic tubing that lies around on the surface of the ground. The first car on the island arrived in 1955 for the district nurse's use, though now there are a number of cars, vans, motorbikes and tractors jolting over the rough tracks. Islanders are exempted from paying road fund tax which, since there is only one bit of

PLACES TO VISIT IN THE GLENS AND NORTH-EAST ANTRIM

Rathlin Island
Unspoiled offshore island with 100 inhabitants. Large bird sanctuary on the western cliffs near lighthouse. Neolithic axe factory. Fishing, sub-aqua diving, excursions round island in fine weather. Overnight accommodation, restaurant, pub, food shops. Tented camping permitted. The harbour is 50 minutes by boat from Ballycastle.

Fair Head and Murlough Bay
Views of Rathlin and Scotland from the top of the 626ft cliffs of Fair Head are worth the mile walk from carpark, past a well preserved crannog, a fortified artificial island in one of three lakes. Birds of prey and wild goats frequent the heights.

Beautiful Murlough Bay has good parking and picnic facilities.

Bonamargy Friary, Ballycastle
Ruined Franciscan friary with substantial remains of gatehouse, church and cloister. MacDonnell vault preserves interesting tombs of the Earls of Antrim, and the tomb of Sorley Boy MacDonnell (died 1590).

Glenariff Forest Park
Spectacular glen walk, waterfalls, waymarked mountain trails, views. Visitor centre with restaurant.

Watertop Open Farm
A 500-acre farm bordering Loughareema, the 'vanishing lake'. Ornamental game birds, trout lake, small museum. Pony-trekking in Ballypatrick forest.

road to speak of, is only fair.

The cliffs of Rathlin are home to vast numbers of seabirds. The 350ft cliff towering 100ft over the west lighthouse above **Bull Point** is the best place from which to see them, crowded in tens of thousands on to ledges and majestic rock stacks that reverberate with their shrieks. The lighthouse light is actually at the foot of a square four-storey tower which has chimney pots and sash windows. It was completed in 1919 — the year the south lighthouse, an automatic light at Rue Point, was built. Most Rathlin caves can be visited only by boat in a flat calm. The high caves before Bull Point are jammed to the roof with iron girders, steel plates and chunks of engines from ancient wrecks, wrenched from the seabed by Atlantic storms — an awesome reminder, on a sunny day, of the ferocious winter storms that lash these parts. The most famous cave is **Bruce's Cave**, below the east lighthouse at the other end of the island. Robert the Bruce hid here in 1306 after his defeat by the English at Perth, and it was a Rathlin spider whose arachnoid energies gave the despondent warrior new heart and sent him back to Scotland to win the Battle of Bannockburn. The east lighthouse, looking, one feels, as a lighthouse ought to look — a tall confident black-and-white cylinder — was erected in 1856. Concrete slabs lying in grass east of the lighthouse enclosure and marked with the name 'Lloyds' are the remains of the Marconi wireless mast of 1898.

Some 6,000 years ago a Neolithic axe factory on Rathlin was producing distinctive axe heads of porcellanite which have been found all over Ireland and in parts of England. It was one of three main axe factories in the British Isles. The others were at Tievebulliagh near Cushendall, County Antrim, and at Langdale in the Pennines. Stone Age men discovered a small outcrop of this rare, very hard, fine-grained blue stone in **Brockley** townland on the west side of the island. North of Brockley at **Doonmore** is an ancient rath with some extremely thick stone walls on the top. At **Knockans**, south-east of Brockley, a stone sweat house, a kind of early sauna, is close to the scant remains of a monastic settlement.

The island's main monastic site, where St Comgall of Bangor established a foundation in the sixth century, is in the Church Quarter near Rathlin's two churches. The small Anglican parish church, which was rebuilt in 1815, has a lovely position close to the water, backed by whin-covered slopes. Inside is a memorial to the Rev. John Martin, who was rector here in 1723–40, and monuments to members of the Gage family, resident landlords of Rathlin from the eighteenth century. Mrs Catherine Gage, who died in 1862 is commemorated by two shapely maidens in diaphanous gowns of gleaming white marble. The Gages have gone now but they built the long low manor house that extends along the waterfront at Church Bay. A short distance back up the track is a modest little Catholic church of 1865, Rathlin's main place of worship, next to the priest's house. It has a pretty grotto in the garden.

From Ballycastle the A2 runs east across the Antrim plateau, past the forest of Ballypatrick, past Watertop Farm which opens to visitors and has pony-trekking facilities, across one end of the 'vanishing lake' of **Loughareema**, and down to Cushendall. After heavy rain the lake can flood the road and then it suddenly runs completely dry. The water drains away rapidly through

Murlough Bay

porous chalk under the mud and the lake vanishes. Last century, when this inland road was just a track, it was not unknown for coach horses to gallop into a watery grave at Loughareema, taking the passengers with them.

If you are not to miss the exhilarating heights of **Fair Head**, you must turn left off the A2 3 miles from Ballycastle and follow the lane up to a small National Trust carpark. The cliff top is about a one-mile walk north from here across heathery boggy scrub. You can follow the Trust's yellow circle markings for a bit but after half a mile their route swerves round to the east, away from the cliff edge. Buzzards and peregrine falcons frequent the desolate tableland and you may see flocks of red-legged choughs. Walking north you pass, on the left, **Lough na Cranagh**, the largest of three lakes in the vicinity. The oval-shaped island in the middle is in fact an artificial lake dwelling, a crannog, with a stone revetment 6ft above the water level. From the headland is a superlative view of Rathlin and the hills and islands of Scotland, very close indeed across the narrow North Channel. Grey Man's

Path, a convenient short cut for wild goats foraging on the cliffs, plunges dramatically down a steep gully. It is actually less difficult to negotiate than it looks.

Murlough Bay, the loveliest of all the bays along the Antrim coast, is in the lee of this great headland. Unless you want to walk to it, you should return to the carpark and drive round via Ballylucan where the turning is well signposted. The contrast between the scrubby top of Fair Head and this lush green place is most striking. Below the chalk escarpment, buttercup meadows and trees run down nearly to the water's edge, with sheep and a few cows grazing the slopes. The main carpark is up above the bay but there is a smaller one on a hairpin bend further down, past the stone cross memorial to Sir Roger Casement, who was executed for treason in 1916.

Regarded by Irish nationalists as a martyr, Casement had a brilliant career in the British colonial civil service; in particular, he reported on labour conditions in the Belgian Congo and Peru. In 1911 he accepted a knighthood. However, he believed that the war with Germany offered a genuine opportunity for a successful Irish rebellion, and he went to Berlin to negotiate for military aid against Britain. At the height of the war he returned to Ireland with a shipload of armaments and was landed from a German submarine on the Kerry coast. But the plot was frustrated and he was arrested and hanged at Pentonville. In 1965 his remains were taken to Dublin after representations by the government of the Irish Republic, and buried alongside O'Connell and Parnell at Glasnevin. The Murlough Bay memorial was erected by his cousin, Mrs Parry of Cushendun. It commemorates three other men with local connections including Casement's friend, F.J. Bigger, a Belfast solicitor and antiquarian.

A scenic road, very steep and winding, runs from Murlough Bay past **Torr Head**, where a modern Celtic cross commemorates Shane 'The Proud' O'Neill, killed in 1567 by the MacDonnells who, like other Ulster clans at the time, had tired of his bullying. The road wriggling from here down to the National Trust village of Cushendun is hedged with wild fuchsia and honeysuckle.

Two of the 'Nine Glens' of Antrim, Glentaisie and Glenshesk, cut north to the bay at Ballycastle. Better known, however, are the Glens running west to east, bisecting the mountainous region all the way from Cushendun down to Larne. The physical isolation of the small communities of farmers and fishermen, which has left

Cushendun

Exploring the caves
at Cushendun

the Glens with a wealth of myth and legend, was alleviated in 1834 when a Scottish engineer, William Bald, blasted a road out of the chalky cliffs for of distance of 28 miles up the eastern seaboard, passing by the foot of each of the Glens. The road was later extended to Ballycastle. Names of the traditional nine Glens with their popular translations are, from north to south: **Glentaisie**, Taisie's glen — Princess Taisie, daughter of the king of Rathlin, who escaped being kidnapped by a Norwegian king when her fiancé, 'Long Nails' Congal, beat off the invader's boats in 200BC; **Glenshesk**, sedgy glen; **Glendun**, brown glen; **Glencorp**, glen of the slaughter; **Glenaan**, glen of rush lights; **Glenbally-eamon**, Eamonn's townland glen; **Glenariff**, ploughman's glen; **Glencloy**, glen of hedges; and **Glenarm**, meaning—apparently — glen of the army.

Cushendun (population 50), once a highly fashionable water-ing place, is admired for the quaint Cornish architecture which Ronald McNeill, first (and last) Lord Cushendun, and his Cornish wife, Maud, commissioned from the famous Clough Williams-Ellis (1883–1977). The square with small white-washed terraces is approached through large gate pillars. It was built in 1912. A row of cottages with hanging slates on the upper storey, facing the sea, was erected in memory of Maud in 1925. Williams-Ellis, remembered for Portmeirion in North Wales, also designed Lord Cushendun's large Neo-Georgian house, Glenmona Lodge, set among trees in the middle of the bay. Now a home for the elderly, it has an eccentric five-arch arcade at the front. The white Georgian house at the north end of the beach, Rockport Lodge, was the home of a local poetaster, Moira O'Neill, whose real name, Nesta Higginson, suited her verses much better than the romantic alias she adopted. The ivy-covered ruins of a MacDonnell castle above Rockport House off the Torr Head road was where Shane 'The Proud' was killed by Sorley Boy MacDonnell and his head sent to be spiked at Dublin Castle. Cave House, another substantial Cushendun mansion, occupies a completely secluded position in an amphitheatre of cliffs at the end of a red sandstone cave 60ft long. The only approach is through this cave. John Masefield knew the house well. He married a daughter of the Crommelin family who built the house in 1820. It is now a religious retreat.

Craigagh Wood, west of the village, conceals a rock where Mass was said in the eighteenth century. It is carved with a crucifixion scene and is said to have been brought here from

Carnlough, a typical Glens village

Iona. The Gloonan Stone nearby, opposite the Catholic church, has two hollows made, they say, by St Patrick's knees. The name is from the Gaelic *gluire*, meaning 'knees'. An immense red stone viaduct with three arches, built by Charles Lanyon in 1839, carries the A2 over the tawny-coloured Glendun river. This glen has the wildest scenery of all the Antrim Glens, and the walk up to the waterfalls is memorable. The B92 from Cushendun rejoins the A2 to Cushendall south of the viaduct.

Ossian's Grave, on the north-east slopes of the pointed 𝝅 mountain of **Tievebulliagh** (1,320ft) is signposted to the right (west) a mile before Cushendall. There is a carpark behind a house about half a mile up the lane from where a short walk brings you to an atmospheric little meadow with what is actually a Neolithic court grave in the centre. The site of Tievebulliagh's ancient porcellanite axe factory is near the summit. From Ossian's Grave there are lovely views to Glendun, Glenaan and Scotland, and to the south-west is **Trostan** (1,817ft), highest mountain on the plateau. The warrior-bard who gave his name to what is known as the 'Ossianic Cycle' was the son of Finn McCool. The legends about Finn and his warrior band, the Fianna, originate from the third century. James Macpherson (1736–96), who translated and popularised them in the 1760s, added quite a few elements of his own but the tales are none the worse for that.

Ossian is said to have returned from the fabulous kingdom of *Tir na nOg*, the land of the ever-young, to find St Patrick preaching Christianity to the Celts. Despite the saint's best efforts, Ossian preferred the old gods and died unconverted.

Three glens converge at **Cushendall** (population 800) where the river meanders past a golf course into the bay. The red sandstone curfew tower on the corner of Mill Street was built in 1809 by Francis Turnly, a nabob of the East India Company, as 'a place of confinement for idlers and rioters'. North of the village, Tieveragh Hill is a small curiously rounded volcanic plug which is one of the best known 'gentle' or supernatural places in the Glens, a haunt of the 'wee folk'. A cliff path north from the beach leads after a mile to the delightful ruins of thirteenth-century **Layde Old Church**, chief burial place of the MacDonnells after Bonamargy. It was rebuilt at least three times and served as a parish church until 1790. Fine stones in the graveyard include a cross in memory of Dr James MacDonnell, a pioneer in the use of chloroform for surgical operations. He was also one of the organisers of the famous Belfast festival of Irish harpers in 1792.

Going south, flat-topped **Lurigethan** (1,153ft) looms on the right. Straight ahead are the fragmentary walls of a sixteenth-century castle on the cliff just before you pass under Red Arches. **Red Bay** boatyard, which builds wooden boats, has fishing boats and tackle for hire. Iron ore was mined in upper Glenariff until the end of last century and was loaded at Red Bay. The shell-strewn sand on the beach here has a noticeable red tinge to it. Between Red Bay pier and Waterfoot village are several interesting caves. The biggest one, Nanny's Cave, is 40ft long and was inhabited by Ann Murray who was aged 100 when she died in 1847. She supported herself by spinning and knitting and was known to the revenue men for selling 'poteen' (illicit whiskey). In the eighteenth century the children of Red Bay learned reading and writing inside another of these caves. The 'school' cave can be entered just beyond Red Arch. **Waterfoot**, also called **Glenariff** (population 300), hosts the *Feis na nGleann*, one of the liveliest of the *Feisanna*, competitive festivals of Irish sport and culture, which are held in summer in various parts of Northern Ireland. The waterfalls and woodlands of **Glenariff Forest Park**, best known of all the Antrim Glens, should not be missed. In spring and early summer the upper glen is luxuriant with wild flowers, and there is a superb view from the café in the visitor centre.

Extinct volcano, Slemish, where St Patrick herded swine

The A2 now follows every indentation of the coast round **Garron Point**, where there is a marked change in the rock from red sandstone to limestone. After the chalky White Lady formation, watch out at a bend in the road for a large limestone rock with a bronze inscription, a rather dreadful poem, by Frances Anne Vane Tempest, Marchioness of Londonderry (1800–65). Immediately round the point a lane winds up to Garron Tower, a castellated blackstone mansion overlooking the sea, where she entertained on a grand scale. The house is now a boarding school.

The quarries above **Carnlough** (population 1,450) are worked out now but until the 1960s the sturdy white bridge over the main road carried a railway which brought limestone down to the harbour. The bridge, an adjacent clock tower and old courthouse, all made of large squared blocks of limestone, were built by the Londonderrys in 1854. The Marchioness was not able to resist having a few words about herself inscribed on a plaque which was set into the bridge on the south side, to be seen and read from the carriages passing underneath. The Londonderry Arms hotel, built about the same time, was briefly owned by Winston Churchill who came on a visit while he was Chancellor of the Exchequer. Inside is a collection of mementoes of Arkle, a famous horse who won the Cheltenham Gold Cup three times. The harbour has recently been improved and is a port of call for yachtsmen visiting the Glens. Lobsters and crabs are caught here and flatfish spearing is advertised on the main road. Carnlough has a nice sandy beach, a tourist office in the post office and, like most of the villages down this coast, camping and caravan sites

Glenarm (population 650), which exports limestone and powdered chalk from the harbour, developed after Randal MacDonnell built a hunting lodge in the glen in 1603. When Dunluce on the north coast was abandoned, the lodge was enlarged and Glenarm became the principal seat of the Earls of Antrim. To view Glenarm Castle, a theatrical pile of turrets and cupolas, you must gain access to the glen through a stone arch at the top of the village street, with parking beyond. The castle is clearly visible across the river. There was a major rebuilding around 1750, and the Tudor parts are nineteenth-century. The main entrance to the private demesne is a barbican archway with fake portcullis slits and boiling oil holes. A stone crest dated 1636, from the original castle, is set in the front. The lower glen is planted with Forest Service conifers but the woodlands of the upper glen, covenanted to the National Trust by the fourteenth earl in 1980, are pleasant enough. The village itself has a self-possessed air, a nice place to explore on foot.

South of Glenarm, the road hugs the shore past a tumbled heap of limestone known as the Madman's Window, and on down past **Ballygally Castle**, an engaging plantation castle which is now a hotel. Apart from sash windows, it is unchanged since it was built in 1625. After Drain's Bay, with a view of the Maidens' lighthouses out to sea, the road snakes through Blackcave

PLACES TO VISIT FROM BALLYMENA

Slemish Mountain
A place of pilgrimage on St Patrick's Day (17 March), this hill is where the saint herded swine for 6 years. View of ancient ruined Skerry church from summit. Picnic site, toilets.

Gracehill
Moravian settlement founded in 1746 by the Rev. John Cennick. Square village green surrounded by eighteenth-century buildings — church, schoolhouse, separate communal dwellings for unmarried sisters and brethren. Moravian burial ground. Pleasant walk across Main river to view Flemish-style Galgorm Castle (private), once home of a famous local black magician, Dr. Alexander Colville.

Chester Alan Arthur Ancestral Home, Cullybackey
The father of US President Arthur emigrated from this farmhouse, now restored, with clay floors, open flax-straw thatched roof and early furniture. Display of agricultural machinery in farm building. Demonstrations in summer of traditional crafts such as quilting, lace-making and crochet.

Toomebridge Eel Co-operative
Largest eel fishery in the British Isles. Informal, friendly fishermen —visitors are welcome to call in.

Tunnel and into Larne. However, at Glenarm you have the option of turning inland to see something of the mid-Antrim region. The road joins up with the A42 which runs across the shallow valley of the Braid river, through Broughshane and into Ballymena, biggest town in County Antrim.

The flat landscape around Broughshane is relieved by **Slemish**, a small extinct volcano (1,437ft) which can be seen from a great distance. Evidence from St Patrick's writings suggests that this solitary hill is where Ireland's patron saint herded swine as a boy slave. Captured on the coast of Britain by pirates, Patrick was brought to the north of Ireland where he worked for 6 years for Miluic, chieftain at Slemish, before making his escape. He returned in 432, a grown man, to convert the Irish to Christianity. Slemish is a place of pilgrimage on St Patrick's Day (17 March) though not particularly well signposted. An easy way to get to it is to go into Broughshane, passing the Carncairn daffodil nursery on the right, and then turn left on to the Ballyclare road (B94). After a mile turn left, right after 3 miles, right after 700yd, and a lane runs up between dry-stone walls to a carpark. From the top, a scramble of less than 700ft, look north to the ruins of old Skerry church on a hill where Miluic's fort once stood .

Several well known daffodil breeders have lived at **Brough-shane** (population 1,500), and the village gardens in spring are bright with drifts of daffodils and narcissi. Rare bulbs directly descended from daffodils created by Guy Wilson, a distinguished Broughshane hybridist, can be obtained from the Carncairn nursery.

The seventeenth-century settlers of **Ballymena** (population 28,250) came mostly from south-west Scotland. The Bard of Dunclug, David Herbison (1800–80), who was born in Mill Street, captured the lowland accent and intonation in his ballads and songs. That distinctive voice, only slightly modified, still predominates. The town's prosperity was based on the linen industry which, with other textiles and some engineering, continues in a small way. Now this whole area, including **Ballymoney** (population 5.700) to the north, is overwhelmingly agricultural. Crowds up to 3,000 attend Ballymena's four weekly livestock markets, and the Saturday variety market has been going strong since 1626 when the Adair family obtained patents from Charles I. Local blackstone, the basalt which covers most of the Antrim plateau, is characteristic of the town's solidly built banks and sober churches. The People's Park was given to the town by the Adairs whose best known member, Dr Robert Adair, was the 'Robin' of the love song *Robin Adair*. Eaton Park is named after the family of Timothy Eaton, founder of the Canadian chainstore. Ballymena Academy (emblem: the industrious ant) has produced judges, doctors, and outstanding athletes such as Mary Peters, pentathlon gold medallist in the 1972 Olympics in Munich, and Willie John McBride, Irish international and captain of the British Lions rugby team. The school's most infamous pupil was Roger Casement.

The centre of **Gracehill** (population 450), just west of Ballymena, is much as it was in the eighteenth century when a small band of Moravians (United Brethren) settled here. The village is built round a green, with separate houses for the brothers and sisters who lived by making clocks and lace. The church (1765) contains interesting stained glass windows and a central pulpit. A long path down the middle of the grassy cemetery separates the graves of men from those of women, a Moravian burial custom which is still observed.

Just beyond **Cullybackey** on the B96 to Portglenone, the **ancestral home** of **Chester Alan Arthur**, president of the

United States 1881–5, is signposted up a lane to the right, an awkward sharp turn. His father, who later became a Baptist clergy man, emigrated from here in 1816 and settled in Vermont. Arthur himself, a physically huge man, enjoyed good living, fine suits and was an excellent salmon fisherman. Baking and traditional crafts, such as crochet and quilt-making, are demonstrated in the thatched cottage during the summer months.

Until the mid-eighteenth century, **Portglenone** (population 200) had the only bridge across the 35-mile-long Lower Bann, apart from Coleraine near the estuary. In the seventeenth century a drawbridge was pulled up at night to protect the settlement from 'tories', or outlaws, lurking in the forests on the opposite bank. At 48 Main Street, facing a pleasant elongated market place, a plaque records that Timothy Eaton, who later emigrated to Toronto and made a fortune from retailing, learned the drapery business in this shop 1847–52. He worked 16 hours a day and slept under the counter.

South of Portglenone, at **Toomebridge** (population 450) where the Bann flows out of Lough Neagh, is a large eel fishery ✳ where visitors can call in. Demand in Europe for Lough Neagh eels is insatiable. At the height of the fishing season every day 7 tons of brown eels are flown to Holland from Belfast International. Elvers, baby eels that look like little silver matchsticks, are a sought-after delicacy; but they are not appreciated in Ireland, and most of them are allowed to grow to maturity in the lough. Large quantities are collected at Coleraine and brought to Lough Neagh by lorry. Left to their own devices, elvers take a year to make their way up the Bann. Salmon, on the other hand, swim up in a month. If you take a trip along the Bann after 1 May, there are dramatic piscatorial scenes of anglers tussling with these beautiful fish at every lock and weir.

FURTHER INFORMATION

Visiting Places of Interest

1. Important monuments in the care of the Department of the Environment (DOE) have full-time caretakers, and there is a modest entrance charge. Most other state monuments have year-round free access. Current admission charges for popular attractions and much other practical information is published in *Stop and Visit*, an annual brochure produced by the Northern Ireland Tourist Board (NITB). Thankfully, Northern Ireland has not yet got round to fully exploiting its treasures for cash. This easy-going approach can occasionally require persistence by the visitor when faced by a bolted gate or the locked door of a country church. However, local people nearly always know of someone with a key who will be genuinely pleased to show you round.

2. Contact telephone numbers are given below for attractions to which there is greater access as the summer wears on, and particularly where times seem likely to alter. Sometimes you can tack on to pre-arranged group visits, and opening hours may be extended for special events or exhibitions. As a general rule, the more complicated the hours, the more they are subject to change. To give the minutiae of National Trust (NT) arrangements would occupy too much space; current hours and charges can be got from tourist information offices or from the Trust direct (see addresses). A main point to remember is that no NT houses open in the morning; they do open on bank holidays — again afternoons only.

3. Some privately owned mansions occasionally have open days on bank holidays and summer weekends, though these tend to be advertised at short notice. Visits are sometimes arranged to others under the ægis of the Ulster Architectural Heritage Society (see addresses).

4. State forests are open daily from 10am to sunset. They include nine forest parks which have a wide range of leisure facilities. Admission charges vary. Full information from: Forest Service, Dundonald House, Upper Newtownards Road, Belfast BT4 3BS. ☎ (0232) 650111. Outside office hours, try 'phoning individual forest parks (numbers given below).

Attractions Open to View

Chapter 1 — In and Around Belfast

A Belfast street map showing the location of most places mentioned below, and walking tours of central areas of the city, are available free from the tourist information centre in High Street (☎ 246609). From Easter to September Belfast's bus company, Citybus, runs a 3^1/$_2$-hour tour each weekday afternoon, leaving from Royal Avenue at 2pm. Other tours cover the surrounding countryside. Details from: Citybus, ☎ 246485. (Phone numbers are all Belfast exchange — STD 0232).

Belfast City Hall
For free tour (Wednesday morning only) ☎ 220202 ext. 227 (must book).

Botanic Gardens
Open daily until dusk. Palm house and tropical ravine open weekdays 10am-5pm, weekend 2-5pm; in winter (October-March) they close an hour earlier.

Crown Liquor Saloon
Open pub hours.

Harbour Office
Advance booking essential. Weekdays only. ☎ 234422 ext. 205

Harland & Wolff Shipyard
Access difficult unless you can demonstrate a professional interest. Write to Public Affairs Office, Harland & Wolff, Queen's Island, Belfast BT3 9DU; ☎ 58456. The main Citybus tour includes Belfast docks.

Linen Hall Library
Open weekdays 9.30am-6pm (8.30pm Thursday), and Saturday to 4pm. Library tour Saturday 11am. ☎ 321707.

Public Record Office, Balmoral Avenue
Public search room open weekdays 9.30am-4.45pm. ☎ 661621.

Queen's University of Belfast
Grounds always open.

Transport Museum, Witham Street
Open Monday-Saturday 10am-5pm. Nominal charge. ☎ 51519.

Sinclair Seamen's Church, Corporation Street
Usually only open for Sunday services, otherwise try ☎ 232081.

Ulster Museum
Open Monday-Friday 10am-5pm, Saturday 1-5pm, Sunday 2-5pm. ☎ 668251.

Zoo
Open from 10am all year except Christmas Day. Latest admissions at 5pm (3.30pm in winter).

Near Belfast

Ulster Folk and Transport Museum, Cultra
Open Monday-Saturday 11am-6pm, Sunday 2-6pm. Closes at 5pm October-April. Modest charge, helpful leaflet. ☎ Belfast 428428.

Carrickfergus Castle
Open Monday-Saturday 10am-6pm, Sunday 2-6pm. Closes at 4pm October-March. Admission charge. ☎ (096 03) 62273.

President Andrew Jackson Centre, Carrickfergus

Open daily 10am-5pm, and 6-8pm June-August. Admission charge.
☎ (096 03) 64972 (caretaker).

Shane's Castle Railway and Nature Reserve

Open noon-6pm every Sunday April-September, plus Saturday and some weekdays June-August. Special events. Admission charge.
☎ (084 94) 63 380.

Pogue's Entry, Antrim

Visible from road but ask for the key at Simpson's newsagents, 32 Church Street, Antrim.
☎ (084 94) 63280.

Castle Upton, Templepatrick

Admission charge to grounds. Group visits to house by arrangement ☎ (084 94) 32466.

Talnotry Bird Garden and Tea Room, Crumlin

Open 2-6pm from Easter to September at weekends and public holidays. Visits arranged at other times, year round. ☎ (084 94) 22900. Admission charge.

Lisburn Museum, Market Square, Lisburn

Open Tuesday-Saturday 11am-4.45pm; the museum closes for lunch (1-1.45pm) and is not open on Saturday in winter.
☎ (084 62) 72624.

Hillsborough Fort

Open Tuesday-Saturday 10am-7pm, Sunday 2-7pm. It closes at 4pm October-March. Grounds always open until dusk.
☎ (0846) 683285 (DOE).

Chapter 2 — Ards Peninsula and St Patrick's Country

The car ferry between Strangford village and Portaferry runs continuously all day throughout the year except on Christmas Day. Last ferry from Portaferry side 10.45pm (11.15pm on Saturday); last ferry from Strangford 10.30pm (11pm Saturday); ☎ (039 686) 637.

Ballycopeland Windmill, Millisle

Open Tuesday-Saturday 10am-7pm, Sunday 2-7pm. In winter (October-March) open only on Saturday (10am-4pm) and Sunday (2-4pm).
Admission charge (DOE).

Grey Abbey Ruins

Open Tuesday-Saturday 10am-7pm, Sunday 2-7pm. Winter access same as Ballycopeland.

Mount Stewart House and Gardens

Open weekend afternoons (2-6pm) April-October, plus Friday afternoons in May and June. In July and August open Tuesday-Sunday from noon to 8pm.
☎ Greyabbey (024 774) 387/233 (NT).

Castle Ward

House open weekend afternoons April-October, plus Wednesday-Friday pm in May and June, plus every day except Tuesday in July and August from noon to 8pm.
☎ Strangford (039 686) 204 (NT).

Inch Abbey Ruins, and Holy Wells at Struell

Always accessible (DOE).

Saul Church
Site of St Patrick's first church.
Open daily.

Quoile Castle and Pondage Centre
(National nature reserve off A25 1¹/₂ miles north of Downpatrick).
☎ (0396) 5520.

Down Museum and St Patrick Heritage Centre, Downpatrick
Open most weekdays plus bank holidays and weekend afternoons.
Town trails available.
☎ (0396) 5218.

St Patrick's Grave, Downpatrick
In cathedral old graveyard. Always accessible.

Chapter 3 — Mournes and Mid-Down

Rowallane Gardens, Saintfield
Open from 9am every day April-September but not on weekend mornings. Admission charge.
☎ (0238) 510131 (NT).

Dromore Cathedral
Ask at the rectory opposite for access.

Legananny Dolmen
Like most prehistoric monuments, always accessible (DOE).

Dundrum Castle
Grounds always accessible. The keep is open Tuesday-Saturday 10am-7pm, plus 2-7pm on Sunday. It closes at 4pm in winter (DOE).

Murlough Sand Dunes
Permanent access.
NT interpretative centre.

Castlewellan Forest Park and Arboretum
☎ (039 67) 78664 (head forester).

Cornmill, Annalong Harbour
Open most days from Easter.
Admission charge.
☎ (039 67) 68746.

Fairy Thorn
Near Kinnahalla youth hostel.
Visible from main road.

Greencastle Ruins
Always accessible.

Tollymore Forest Park
☎ (039 67) 22428.

Chapter 4 — County Armagh and Newry

Armagh City
Armagh County Museum
Open 10am-5pm Monday-Saturday, closed for lunch (1-2pm) and most bank holidays.
☎ (0861) 523070.

Royal Irish Fusiliers Regimental Museum
Open weekdays, limited hours.
☎ (0861) 522911.

Planetarium
Hall of astronomy open Monday-Saturday 2-4.45pm. Star shows every Saturday at 3pm and on most days except Sunday in July and August. ☎ (0861) 523689.

Anglican Cathedral
Open 10am-5pm weekdays, and at weekends. At other times ask at no.3 Vicar's Row. Access to the cathedral library is limited to 2-4pm on weekdays (but no access in July or August, nor on bank holidays); those interested in the collection can write to the Keeper,

Public Library, Abbey Street,
Armagh, or ☎ (0861) 523142
between 2-4pm.

Catholic Cathedral
Always open.

Armagh Friary Ruins
Always accessible.

Navan Fort
Off A28, always accessible.

Gosford Forest Park
 Near Markethill. ☎ (0861) 551280.

Tandragee Castle
(10 miles east of Armagh).
For free weekday tour of the Tayto
crisp factory ☎ (0762) 840249.

North Armagh
Oxford Island, Lough Neagh
Permanent access to nature
reserve. The information centre is
open Monday-Friday 9am-5pm and
on Sunday from 10am.
☎ (076 22) 22205

Ardress House
Seven miles west of Portadown.
Open weekends from April, plus
Friday and Monday from June, plus
other days in high summer. Always
closed on Tuesday.
☎ (0762) 851236 (NT).

The Argory
Signposted at Moy. Open
weekends from April, plus Friday
and Monday in June. In July and
August open every day except
Monday. ☎ (086 87) 84753 (NT).

Newry Area
**Newry Museum and Arts
Centre**
Open Monday-Friday 11am-4pm,
and Saturday 11am-1pm.
☎ (0693) 61244.

Slieve Gullion Forest Park
☎ (069 384) 226 (head forester).

Killevy Churches
Permanent access.

Chapter 5 — Fermanagh and the
Clogher Valley

The Lakeland Visitor Centre at
Enniskillen, ☎ (0365) 23110,
supplies current opening hours,
information on boat hire etc, for the
whole of Fermanagh. The Clogher
Valley region is well served by the
big Killymaddy tourist centre on A4
west of Dungannon. ☎ (086 87)
67323.

Lough Erne Islands
Local boatmen take visitors out at
any time of the year. In summer
regular passenger cruises leave
from the Round 'O' jetty,
Enniskillen. Public ferries (DOE) to
Devenish and White Island are
mentioned below. Hire craft range
from eight-berth cruisers with all
mod cons, to motor launches and
rowing boats hired by the day or
half day. Public moorings and
jetties are free, and so are most
other jetties and harbours. Visitors
with their own boat will find plenty of
slipways. If you want to land on an
island but cannot see a jetty, you
are advised to use a dinghy. The
water may be shallow. Some
islands are privately owned and
visitors should respect 'private'
notices by not landing there. A free
navigation chart is produced by the
Erne Charter Boat Association but
the best maps are the Ordnance
Survey outdoor pursuits maps, one
for the upper, the other for the
lower lough (see bibliography —
maps).

Devenish Island

Public ferry leaves from Trory April-September 10am-7pm daily except Monday.

White Island

Public ferry from Castle Archdale marina June-August 10am-7pm Tuesday-Saturday plus Sunday 2-7pm. Ferryman makes other crossings on request.

Marble Arch Caves

Open daily from spring to October. Heavy rain can affect water levels and occasionally obliges the warden to close the caves. If in doubt contact him on ☎ (036 582) 777 before setting out.

Museums at Enniskillen Castle

County Museum ☎ (0365) 25050 — opens Monday-Saturday from May to September 10am-5pm but closes for lunch (12.30-2pm); in July and August it also opens on Sunday afternoons; in winter open weekdays only. Regimental Museum ☎ 23142 — opens weekdays only (closes at lunchtime).

Florence Court

House open April-September daily noon-6pm except Tuesday ☎ (036 582) 249 (NT).

Castle Coole

☎ (0238) 510721 (NT) to enquire about access to the mansion.

Monea Castle

Always accessible.

Belleek Pottery

For weekday tour of works ☎ (036 565) 501. Pottery is closed at Easter and first half of August.

President Grant Ancestral Home and Farm, Ballygawley

Open Easter-September until 8pm Monday-Saturday, plus 2-6pm on Sunday. Open until 3pm in winter (Monday-Thursday only). Admission charge. ☎ (066 252) 7133 (on-site warden/farmer).

Chapter 6 — Sperrins and the North West

Tyrone Crystal, Dungannon

For free weekday tour of glassworks ☎ (086 87) 253 35. Factory shop sells imperfect glass.

Wellbrook Beetling Mill, Cookstown

Open April-September weekends 2-6pm, plus weekday afternoons (except Tuesday) from June-August. ☎ (064 87) 48788 (NT).

Springhill House, Moneymore

Similar hours as Wellbrook. ☎ (064 87) 48210 (NT).

Ulster-American Folk Park, Omagh

Open everyday April-September, and on weekdays in winter (except Christmas etc). ☎ (0662) 3292/329.

President Wilson Ancestral Home, Strabane

Open daily all year — call at farm adjacent. Admission charge.

Londonderry City

The tourist office opposite the Guildhall is open weekdays all year, plus Saturday May-end August. Plan of the city walls available. ☎ (0504) 267284.

Walls of Derry
Permanent access.

St Columb's Cathedral
Opening times, and the verger's address, are posted at the door.

Long Tower Church
Always open.

St Eugene's Cathedral
Always open.

Near Limavady
Mussenden Temple, Downhill
Access to grounds all year. Temple is open most days. To visit crypt ask at Bishop's Gate lodge.
☎ (0265) 848281 (warden).

Roe Valley Country Park
Always open. Visitor centre open weekdays plus Saturday and Sunday afternoons.
☎ (050 47) 2074 (warden).

Dungiven Priory
Always accessible. O'Cahan tomb is visible from outside (DOE).

Chapter 7 — Causeway Coast, Glens and Mid-Antrim

Giant's Causeway
Permanent access. To identify geological features buy the NT leaflet (includes a good map) at the Causeway Centre, open daily 10am-5pm with extended evening hours June-October. ☎ Bushmills (026 57) 31855/ 31582.

Dunluce Castle
Open Tuesday-Saturday 10am-7pm, Sunday 2-7pm. Closes at 4pm in winter (October-March). Admission charge (DOE).

Old Bushmills Distillery
For free weekday tour (except Friday pm) ☎ (026 57) 31521. Ulsterbus operates an open-top bus, the Bushmills Bus, between Coleraine and the Causeway from end June to end August.

Carrick-a-rede Rope Bridge
In position from late April to September only.

Rathlin Island
Daily crossings Easter-September. Tourist office at Ballycastle ☎ (026 57) 62024/62225 — can arrange crossings at other times. Mail boat leaves Ballycastle harbour every Monday, Wednesday and Friday at 10.30am. Rathlin Guesthouse can also arrange passage.
☎ (026 57) 63916.

Bonamargy Friary
Always accessible.

Glenariff Forest Park
☎ (026 673) 232 (head forester).

Watertop Open Farm
Open daily June-September. Admission charge.
☎ (026 57) 62576 for details.

Safari Park, Dervock
Admission charge.
☎ (026 57) 41474.

President Arthur's Ancestral Home, Cullybackey
Open afternoons Easter-September except Sunday. Admission charge. For details telephone tourist office in Ballymena. ☎ (0266) 44111.

Toome Eel Fishery,
Toomebridge. ☎ (0648) 50618.

Events

This brief list gives a flavour of regular events in the province. The tourist board publishes a fuller list.

St Patrick's Day (17 March) — processions and pilgrimages.

Horse Ploughing Match, Ballycastle (mid-March) — heavy horses.

Country Music Festival, Belfast (Easter) — international Country and Western.

Sealink Classic Fishing Festival, Fermanagh (mid-May) — coarse fishing.

Ballyclare Horse Fair (late May).

Royal Ulster Agricultural Society Show, Belfast (late May).

Black Bush Amateur Golf Tournament , Causeway Coast (early June) — played over four courses.

Fleadh Amhran agus Rince, Ballycastle (late June) — traditional Irish song and dance.

Game and Country Fair, Bangor (late June) — field sports.

Belfast/Dublin Maracycle (late June) — two huge teams pass each other *en route* to the other city.

International Rose Trials, Belfast (July-September) — Rose Week and finals for catalogued roses is in late July.

Hilltown Booley Fair, Mourne Mountains (early July) — mountain sheep fair, traditional music.

'The Twelfth' (12 July) — numerous large parades in main towns on the anniversary of the Battle of the Boyne (1690).

Sham Fight, Scarva, County Down (mid-July) — 200-year-old pageant with horseback joust between two seventeenth-century kings, a symbolic re-enactment of the Boyne.

Lughnasa Medieval Fair, Carrickfergus Castle (late July) — Lughnasa (Lammas) was one of the quarterly feasts of the old Irish year.

All-Ireland Road Bowls Finals, Armagh (early August).

Ancient Order of Hibernians' parades (15 August) — processions, mainly in rural areas, to mark the Feast of the Assumption.

Ulster Grand Prix, Dundrod near Belfast (late August) — international motorcycling.

Ould Lammas Fair, Ballycastle (late August) — oldest traditional fair in Ireland.

North West Arts Festival, Londonderry City (November).

Belfast Festival at Queen's , Belfast City (November) — UK's largest arts festival after Edinburgh.

Accommodation

Northern Ireland — All the Places to Stay is available in a new edition each year and is good value. It gives over 800 addresses, with prices, of hotels, guesthouses and farmhouses in the province — all inspected and approved by the Northern Ireland Tourist Board (NITB). A separate section describes self-catering accommodation and youth hostels. Main tourist information centres offer an accommodation booking service. *Camping and Caravan Parks*, another NITB annual booklet, lists about a hundred caravan sites with prices and details of facilities. You can order them by post (see addresses) or through bookshops. If you want to leave dry land for a week or two, ask the NITB for details of cruising holidays on Lough Erne .

Activity Holidays

Fishing, sailing and other water-based sports are the most popular activity holidays. Golf, pony-trekking, walking the Ulster Way, bowling, bird watching and landscape painting also have enthusiastic followings. The tourist board publishes a free series of detailed information bulletins on subjects such as game fishing, sea fishing, shore fishing, sub-aqua diving, golf, riding and cycling. Other leaflets cover boating on the Bann river and coarse fishing, and the Sports Council produces a set of leaflets on manageable sections of the 500-mile Ulster Way.

Travelling in Northern Ireland

By Car
The rules of the road — speed limits, seat belts, drink/drive laws, driving on the left, not parking on double yellow lines, an ordinary driving licence, etc — are the same as in Britain, and the AA and RAC breakdown services operate similarly. Cars bearing large red 'R' (Restricted) plates identify drivers who have passed their driving test within the past 12 months and are meant to keep to low speeds.

One additional parking rule concerns the province's 'control zones', usually in town centres and indicated by prominent yellow signs 'control zone — no unattended parking'. A parked car in a control zone is considered a security risk unless someone is sitting in it. Belfast city centre is partly pedestrianised with pay carparks within easy walking distance of shops. Most other towns have capacious carparks, usually free.

Car Rental
Visitors are advised to ask the hire firm for the total cost, since insurance and VAT may be added to the quoted price. Picking up a car from airport branches of main firms may increase your bill so compare the airport and city rates. The tourist board publishes a list of car hire firms. If you plan to cross from Northern Ireland to the Republic or vice versa, check the rental insurance position. In addition, note that it is cheaper to do a round trip and to deposit the car where you collected it. Rental

firms make a substantial surcharge if the car is dropped off on the other side of the border.

Public Transport

The province has a good bus network. Express buses from Belfast run to all main towns, including Larne (for boats to Scotland). In July and August there are day and half-day tours from Belfast to popular holiday spots. 1-day and 7-day unlimited travel bus tickets are available. A 15-day Irish Overlander ticket allows unlimited travel on scheduled bus and rail services throughout Ireland (not valid for coach tours or on Belfast Citybus services). Contact: Ulsterbus, 10 Glengall Street, Belfast BT12 5AH; ☎ (0232) 220011. This is the central enquiry number. Belfast has two 'main' bus stations, one behind the Europa Hotel, the other in Oxford Street. Phone to check if you have any doubt. It is easy to go to the wrong one. There is a regular bus service from Belfast International Airport to the city centre.

For Citybus services (i.e. Belfast area only) ☎ 246485. All routes radiate out from City Hall, and if you wish to get right across the city you have to change at City Hall. Routes and bus numbers are listed on the reverse of the city map available from the tourist office in High Street.

Trains from Belfast Central Station (☎ 230310/230671) run north to Londonderry and south to Dublin. The Dublin-Belfast non-stop express takes 2 hours. The Belfast-Bangor line is used mostly by commuters. The Larne boat train leaves from York Road Station. The two stations have no rail link but a special bus runs between them Monday-Saturday. Other buses from York Road end up within easy walking distance of Central Station. Note: there are no left luggage facilities at Central Station.

Taxis

Main stations, ports and Belfast International Airport have the usual taxi services. Air passengers wishing to go by train to Londonderry may find it convenient to join the train at Antrim station. Sharing a cab from the airport to Antrim is sometimes possible. In Belfast not all the London-type black cabs you see around have meters. If the cab does not have a yellow disc on the windscreen, ask the fare first.

Money

Most banks are open 10am-3.30pm Monday-Friday except at lunchtime (12.30-1.30pm), and automatic cash dispensers are in general use. Access and Barclaycard are the commonest credit cards. Diners' Club and American Express are not widely accepted. For travelling around and staying at small hotels or farmhouses, you need cash (sterling only) though cheques (with bank card) are usually acceptable.

Maps and Books

The handiest map is the Ireland North Holiday Map ($1/4$" to 1 mile) from the Ordnance Survey (OSNI). The old series of $1/2$" maps covering

Northern Ireland on four sheets is still available from OSNI (see addresses) but the modern 1:50 000 (1¼" to 1 mile) maps are excellent. OSNI also produces 1:25 000 (2½" to 1 mile) outdoor pursuits maps, two for the Lough Erne lakes, and one for the Mournes. The Erne maps are particularly useful for making sense of the maze of small roads round the lake shore. There are a number of road maps of the whole island: for example, the 1" to 10 miles Bartholomew touring map, the map at the back of the AA members' handbook (Ireland edition) to the same scale, and the Bord Failte (Irish Tourist Board) map. For a comprehensive list of Northern Ireland Tourist Board publications write to: Tourist Information Centre, 48 High Street, Belfast BT1 2DS. ☎(0232) 246609. Out of a long list of books that have been consulted the following very brief selection is recommended for further reading:

Historical
Bardon, Jonathan. *Belfast*. Notably, eighteenth- and nineteenth-century development, illustrated. Blackstaff 1982.

Beckett, J.C. *The Making of Modern Ireland 1603-1923*. The best introduction. Faber paperback 1985.

Benn, George. *History of the Town of Belfast*. First published 1823 facsimile edition by Davidson Books, Ballynahinch 1979.

Chadwick, Nora. *The Celts*. Pelican 1981.

Clark, Wallace. *Rathlin — Disputed Island*. Volturna paperback 1971.

Curl, James Stevens. *The Londonderry Plantation 1609-1914*. Large scholarly hardback, lavishly illustrated. Phillimore 1986.

Macrory, Patrick. *The Siege of Derry*. Good readable account of the great siege in historical context. Hodder and Stoughton 1980.

Architecture/Antiquities
Brett, C.E.B. *Buildings of Belfast 1700-1914*. Well illustrated. Friar's Bush 1985.

Hamlin, Ann. *Historic Monuments of Northern Ireland*. HMSO 1983.

McCutcheon, W.A. *The Industrial Archaeology of Northern Ireland*. Large scholarly hardback, handsomely illustrated.

Rogers, Mary. *Prospect of Erne*. Comprehensive popular descriptions of Lough Erne islands, antiquities, people. Watergate Press 1971.

Rowan, Alistair. *North-West Ulster*. Covers Londonderry, Donegal, Fermanagh and Tyrone. Pevsner series. Penguin hardback 1979.

Others
Donnelly, Daniel J. *On Lough Neagh's Shores*. A study of the fishing community. Published by the Donnelly Family, Galbally, County Tyrone 1986.

Morton, H.V. *In Search of Ireland*. Methuen 1930.

Praeger, Robert Lloyd. *The Way That I Went*. Natural history of Ireland by botanist/geologist.1937.

Allen Figgis, Dublin, paperback reprint 1980.

Rogers, R. *Irish Walk Guides: the North-East*. Gill & Macmillan paperback 1980.

Warner, Alan. *On Foot in Ulster — a Journal of the Ulster Way*. Appletree paperback 1983.

How to Get to Northern Ireland

By Air - GB Direct to Belfast International :
London (Heathrow): British Airways (BA) ☎ 01-897 4000; British Midland ☎ 01-581 0864. *London (Gatwick)*: Dan Air ☎ 01-680 1011. Also direct flights from: *Birmingham* (BA ☎ 021-236 7000); *Bristol* (Dan Air ☎ 0345 100200); *Cardiff* (Dan Air ☎ 0345 100200); *East Midlands* (British Midland ☎ 0332 810552); *Glasgow* (BA ☎ 041-332 9666 and Air Ecosse ☎ 0224771177); *Leeds/Bradford* (Air UK ☎ 0345 666777); *Manchester* (BA ☎ 061-228 6311); *Newcastle-on-Tyne* (Dan Air ☎ 091-261 1395). Summer flights with British Midland from Jersey.

By Air - GB Direct to Belfast Harbour Airport in City Centre
Birmingham (Jersey European ☎ 0253 404314); *Blackpool* (Jersey European ☎ 0253 404314); *Edinburgh* (Loganair ☎ 031-333 3338);*Exeter* (Jersey European ☎ 0392 64440);*Glasgow* (Loganair ☎ 041-889 3181); *Isle of Man* (Manx Air ☎ 0624 824313 and Jersey European ☎ 0624 822162); *Liverpool* (Manx Air ☎ 061-436 1010); *Manchester* (Loganair

☎ 061-832 9922); *Teesside* (Jersey European 0253 404314). Loganair also run summer flights from Blackpool.

Other Direct Air Links with Northern Ireland:
Amsterdam-Belfast International (NLM ☎ (20)434242); *Dublin-Londonderry* (Shannon Executive ☎ Dublin 379900); *Glasgow-Londonderry* (Loganair ☎ 041-889 3181). In addition there are direct charters to Belfast from New York and Toronto.

Car Ferry Services
Liverpool-Belfast (Belfast Car Ferries ☎ 051-922 6234); *Scotland (Stranraer)-Larne* (Sealink ☎ 0776 2262); *Scotland (Cairnryan)-Larne* (Townsend Thoresen ☎ 058 12 276); *Isle of Man-Belfast* (IoM Steam Packet Co. ☎ 0624 72468). Ferry services to the Irish Republic are from France (Le Havre, Cherbourg and Roscoff) and from Britain (Swansea, Pembroke, Fishguard, Holyhead and Liverpool).

Useful Addresses

Northern Ireland Tourist Board
48 High Street
Belfast BT1 2DS
☎ (0232) 231221.
(For accommodation booking service or a publications list phone the information centre on 246609 at the same address).

Northern Ireland Tourist Board
(US office)
40 West 57th Street, 3rd Floor
New York
NY10019
☎ (212) 765 5144

*British Tourist Authority offices in
North America are at:*
875 N. Michigan Ave.
 Suite 3320
Chicago
IL 60611
☎ (312) 787 0490
        and
World Trade Center
350 S. Figueroa Street
Suite 450
Los Angeles
CA 90071
☎ (213) 628 3525
        and
Cedar Maple Plaza
2305 Cedar Springs Road
Dallas
TX 75201
☎ (214) 720 4040
        and
94 Cumberland Street
Toronto
Ontario M5R 3N3
☎ (416) 925 6326

National Trust (s.a.e.)
Rowallane, Saintfield
Ballynahinch
County Down BT24 7LH
☎ (0238) 510721

Youth Hostel Association (YHANI)
56 Bradbury Place
Belfast BT7 1RU
☎ (0232) 324733.

Royal Society for the Protection of
 Birds
Belvoir Park Forest
Belfast BT8 4QT
☎ (0232) 692547

Ulster Architectural Heritage
 Society
181a Stranmillis Road
Belfast BT9 5DV
☎ (0232) 660809 morning.

Sports Council
House of Sport
Malone Road
Belfast BT9 6RZ
☎ (0232) 661222.

Ordnance Survey (NI)
Colby House
Stranmillis Court
Belfast BT9 5BJ
☎ (0232) 661244.

Archaeological Survey
Historic Monuments & Buildings
Branch, DOENI,
66 Balmoral Avenue
Belfast BT9 6NY
☎ (0232) 661621.

Fisheries Division
Dept. Agriculture
Stormont
Belfast BT4 3PW
☎ (0232) 63939.

Forest Service
Dept. Agriculture
Dundonald House
Upper Newtownards Road
Belfast BT4 2SF
☎ (0232) 650111.

Comhaltas Ceoiltoiri Eireann
25 Gortahar Road
Rasharkin
County Antrim BT44 8SB
☎ (026 653) 310 (evenings)
(*Fleadh* information).

Automobile Association
Fanum House
Great Victoria Street
Befast BT2 7AT
☎ (0232) 244538.

Royal Automobile Club
RAC House
79 Chichester Street
Belfast BT1 4JR
☎ (0232) 240261.

INDEX

Accommodation 25
Activity holidays 26, 27
Addresses 235
Aghalurcher
  old church 152
  –parish church 142
Aghory 129
Agriculture 12
American/Canadian
  links 21, 49, 99, 105,
  108, 112, 114, 117,
  137, 169–72, 174,
  176, 177, 221, 223
Annalong 93, 94–5, 98,
  227
Antrim 47, 50–1, 226
Ardboe cross 16, 165,
  167, 168
Ardglass 14, 75, 82
Ardress House 129,
  130, 131–2, 228
Ards peninsula 57, 226
Argory, the 129, 131,
  132, 228
Armagh city 19, 24,
  122ff, 227–8
Arthur ancestral home
  221, 222, 230
Attical 96
Augher 137, 138, 139
Aughnacloy 136–7

Ballinderry 52, 53
Ballintoy 204
Ballyarnet Field 185
Ballycastle 206–9
Ballycopeland windmill
  66, 67, 70, 226
Ballygally castle 220
Ballygawley 137, 229
Ballyhalbert 68
Ballyhornan 81
Ballykeel dolmen 119
Ballykelly 185–6
Ballylumford 49, 50

Ballymartin 95
Ballymena 20, 203,
  221, 222
Ballymoney 20, 112,
  202, 222
Ballynahinch 83, 85–6
Ballywalter 57, 67
Banagher old church
  189–91
Banbridge 101, 103
Bangor 57
Bann river 13, 20, 110,
  111, 187, 194, 223
Barnes Gap 173
Baronscourt 174
Bawns 19
Beaghmore stone
  circles 168, 169, 174
Belfast 30ff, 225ff
  –Albert Mem. 34,37
  –Barnett's park 44
  –botanic gardens 39
  –castle 40
  –Cave Hill 40–3
  –churches 37, 38
  –city hall 30, 32, 35,
  41
  –Dixon park 42
  – entertainment 24
  –Giant's Ring 43, 44
  –Harbour Office 30
  –history 30
  –opera house 35, 36
  –palm house 39, 40
  –public houses 36
  –Queen's University
  38, 39
  –Shaw's Bridge 44
  –shipyard 34, 35, 41
  –Stormont 42
  –Transport Museum
  40
  –Ulster Museum 40
  –zoo 42

Bellanaleck 151
Bellarena 191
Belleek 157, 158, 159
Benbane Head 197,203
Benburb 135, 137
Bessbrook 18, 115,119
Binevenagh 161, 187,
  191
Birches, the 112
Black Bog 172
Black Pig's Dyke 113
Blackwater river 135
Bloody Bridge 92
Boa island 15, 149, 150
Boho 156
Bonamargy friary 208,
  211, 230
Bovevagh 191
Boyne, battle 23
Brackenridge's Folly
  141
Brandy Pad 92
Brookeborough 141
Broughshane 194, 221,
  222
Bushmills 27, 201, 230
Bush Town 97–8

Caledon 136
Camlough 119
Cappagh 169
Carlingford lough 96,
  97, 114, 116
Carnlough 217, 220
Carrick-a-rede 201,
  205–6, 230
Carrickfergus 46, 47–9
  –castle 16, 45, 48,
  53, 225, 226
Carrowdore 73
Castle Archdale 146,
  160
Castle Balfour 18
Castle Caldwell 146,
  159–60

Castlecaulfield 18, 164
Castle Coole 19, 154,
    155, 158, 229
Castlederg 175
Castlerock 193
Castle Ward 19, 75–6,
    78, 226
Castlewellan 86,
    89–91, 227
Chapeltown 81
Charlemont Fort 132,
    162, 164
Clandeboye 62
Cleenish island 151
Climate 9
Clogher 140, 141
Clogher Valley
    134–142, 228
Clonduff 98
Clonfeacle parish
    church 136
Clough castle 86
Coagh 112
Coalisland 163
Coleraine 13, 18, 111,
    193–4
Comber 64, 70
Coney island 111
Cookstown 162, 165
Copeland islands 64,66
Correl Glen 159
Craigagh Wood 216
Craigavon 106
Cranfield 97
Crawfordsburn 62
Cregganconroe 168
Creggandevesky 169
Crom castle 146, 151
Crossmaglen 119
Crumlin 52, 53, 112,
    226
Cuilcagh mountains
    142, 155, 156
Cullybackey 221, 222
Cushendall 218
Cushendun 214, 215,
    216

Dalriada, kingdom of
    204
Dalway's Bawn 19
Dane's Cast, the 113

Derrygonnelly 158–9
Derrylin 154
Derry — see
    Londonderry
Derrymore House 120,
    121
Dervock safari park
    203, 230
Devenish island 16,
    145, 146, 149
Donaghcloney 103–4,
    105
Donaghadee 64–6
Donaghmore (Tyrone)
    16, 164, 165
Douglas Bridge 175
Downhill 191–3
Downpatrick 78–80,
    227
Draperstown 161, 189
Driving — see
    Travelling
Dromara 100
Dromore (Down) 86, 87,
    102, 104, 227
Drumballyroney 99,100
Drumbeg church 45
Drumbo 46
Drumbridge 45
Drumena cashel 90
Drumlins 9, 69
Drum Manor forest park
    168
Drumquin 172
Drumskinny stone
    circle 160
Dundrum 86, 87, 88,
    100, 227
Duneight motte 87
Dungannon 162–3,165,
    229
Dungiven 161, 187,
    189, 190, 230
Dunluce castle 200–1,
    202, 230
Dunnaman 95
Dunseverick castle
    203–4

Edenderry 44
Eglinton airport 185
Ely Lodge 157

Enniskillen 24, 142–6,
    158, 229
Errigal Keerogue 137

Fair Head 12, 195, 211,
    213
Favour Royal 138
Festivals 22, 24
Finnis 100
Fintona 172
Fivemiletown 141
Flight of the Earls 17
Florence Court 19, 151,
    155, 158, 229
Food & drink 26, 130
Forest parks 27
Foyle river 13

Galloon island 149, 152
Garrison 159
Garron Point 219
Giant's Causeway 195,
    197, 198, 201, 230
Giant's Ring — see
    Belfast
Gilford 101
Glenariff — see
    Waterfoot
Glenariff forest park
    211, 218, 230
Glenarm 220
Glendun 217
Glenoe 49
Glenelly river 172, 173
Glenshane Pass 161
Glens of Antrim 20,
    201, 214
    –names 216
Gobbins, the 50
Goblusk bay 160
Gortin 172–3
Gosford 121, 128
Goward dolmen 98
Gracehill 221, 222
Grant ancestral home
    137, 229
Greencastle 96–7, 98,
    227
Greyabbey 57, 70–1,
    226
Groomsport 64

Hare's Gap 91
Harry Avery's castle
    18, 174
Helen's Bay 62
Hen island 74
Hezlett House 193
Hilden 54
Hillsborough 19, 53,
    54, 55, 56, 129, 226
Hilltown 92, 98
Historic monuments 14
Holywood 59, 60

Inch Abbey 70, 78,
    80, 81, 226
Industry 12
Inishkeen 150
Inishmacsaint 147, 149
Inishrath 151
Irvinestown 160
Islandmagee 49

Jerrettspass 112
Jonesborough 116,119

Katesbridge 98, 100,
    101
Kearney 66
Kesh 160
Kilbroney 118
Kilclief castle 75
Kilfeaghan dolmen 96
Kilkeel 14, 92, 94, 95
Killadeas 146, 150
Killard Point 81
Killevy churches 115,
    119, 228
Killough 82
Killyleagh 57, 74–5
Killymoon castle 166
Kilmore (Arm.) 129, 130
Kilnasaggart Stone 119
Kilroot 49
Kinbane castle 203,
    204
Kingdom of Mourne 83,
    92
Kircubbin 70
Kirkistown castle 68–9
Knocklayd mountain
    208
Knockmany 138,
    139–40

Knockmore cliff 157
Knockninny hill 154

Lagan
  –river 100, 103
  –valley 20
  –towpath 44–5
  –regional park 29, 42
Lambeg 23, 54
Larne 11, 49
Larrybane Head 206
Layde old church 218
Legananny dolmen 86,
    100, 102, 227
Limavady 21, 186, 188
Linen 13, 54, 108, 189
Lisbellaw 142
Lisburn 53–6, 163, 226
Lisnaskea 152, 154
Literature 24
Londonderry city 18,
    22, 24, 161, 178ff,
    229ff
Loughareema 211,
    212–3
Lough Erne 9, 133,
    142,158
  –Lower 146, 152
  –Upper 150
Lough Foyle 161, 178
Loughgall 131
Lough Macnean 157
Lough Melvin 159
Lough na Cranagh 213
Lough Navar forest
    viewpoint 158, 159
Lough Neagh 9, 13, 45,
    50, 111–12, 168,
    223, 228
Loughry Manor 167
Lurgan 106, 107–8
Lurigethan mountain
    218
Lustybeg island 149,
    150
Lustymore island 150

Maghera 189
Magherafelt 189
Magherally old church
    100
Magheralin 103, 105

Maghery 111
Magilligan Point 191
Mahee island 73, 74
Maps 233
Marble Arch caves
    133,153, 155, 158,
    229
Markethill 121
Marlbank Loop road
    156
Massforth (Kilkeel)
    95–6
Millisle 66
Moira 105
Monea castle 14, 17,
    158, 229
Monea parish church
    147
Money 233
Moneymore 19, 165,
    188
Mountjoy castle 163
Mountsandel 194
Mount Stewart 70, 71,
    72, 73, 226
Mourne mountains 10,
    83, 88, 91
Moy 132, 135
Moyry castle 119
Mullaghcarn mountain
    172
Murlough bay (Antrim)
    211, 213, 214
Murlough nature
    reserve (Down) 86,
    87, 227
Mussenden Temple
    187, 192–3, 230
Narrow Water castle
    116
Navan Fort 106, 128,
    228
Nendrum monastic site
    73
Newcastle 24, 88
Newry 20, 24, 113–16,
    228
Newtownards 60, 63–4
Newtownstewart 18,
    161, 174
Noon's Hole 156

Omagh 24, 171, 172
Ossian's Grave 217
Oxford island 111, 129, 228
Parkanaur forest park 164
Peatlands park 112
Place names 20
Plumbridge 173
Pomeroy 169
Portadown 106, 109, 110
Portaferry 69, 75
Portavogie 14, 68
Portballintrae 202
Portbraddan 204
Portglenone 223
Portora castle 146
Portrush 24, 26, 28, 197, 200
Portstewart 199
Poyntz Pass 112

Queen's University, Belfast 20, 39, 225
Quoile river 80

Raholp 77
Ramore Head 200
Rathfriland 21, 99
Rathlin island 209–12, 230
Red Bay 218
Richhill 56, 129
Ring of Gullion 118
Roe
 –river 185
 –valley 161, 187, 188
Rostrevor 28, 117
Roughan castle 165
Rowallane gardens 83–5, 86, 227

Safari park 203, 230
Saintfield 83, 227
St John's Point 82
St Patrick's Grave 78, 79, 227
St Patrick's Memorial 77

St Angelo airfield (Enniskillen) 160
Sampson's Tower 186
Saul 76–7, 227
Sawel mountain 161, 173
Scarva 23, 112, 113
Scrabo Tower 63
Seskinore 172
Sess Kilgreen 137
Shane's castle, Antrim 50, 53, 111, 226
Share Centre 154
Sheep island 204
Silent Valley 93–4, 98
Sion Mills 18, 174, 176
Skerry church 222
Skerries (islands) 200
Sketrick island 74
Slemish mountain 219, 221
Slidderyford dolmen 87
Slieve Beagh 137
Slieve Croob 100
Slieve Donard 9, 83, 93
Slieve Gallion 166, 187
Slieve Gullion 115, 118–9, 228
Spanish Armada 27, 40, 201
Spelga dam 97
Sperrin 173
Sperrins (mountains) 9, 161, 163, 168
Springhill House 17, 165, 188, 229

Strabane 21, 161, 175, 176, 177
Strangford 69, 75
 –ferry 68, 69, 226
 –lough 14, 69–70
Struell Wells 78, 81, 226

Tandragee 122, 228
Templepatrick 51, 226
Tempo 141, 146
Tievebulliagh mountain 217

Tieveshilly hill 69
Tieveragh hill 218
Tollymore forest park 91, 92, 98, 227
Toomebridge 191, 221, 223, 230
Torr Head 9, 214
Travelling in N.I. 10, 11
Travelling to N.I. 235
Trostan mountain 217
Tullahoge 164–5
Tully castle 18, 159
Tyrella strand 82

Ulster-American Folk Park 21, 171–2, 174, 229
Ulster Folk & Transport Museum 13, 34, 53, 60–2, 225
Ulster Museum 40, 73, 195, 225
Ulster Way footpath 29, 45
United Irishmen 36, 41, 46, 51, 83
University of Ulster campuses 185, 193, 194
Upperlands 21, 189

Victoria Bridge 174
Walworth House 186
Waringstown 103, 104
Warrenpoint 116–17
Washing Bay 111, 164
Waterfoot 218
Watertop Farm 211, 212, 230
Wellbrook beetling mill 165, 166, 168, 229
Whitehead 50
White island 148–9
Whitepark bay 204, 207
White Rocks 199, 200, 201
Wilson ancestral home 174, 177, 229